A Strategy For Reaching Secular People

The Intentional Church in a Post-Modern World

Ernan A. Norman, D. Min.

Bloomington, IN  Milton Keynes, UK

authorHOUSE®

AuthorHouse™
1663 Liberty Drive, Suite 200
Bloomington, IN 47403
www.authorhouse.com
Phone: 1-800-839-8640

AuthorHouse™ UK Ltd.
500 Avebury Boulevard
Central Milton Keynes, MK9 2BE
www.authorhouse.co.uk
Phone: 08001974150

First published by AuthorHouse 4/30/2007

ISBN: 978-1-4343-0577-0 (sc)

Library of Congress Control Number: 2007902396

Printed in the United States of America
Bloomington, Indiana

This book is printed on acid-free paper.

I dedicate this book first and foremost in memory of my mother and father, Elmer Norman and Leila Elfreda Norman. I especially dedicate this book to my mother, who not only birth me physically, but who brought me up single handedly in the Faith, and who introduced me to Jesus.

I also dedicate this book to my dear wife, Velvia, and our three children Joy, Joshua and Jewel.

This book is also dedicated to all my brothers and sisters, who have the same testimony about mother as I have.

This book is finally dedicated to all evangelists, pastors, lay-workers and missionaries who share a like passion for reaching lost people for Christ.

TABLE OF CONTENTS

CHAPTER 4

A BIBLICAL AND THEOLOGICAL RATIONALE FOR REACHING SECULAR PEOPLE

CHAPTER 5

THREE MODELS FOR REACHING SECULAR PEOPLE

CHAPTER 6
A SUGGESTED STRATEGY
　TO REACH SECULAR PEOPLE

PREFACE

I introduce this book (to all those who will read it) with great humility. While it is written based on the need that presents itself within the Seventh-day Adventist Church as I perceive it (I have served in active pastoral ministry, and engaged in evangelistic work as a Seventh-day Adventist minister for more than seventeen years, and I am currently an assistant professor of theology and religion at Atlantic Union College), I do hope that those not of my faith-persuasion will find the principles and ideas helpful to themselves as well. A number of issues that I address in the model of the intentional church will differ somewhat with popular church growth theory. I pray that none of those ideas will be a hindrance to anyone searching for new ways of reaching lost people in our secular-postmodern age. Within the pages that follow are principles that are unique and others that may not be as unique. It is my prayer that all who are sincerely engaged in the work of saving lost people will find this book to be a source of fresh perspectives and a cause for stimulation, adding to what they already have, contributing to that which has proven to be successful, and supplying added relevance to mission endeavors.

Perhaps you are now asking, "Why another book on reaching secular people for Christ?" This is a very good question which deserves an answer. This book grew out of my experience both as a pastor and as a student whose passion for this subject led me to write my doctoral dissertation on a strategy for reaching secular people. The idea for this book was born when the committee who guided me through the dissertation process and finally before whom I defended my dissertation, encouraged me at the time to consider publishing a book on the subject. Not only the doctoral committee members, but also individuals from a wide variety of backgrounds and places with whom I have had opportunity to converse, have expressed the need for such a book. There is an obvious need to find some relevant ways of reaching people in our society who no longer espouse a Christian worldview and who no longer have a favorable attitude toward the Church and the Christian faith. Times have changed. We are now living in what is often referred to in this book as a postmodern age. The challenge to the Gospel has become obvious, as evangelism and church growth is stymied. Despite a so-called return to the supernatural and a sudden quest for spirituality in a highly secular society, the good news of the Gospel as traditionally presented to the masses is met with great skepticism and even avoided.

A recent experience that I had testifies to the fact that individuals within our churches are concerned and are seeking for answers as to how we can address this need to reach secular people. While sitting in my office and making preparations to teach a class, there was a knock on my door. One of my fellow professors came to see me about a concern he had about the method and approach of an evangelistic event that was intended to reach a city of more than three hundred thousand people. Knowing that reaching secular people is my specialty, and that I teach a class on "Witnessing to Secular People," this professor asked me to speak with his pastor for the purpose of explaining to him that traditional approaches that call for large spending yield very little or no returns in a secular society. It is simply a fact that we are not reaching secular people, and that means we are not reaching the majority of people in our urban centers. While our passion for public evangelism must remain strong and our efforts encouraged, there must be a change in the present approach to reaching a secular-postmodern people. New methods, new ideas, new and innovative strategies must now be developed and employed. In this book there is a call for intentional ministry, by intentional people, through an intentional church as a way to reaching our teeming masses who have found themselves at a cultural and spiritual distance from the Christian Church and the Christian Faith. The traditional approaches of yester-year can no longer bridge the gap.

Another important reason why a book on this order is necessary is that wherever I have presented the subject on how to reach secular people, whether in the classroom to my students or to church members in seminar settings, it has always been welcomed with enthusiasm and great passion. When the subject of secularism within the context of modern and postmodern mega-shifts in culture and its implications for the witness of the gospel and the growth of the church in advancing the kingdom of God are explained, it's as if a light goes on in the minds of listeners, awakening a passion and an enthusiasm that springs to life. Many would ask, "When is your book coming out?" Well hear it is, you are holding it in your hands. It is here!

What will you find in this book?

- In this book the subject of secularization and secularism and how these phenomena have affected the lives of the majority of people in our culture and society is addressed. Also highlighted is how the present secular ethos has short circuited the witness of the church and as a result has rendered the traditional methods used for reaching secular-postmodern people ineffective and irrelevant.

- There is a focus on the subject of secularization within the North American context—in particular the United States. The notion that perhaps America is the exception to the secularization thesis is challenged. Despite a high profession of religion (reports of high percentages of people saying that they believe in God or some higher power or consciousness, polling data that seem to suggest that there are high rates of church attendance, etc.) by Americans, it has been shown that this nation is highly secularized as evidenced in the educational institutions, the nature of the religious experience of many to the contrary, and the attitude of many toward substantive Christian religion and the Church.

- A biblical and theological rationale for reaching secular people is discussed using the starting point as the *Missio Dei* (Mission of God). This is further rooted and expanded in the mission of Christ, the example of the Apostle Paul, God's own example of communicating with people, and several statements by Ellen G. White that suggests the need to introduce new methods that find their answer in Christ's method. Implications are drawn for intentional efforts to reach secular-postmodern men and women in our day.

- Three models for reaching secular people are critically evaluated and discussed with an eye to differentiating some of their strengths and weaknesses. The positives are possibilities for our emulation and adaptation and the negatives are highly discouraged. There is a call for a critical contextualization in finding and developing intentional and relevant ways for reaching secular people.

- A suggested strategy for reaching secular people with the Gospel of Jesus Christ by means of the Intentional Church is introduced. While the Intentional Church is discussed from the perspective of a Seventh-day Adventist Christian and minister of the gospel, other fellow Christians may find the broad based principles suggested helpful in their own context as they endeavor in some ways to reach and disciple lost people for Christ and His kingdom. This model is not a hard and fast rule, but is intended to stimulate further investigation and initiative in mission endeavors.

- Finally there are a few appendices, a glossary of terms, and an extensive suggested bibliography that will provide added resources for further study and investigation.

There is hope....

The task of reaching secular people with the gospel will also meet its fulfillment in the words of Christ, *"And this gospel of the Kingdom shall be preached in all the world for a witness unto all nations; and then shall the end come"* (Matt. 24: 14, KJV). In the nations of the West, the majority of the people yet to be reached for Christ are substantially secular, and that presents just as much if not more of a challenge in the preaching of the gospel as in any foreign mission field. Many will be reached as they will have to take a stand for or against Christ and His Truth. The promise is that the gospel will be preached in the entire world, and that includes the secular cultures of our postmodern West. What I also gather from this text is that there is still hope that we will once again be effective in reaching our secular friends, neighbors, and all others, with a clear witness of the Gospel. None will be able to plead ignorance, irrelevance, or neglect. There will be an intentional engagement under the outpouring of the Holy Spirit on the many intensively active agencies that will call all peoples of earth, including secular-postmodern people, to take their stand. Hasten glad day! Read on!

ACKNOWLEDGEMENTS

The development of this book comes with acknowledgement of certain influential people and others near and dear to me. While I do not lay claim to originality in every detail, I do take full responsibility for the content of this book. Many of the ideas and the larger portion are a direct outgrowth of my Doctoral Dissertation on, *A Strategy for Reaching Secular People.* In this regard I wish to give recognition to my mentors, readers, and teachers who served on my committee. I wish to acknowledge Dr. Clifford Jones, Committee chair, mentor, and teacher who provided able guidance and expert editing in the dissertation process and Dr. Jon Pauline, a second reader and systematic, who made helpful suggestions and gave encouragement for "another book" on the subject of reaching secular people. I wish to also recognize Dr. Walter Douglas, a mentor, teacher, and third reader, who gave timely insights and encouragement in my writing of the dissertation.

I must also recognize a dear friend, Dr. Ruthven Roy, whose many conversations, support, and shared passion for the subject of reaching secular people, helped in the reshaping of this study into a book.

Special recognition is given to Dr. Weymouth Spence, Dean of Academic affairs, Atlantic Union College, who kindly consented to the reading of my manuscript and who wrote the endorsement for the back of this book.

It gives me great pleasure to also acknowledge my own brothers and sisters whose encouragement, prayers and suggestions supported me during my journey.

I give full acknowledgment to my immediate family, who witnessed day by day my ups and downs during this process, and whose prayers and undying support and patience, cannot be fully expressed in mere words. My wife Velvia, who provided ardent support, encouragement, and great patience, was my source of strength in times of struggle, and in times of exuberance. My oldest child Joy who was an able reader and who provided much needed editing to many of the new portions that went into the reshaping of this book, is someone of whom I am especially proud. I am equally proud of Joshua, my only son, and Jewel, my younger daughter, whose prayers, support and patience provided an added source of strength and motivation for me. Thank you family for supporting me and for enduring the loss of my presence during the many hours I spent on this book.

Last, but certainly not least, is the honor, praise, and thanks due to my Heavenly Father. His grace, wisdom, and imparted giftedness to me are the reasons why I accomplished this task. Without Him I could have done nothing. Therefore, all praise and all credit ultimately belongs to Him. "To God be the Glory, great things He has done."

CHAPTER 1

INTRODUCTION: A CALL TO INTENTIONAL MINISTRY

In a course outline, "Faith and Mission in a Secularized World," Gottfried Oosterwal stated the following:

"Our spiritual forebears faced the gargantuan task of proclaiming a radically new message to an old, old world. Our generation of the 1990's is confronted with the challenge of communicating an old, old message to a radically new world. That radical newness can best be described by the term secularization."[1]

This observation by Oosterwal introduces what has been the greatest challenge to the church in both a modern and post-modern world—that is, secularization. In a largely secularized society, it has become increasingly difficult for the church to present the gospel in such a way as to influence and reach secular people. As we have entered the twenty-first century, we are also facing a secular mind-set that is impacted by the "postmodern condition."[2]

The postmodern condition points to a situation where in recent decades the seemingly rational, objective, and managed world of modernity has undergone deep, significant shifts. There have been shifts in knowing and understanding what is real in our world. Secular people are now faced with certain prevailing patterns in the postmodern

1

condition, such as endless choices made available by technology. Loss of shared experiences, meanings conveyed as surfaces and images, transient relationships, and plurality of approaches to sexual expression and experiences also confronts them. The postmodern condition also includes an increasingly two-tiered economy with many dead-end jobs, personal spirituality without the necessity of organized religion, random violence and clashes between cultures, and feelings of anger or resentment because somebody has left us with a mess.[3]

The Challenge

The church must now take an old, old gospel message to a radically new world. The problem is that the Christian church no longer has the cultural support it once enjoyed. Thoughtful people will realize that this is due to the steady erosion of Christianity in the face of autonomous rationality and the burgeoning secularity of the West, pushed forward by the rise of urbanization and the steady growth of post-modernism. To this has been added most recently the graphic reality of religious pluralism.[4]

Religious pluralism offers not one, but a number of spheres of saving contact between God and man.[5] This means that "Christ and Christianity, instead of being the centre of the saving and revealing work of God, 'go into orbit' along with other faiths, as one among many planetary responses to the gravitational pull of the Son of divine reality at the centre."[6] Other faiths could be hundreds of possibilities, the major ones being Muslim, Buddhist, Hindu, Native American, Scientologist, Unitarian-Universalist, Jehovah's Witnesses, Bah'ai, Sikh, Wiccan, Eckankar, and New Agers of varying stripes.[7]

All these represent a range of religious alternatives now available to Americans. It has now become apparent that secular post-modern men and women, while increasingly secular, are also open to the spiritual. These people are searching for a satisfying worldview, and are characterized as spiritual secularists.[8]

There is an intense search for a spiritual meaning to life. That search is seen in the religious market place of consumerist options. These options are as varied as sports, interaction with the internet, interest in the rise of the Occultism and Eastern mysticism, New Age with it's emphasis on the individual and inner spirituality, and the proliferation of religious literature concerned with the supernatural and the spiritual world. The evidence of this new spiritual quest is also found in book stores and coffee shops dotting the landscape. The problem is not a lack of interest in spiritual matters, it is a lack of interest in the established, old paradigm church. Secular post-modern people perceive the church as boring, irrelevant, unfriendly, and money hungry. Some even believe that the church lacks intelligence. George Barna states that 91 percent of non-Christians find congregations insensitive to their needs.[9]

The question is, therefore, what should the church be doing in terms of its mission outreach and evangelism to reach secular people in today's world? Tim Wright has suggested that when trying to reach unchurched people, congregations will do well to find experiential, relevant ways to share the truth of the gospel. People not only want to know about God, they want to experience God. The issue is not just truth, but relevance. Does the gospel make sense? Does it have something to say to my life? Can it make a difference?[10]

In my own experience as a pastor in the Seventh-Day Adventist Church, both within the Caribbean and in particular the North American context, where I am presently serving, I have grown steadily in my conviction that the major challenge facing the church today is—how to reach secular post-modern people for Christ. This conviction has deepened as I have engaged in various forms of evangelism and mission outreach. My conviction on this subject has also been validated through wide exposure in my academic journey at Andrews University SDA Theological Seminary. This synthesis of the field and the class room has led to my decision for writing this book on the subject. Therefore, my crucial intent in this book is to suggest a strategy that will allow the church to be intentional in its ministry and mission for the purpose of effectively reaching secular post-modern, unchurched men and women. This is not just another book, and I ask you dear reader to read it with the understanding that it is a sincere outgrowth of my passion for the subject, and reveals my vision for intentional ministry to lost souls that are seeking for the answers to life. It is also my hope that you share this same passion and vision for the church's mission and ministry to a post-modern generation.

Secularization, as is widely agreed, has impacted a growing number of people in North America both without and within the church. The same could be said for other areas of the world, the least of which would be Europe and other parts of the Americas, including South America, Canada, and the Caribbean. Other sectors of our world are not exempt from the growing specter of secular post-modernism. This is due in part to the recent phenomena of globalization. The phenomenal growth in technology and high speed travel has rendered our world a global village. The super -information high way of computer- internet, global cable access, and mass media communication networks that operate via satellite, has help to bring about deep cultural shifts. These cultural shifts are moving people away from their traditional moorings. People are now perceiving and viewing reality differently. We as a church must come to grips with the fact that most of our world has long since moved out of what has been characterized as a pre-modern era to a modern era and now most recently into the post-modern era. With this has come for most people a difference in understanding and knowing what is real in our world. This includes not only the physical realities of life but the metaphysical realities as well. Unfortunately or fortunately, the search for the answer as to what is truth, is open to a litany of voices- a plurality of meanings, each of which hold legitimacy in the post-modern dialogue. As we engage the world and our culture with the claims of the gospel, we must understand that for the most part the people living in our post-modern world and culture are no longer influenced by traditional forms of evangelism and methods of outreach. Consequently, the church must be intentional and culturally relevant in ministry, worship, and outreach if it hopes to ever reach them for Christ.

Historically, the successes of the traditional forms of evangelism and outreach as carried on by the Seventh-Day Adventist Church, has been in the area of other professed Christians coming out of "Babylon," or of individuals who are already friends of the church or close relatives of the members of the church. Very few have come in from the secular world. We have not been able to influence secular post-modern men and women to any degree that would lead them to find Christ or even join our church. This realization has caused some concern among leadership in our higher organization as it has become apparent that baptisms are down among the indigenous people of our society. A failure to reach secular people could only mean a failure to reach Americans themselves, whether first, second, or third generation. As a consequence our growth in membership has been among foreigners from the Hispanic community, the West Indian Community, the African community, and some other non immigrants. These are the individuals who are more likely to be reached by means of the more traditional approach to soul winning. It is a sociological principle that persons, who are seeking to orient themselves in a new place, seeking to make a new home, will often attach themselves to an institution that offers a sense of continuity. Here they can more often than not fill a need for belonging and also meet people more like themselves. This principle seems to operate in any social context. I can recall that in my pastorate on the Island of St.Croix in the U.S. Virgin Islands, we were reaching and baptizing individuals who were from the other Islands of the Caribbean that had migrated to make a new life for themselves in the Virgin Islands. Very few or non from among the citizenry of St.Croix were effectively reached through our evangelistic and other outreach efforts. I have seen this trend throughout my more than fifteen years of personal active ministry- wherever I have pastored a church or a district.

Church growth in terms of baptized membership has become remarkly slow among Caucasians and is slowing among African Americans. This is the case even among children born to immigrants. As Americans have been impacted by the secular post-modern condition that shapes peoples attitudes toward traditional institutions and societal norms, it is evident that we are failing to reach those (first, second, and third generations) whose attitudes toward religion, the church, or truth claims are reflective of the thorough secularization their fore fathers may not have experienced. We are now faced with a whole new mission frontier in our secular, post-modern world, and the challenges it poses for the church as we seek to "finish the work" and prepare a people to meet the soon coming King. Our success or failure here, as

Seventh-day Adventists, will depend on our attitude and willingness to break with tradition and ineffective methods that no longer have a place in the 21st Century Adventist mission paradigms. It is time for change and new visioning that would lead to intentional ministry on all levels of our church growth strategies. We dear not rest contented with the marginal successes of the tried and true methods of yesteryear. The great-commission mandate includes all people (see Matt.28:18-20; Rev.10:11; 14:6). It means, therefore, that the gospel must be taken not only to foreign lands or to those in "Babylon", but also to the secular people in our society. It also suggests that the church will need to be creative and innovative in the ways we try to reach secular people. Gone are the days when the church had the home-field advantage. As Craig Van Gelder has rightly said, "we are experiencing the end of our particular version of Christendom. The post-Christian reality of contemporary culture means that the church no longer has a privileged position and can no longer expect to receive preferential treatment. It is becoming just one more truth claim in the midst of a plurality of alternative truth claims, all of which are seen as relative."[11]

We must now do ministry from the margins, and this will require relevant cultural ways of ministering and preaching the gospel to a vast unchurched population.

The Reason for/and the Limitations of this Book

In light of the foregoing, this book was undertaken with the hope that it would be a source of help by providing ideas and principles that would help pastors, evangelists, and lay people in their efforts to reach secular people. What follows is a suggested strategy that delineates ways the church can be culturally relevant while remaining faithful to the gospel. In this book is a proposed strategy designed for targeting secular people, that would, by God's assisting grace, effectively reach and disciple them for Christ. It is limited to the idea of planting the intentional church that will structure its services, ministry, and discipling process in such a way as to reach and nurture secular people for the Kingdom of God. It is not an attempt to discuss the pros and cons of church planting. The main idea is to show how the church can be intentional by positioning itself strategically for the main purpose of ministering to and reaching the often unreached secular people.

Even though the strategic principles can find general application in unique contexts, this book is focused primarily on the North American context, namely the United States. It is not intended to be a standardized manual for reaching secular people in our mission outreach. It is an attempt to encourage our leaders and pastors to look at how the church can be intentional in reaching secular people. In this book I suggest relevant ways that the church can minister to secular people. The book is intended to provide a framework from which further study and investigation can be undertaken to discover new and innovative ways of reaching out to secular people. No attempt has been made to field-test the suggestions, strategies, or ideas that emerge from this book. The overall content is intended to be of a more descriptive and practical nature. In this book I approach the subject of reaching secular people from the perspective of being intentional in the way the church does ministry. Since secular people are turned off by traditional church programming, it means that the church, in order to reach the secular population in a meaningful way, would have to be intentional in its specific areas of ministry and mission outreach.

The Method

I have addressed this in seven chapters. Chapter 1 is the introduction. Chapter 2 deals with an understanding of secularization by looking at some commonly held definitions and presenting a definition of my own. This chapter also profiles secular people and their traits and ways of thinking. Chapter 3 deals with secularization in America by looking at the secularization process as it affected higher education, the churches, and the religious experience of the American people. It deals with some polling data that shows the decline in church attendance and people's general attitude toward the church and God. It seeks to show that, in spite of a high profession of religion in America, there is still considerable secularity among the population.

Chapter 4 develops a biblical and theological rationale for reaching secular people. This chapter roots that rationale in the concept of the

Missio Dei. It then shows how Christ and Paul in the New Testament carried forward the *Missio Dei* and did so by reaching different audiences by using varying approaches. They adapted their message and teaching to suit the particular audience. Other examples are discussed as to how God spoke to people in language they could understand and thus reached them where they were. The chapter also shows how Christ ministered to the felt needs of people and thus gained an entrance to their greater spiritual need. The chapter finally ends by examining some of Ellen G. White's statements on the need for reaching all classes of people in different ways. Ellen G. White's statements on the need for new and untried methods for reaching people with the gospel are also given in this chapter.

Chapter 5 is an analysis of three models for reaching secular people. Chapter 6 emerges out of this context as a suggested strategy for reaching secular people. It deals with a church-planting concept that is intentional and gives a strategic planning process for its accomplishment. It also gives some broad-based principles and suggestions for various ministries and strategies that can be used for reaching and discipling secular-unchurched people. Chapter 7 is the general summary and reflections of the book.

Chapter 1 Notes

1.   Gottfried Oosterwal, "Faith and Mission in a Secularized World," Department of World Mission, Andrews University Theological Seminary, April 5, 1993.

2.   Darrell L. Guder, *Missional Church: A Vision for the Sending of the Church in North America* (Grand Rapids, MI: Wm. B. Eerdmans, 1998), 37.

3.   Ibid.

4.   Douglas John Hill, "Metamorphosis: From Christendom to Diaspora," in *Confident Witness Changing World: Rediscovering the Gospel in North America*, ed. Craig Van Gelder (Grand Rapids, MI: Wm. B. Eerdmans, 1999), 69.

5. Chris Wright, "The Case Against Pluralism" in *The Unique Christ in Our Pluralist World*, ed. Bruce J. Nicholls (Grand Rapids, MI: Baker Book House, 1994), 32.

6. Ibid., 33.

7. Wade Clark Roof, *Spiritual Market Place: Baby Boomers and the Remaking of American Religion* (Princeton, NJ: Princeton University Press, 1999), 124. See also Barry A. Kozman and Seymour P. Lachman, *One Nation Under God: Religion in Contemporary American Society* (New York: Crown Trade Paperbacks, 1993), 15-17.

8. Guder, 44.

9. George Barna, *The Barna Report 1992-1993* (Ventura, CA: Regal Books, 1992), 69.

10. Tim Wright, *Unfinished Evangelism: More Than Getting Them in the Door* (Minneapolis: Augsburg, 1995), 23, 24.

11. Craig Van Gelder, "Defining the Center-Finding the Boundaries: The Challenge of Re-Visioning the Church in North America for the Twenty-First Century" in *The Church Between Gospel and Culture: The Emerging Mission in North America*, eds. George R. Hunsberger and Craig Van Gelder (Grand Rapids, MI: William B. Eerdmans Publishing Company, 1996), 41.

CHAPTER 2

UNDERSTANDING SECULARIZATION

Secularization is a phenomenon that affects most areas of life in our world. Because it is a force to be reckoned with, especially in the evangelistic efforts of the Christian church, it is critical that an understanding of secularization and the secular mind be established.

The intent of this chapter is to present an understanding of secularization with emphasis on North America. To begin, a definition of secularization is given, followed by a defining of the secular mind, and finally a secular mind grouping.

Definition

Secularization, a process that has affected a complex and massive change in cultural, social, and religious behavior among varying people groups, defies a simple explanation.[1] However, it is possible to focus on some general elements of an explanation and I will do so by looking at some commonly held definitions of secularization and then attempt a definition for the purpose of this book.

A Misleading Definition

The misleading definition of secularization that I now refer to is that definition that sees secularization in purely substantive terms as the gradual decline of religious belief (the "decline of religion thesis").[2]

The decline is usually measured quantitatively, in terms of declining statistics, or qualitatively, in terms of a decline of personal faith from some pre-modern standard. The assumption is that since a common usage definition of Christianity, for example, is concerned with church attendance, membership, and presence at rites of passage, these constitute significant elements of a definition of religion, and that any move away from this institutional participation involves religious decline.[3]

It is also seen in terms of a linear decline of religion (earlier views from the time of Max Weber onward) in social prominence and cultural influence due to the inevitable onslaught of rationality. [4] People are seen as being better educated and less credulous.[5]

"Committed atheists—the sort of people who join rationalist and humanist associations—and some very liberal Christians believe that religion has lost its medieval dominance because modern people are too clever to believe in old superstitions."[6]

Christopher Kaiser sees two problems with this definition of secularization:

1. The growing popularity of religious faith in secularized countries, such as the United States, and the recent resurgence of fundamentalism around the world pose a serious challenge to this form of the "secularization thesis."

2. The decline-of-religion thesis commonly implies (or presupposes) incompatibility between religious belief and technology and science (or some other form of rationality).

Nonetheless, recent studies in the history of science give evidence that religious belief was one of the primary catalysts behind the development of modern science and technology (and rationality generally).[7]

Russell Staples, regarding this subject, points out that the process of secularization is no more considered to be the demise of religion in an absolute sense, but more commonly understood as engendering change in the forms of religion.[8]

> "There is much more inclination to regard religion as a cultural universal, which fulfills important functions in society, and as being more prone to undergo change than extinction. Religions legitimate and motivate and provide systems of meaning and value and community and self-affirmation and opportunity for alternate life-styles. . . . Religions are born and die, elements are added to and subtracted from them, and adherents may switch from one to another; but religion itself continues."[9]

In this connection, Peter L. Berger asserts that secularization does not appear to be as far-reaching and as inexorable as many theories of modern thinkers have assumed. Not only is the Third World full of religious eruptions, some of which have profound political significance, but evidence also from the Soviet Union (not only on the persistence of religion after a half century of government attempts to suppress it, but on the resurgence of religious impulses in the most unlikely places) is most astounding. Berger also states that in the Western world there have been indications in recent years that the reports of God's demise have been somewhat exaggerated.[10]

It is now evident that even though secularization may seem to have been crowding God out of the world as we know it, the new secularization (a product of post-modernism and the new age movement) encourages us to equate God with the cosmos.[11]

Boa and Bowman further points out that the increasing secularization of the West in the years following WWII left a spiritual vacuum into which a variety of religious movements flourished, offering a spiritual experience. This new trend had become evident in the 1960's and the 1970's with the charismatic movement characterized by such phenomena as speaking in tongues, prophesying, and healing ministries etc., at the same time millions of Americans were also turning to Eastern religions to gain spiritual experiences. The 1960's and the 1970's also experienced an explosive growth in the interest of the occult. The occult became a multimillion-dollar market, evidenced by the sale of such things as tarot cards and other paraphernalia as well as books emphasizing such occult themes as Rosemary's Baby (1968) and The Exorcist (1973). This new interest of the new age has adherents today in the millions. People are still incurably religious and are seeking to find personal fulfillment in religious experiences on their own terms- with God as some force or power perhaps, but not as the standard of truth or transcendent ruler of the universe or the lives of men and women.[12]

It is obvious that a linear decline of religion with emphasis on its extinction in the absolute sense cannot be an adequate definition of secularization as it is understood today. Increasing knowledge and maturity cannot alone explain the decline of religion or define secularization. Hence a more generally held common definition of secularization needs to be set forth, one that will explain why religious beliefs are less plausible or credible than they once were.

A Plausible Definition

The following definitions are considered (for the purpose of this study) to be in line with a more plausible meaning of secularization. These definitions must be taken within the context of the evolution of secularization in certain historical processes (particularly the modern and post-modern eras), which provide a setting for its meaning within some general conditions that have affected our present world. A quick look at what is meant by the modern and post-modern periods of our history and culture now becomes necessary.

The Modern Era

The term "modern era" presupposes what is also known as the "pre-modern era." The modern era is generally believed to have begun with the rise of the Enlightenment following the thirty years war. Some historians date the genesis of the modern era from an even earlier period around 1641 when Rene Descartes made his famous statement, *cogito ergo sum* ("I think, therefore I am").[13]

Rene Descartes is thus considered to be the first modern philosopher essentially because he was more concerned with *how* one knows rather than *what* one knows. This shift in philosophical thinking began the age of reason in which naturalism espoused the epistemological concept of knowing before being.[14]

Human nature was considered by definition a thinking substance and the human self an autonomous rational being. Along this same corridor of time came Isaac Newton as a twin bill to Descartes. Newton saw the world in mechanical terms. The scientific framework that Newton provided essentially entailed the world and the laws that operate within it as fixed laws ready to be discovered and analyzed by the human mind. Thus Grenz concludes that "the modern human can appropriately be characterized as Descartes's autonomous, rational substance encountering Newton's mechanical world."[15]

Into this modern era man stepped with the enlightenment emphasizing reason as the supreme and all sufficient means of knowing what is real and true in our world. Reality and truth in this context is an ontological and physical entity existing independently of the knower, waiting to be discovered and verified by means of the scientific approach. Man's rise toward progress and improvement of himself and society became a certainty in the modern view of things. An increase in scientific knowledge along such lines as the social sciences, physics, biology, and technology gave rise to a host of modern inventions and scientific solutions to some of man's nemeses. The society and it's culture resulting from this explosive growth in the scientific revolution lead to a new frontier in the philosophical sense. Whereas in the pre-modern era the world and the cosmos was of a sacral nature (meaning that man understood reality and truth as coming through revelation from an omnipotent God who ordered all things, and the Holy Scriptures as the authoritative guide in man's ability to know what was real and true), the modern era brought a secularizing influence with man an autonomous self and his reason an autonomous guide. Sire rightfully observes that:

"the notion of the autonomy of human reason liberated the human mind from the authority of the ancients. Scientific and technical progress came not from the notions revealed in Scripture but from the assumption that human reason could indeed find it's way toward the truth. Such knowledge was power, instrumental power— power over nature, power to get us what we want. In science, the results were stellar. In philosophy, however, the move from *being* to *knowing,* from the primacy of God who creates and reveals to the primacy of the self that knows on it's own, was fatal. It both set the agenda for modern philosophy from Locke to Kant and sparked, as well, the recoil of postmodern philosophy from Nietzsche to Derrida as humanistic optimism flirted with despair."[16]

The modern period for all intent and purposes was characterized by a spirit of optimism concerning the positive development of the empirical method. It took on the philosophical contours that place man at the center of a new epistemological view of reality. That which could be verified by the use of reason and demonstrable fact was the new way to a certain future. Man had now come of age. The major shift from a pre-scientific world view gave promise of a new age where human beings were the final arbiters of their own *sitz im leben.* Scientific progress furnished the new evidence for a growing consciousness that the old social order shaped by the institution of the religious establishment and it's insistence of the primacy of revelation, and it's faith in a transcendent being who ordered all processes of knowing had failed. Religion in the public polity was increasingly sidelined in favor of the rational and naturalistic ordering of life. Faith as an universal rallying point for all people was increasingly relegated to a matter of private experience. What had now characterized this modern era more than any other aspect of it was the disassociation of religious faith and practice from the new structuring of a new age. The theistic view of a personal God who created, sustained and ordered the universe was basic to the Christian faith but not to the philosophical tenets of the scientific revolution. What was taking shape was a worldview founded on naturalism. Naturalism denied the reality of the transcendent. It is without question that naturalism has been the predominant world view in our modern age. Throughout this period a great deal of secularization as we now know it took place.[17]

It is believed by certain Christian thinkers that this period (known as the modern age) lasted for 200 years, from the fall of the Bastille in 1798 to the fall of the Berlin Wall in 1989.[18] During this period the shaping of modern culture with it's secularizing influences found expressions in the institutional forms that are still with us today. Such developments as the modern nation-states, market capitalism, bureaucratic structures, major systems in technology, and mass media centers have become visible dominant cultural expressions of the drive toward progress and solutions to the problems of life. These were the carriers of the development and construction of what is known as the metanarratives and centers of absolutistic models that grew out of the enlightenment and took root in a modern culture that promised utopia. "For a time" says Van Gelder "toward the end of the nineteenth century, it appeared that the modern project was achieving its aims. The realities of twentieth-century world wars and totalitarian regimes, however, ended this illusion on the European continent and in England....the unraveling of Keynesian economics and capitalistic Fordism in the midst of the radical cultural shifts of the 1960s and 1970s has accomplished the equivalent collapsing of this illusion in North America.[19]

In more recent times the uncertainties and despair throughout our society has been heightened by the obvious collapse of the promissory note undergirding modernism's claim to lead humanity to a certain future of peace and prosperity. This failure of modernity to deliver on what had been promised is further evidenced in the collapse of institutions and the rise in cultural conflicts over issues that define our ethics, our common humanity, and our struggle for cohesiveness. Who can deny the lingering inequities of our capitalist system where in a culture of plenty we are still haunted by grinding poverty and socio-economic injustices? The on going debate over the meaning of the nature and dignity of human life represents one aspect of the culture wars (on such issues as abortion and human cloning) that leaves us politically and socially divided. Recent developments that serve to undermine the traditional family unit of male- female, is now realized in the legal right granted by certain municipalities allowing homosexual couples to be united in same-sex marriages. What is even more telling in this regard is the right given to these same-sex couples to be able to adopt children and raise them in a family structure with values that are without question a major departure from the sacred norm of the traditional nuclear family. This small sampling indicates the unfortunate decline in some of our moral and cultural values. Our present moral crisis serves as an indicator that modernism and the enlightenment project has failed to live up to it's claims.

The general consensus among trend watchers and contemporary culture commentators is that the modern project is weakening and has indeed weakened. It is no longer tenable to espouse a view that says "we can bring rational management to improving the quality of life through technological developments. The confident claim of objectivity in both reason and method, which under girded the project for so many decades, has been shown to be but yet another paradigm of social construction subject to the same relativity of all social constructs."[20]

The so-called meta-narratives, which were once accepted as normative, are now being met with greater skepticism. One such meta-narrative is the idea of "unlimited development," which has been delegitimated, or deprived of it's authoritative acceptance, due to certain of the following: "environmental pollution, the depletion of natural resources, fear of global warming and increasing depletion of the ozone layer, serious accidents at facilities such as chemical factories and nuclear power plants, increased poverty in the world because of unequal development, and the observation that developed nations seem to reach an optimum point in development at which economic decline sets in and the overall quality of life begins to deteriorate."[21]

This growing incredulity toward the meta-narratives and "absolute social constructs" that dominated the modern period is what is called the "legitimation crisis." This crisis is said to reach into all areas of contemporary life. What we are faced with in this cultural shift is a plurality of beliefs and values. With no particular or universal value system that provides the grounds for all values in society, it is no longer possible to legitimize any particular set of values or any value system. This mega-shift away from the certainties that characterized most of the modern period has lead to the belief that we are entering into a new cultural and philosophical approach to truth and reality called postmodernism. To this next era we now turn our attention.

The Postmodern era

The postmodern era is characterized by an ethos variously referred to as postmodernism. Post- modernism is in turn considered to be a reaction against modernism- to the expectations or underlying assumptions of the modern era. The Modern period as discussed above, failed to deliver on its promise of utopia. Our society, instead of being in a state of uninterrupted progress and development (with peace and security) is anything but. Not that every thing in the modern world was or is negative or a failure. There has been much improvement in the quality of life, and much that is positive arising out of the developments of the cultural and scientific revolutions of the modern era. Some of these benefits include better health care through advanced medical technology, quicker and easier travel through improved modes of transportation, the development of urban centers of learning through universities, and information systems that opened up access to knowledge in all areas of life, our world, and the universe. David Wells has further observed that our technological achievements have made our world a lot more comfortable, somewhat safer and more productive. Modernization has "enlarged our knowledge of the world, secured freedoms once only dreamed of, expanded rights, opened the doors of education, lifted hopes, and mightily multiplied our prosperity."[22]

On the flip side however, there has been the negative fallout to the apparent successes and advancements in the modern experiment. The intentional exclusion of faith as a thought shaping view of life in favor of the certainties of the scientific and empirical methods of discovery has exacted a heavy spiritual toll that has left us empty, disillusioned and psychologically bereft. Alas, the outcomes of our modern way of life has ripened into fragmented communities, cultural conflicts, a cosmic loneliness, greater anxiety as we view the forces of history as out of control, a crime ridden society, a disruption in the cohesiveness of families, human relationships,   and a confused state of values clarification. In order to more fully comprehend the postmodern ethos, one will have to grapple with the costs and the losses that have been and are even now being suffered in our present flux in culture due to the modern experiment. Wells has articulated well the difficulties that modernization has heaped upon us throughout most of the twentieth century. Wells notes for example that even though the average family income in America had increased by two-thirds in constant dollars between 1945 and 1973, and unemployment had dropped from a high in the depression of one in three to less than one in ten by 1993, and that even though the American Way of Life had become a byword in many parts of the world, study after study conducted during this same period suggested that newly prosperous Americans who had the money and the leisure time to buy and do the things that had only been a dream for their parents, (newly prosperous Americans) had become increasingly less satisfied with their lives.[23]

> "City streets" says Wells, "became less and less hospitable at night, drugs became more and more prevalent, inner cities began to rot, and a whole generation of baby-boomers became painfully alienated from their parents and their society. As economic welfare increased in this country during the postwar period....psychological well-being declined."[24]

The hunger for more in the hour of plenty that many thought would have displaced the emptiness in the human spirit that modernization had inflicted led to sore disappointment. While it is true that we now enjoy increased prosperity, the means by which this prosperity has come- "the reorganization of our world by the processes of modernization-has diminished our souls."[25]

How then do we attempt a definition of postmodernism as it relates to our understanding of secularization? Keeping in mind that secularization as we have experienced it and understood it grew out of the driving forces of modernization, makes it critical that we understand that although the foundations of modernity are crumbling (and to some extent have already crumbled), the superstructure seems to be intact. For while the crumbling foundations of modernity are evident in the human and societal conditions as highlighted above, the modern worldview is still a force in the mass media, the formative educational institutions, and our popular Western consciousness. Indeed, says R. Albert Mohler, Jr., "modern assumptions still frame the thinking of most North Americans and Europeans-and it is still a powerful mission movement around the globe."[26]

Wells insightfully points out that while Enlightenment dogma about inevitable progress no longer holds a place in our new culture and is disappearing in the quick sands of self-doubt, most Enlightenment ideas on the other hand, fit comfortably in our new culture.[27]

What does all this mean as we attempt to explain something of the postmodern condition? It means, as Mohler has observed, that postmodern philosophy is some what "limited in reach to the elite academic circles common to the ideological left and the so-called New Class of post—World War II intellectuals in the knowledge industry. It is not yet formative in the worldviews of most individuals in mass culture." Yet Mohler contends that something significant and enduring has happened in the Western mind. "Modernity" says Mohler, "is giving way to something new—something *post-the-modern*." Mohler goes on to explain that "the so-called death of the meta-narrative, the demise of the grand explanatory theory or universal truth, ensures that postmodernism will not be a single, unified reality."[28]

Postmodernism (because of it's aversion to uniformity and absolute certainties) poses a challenge on any attempt at defining it. In defining the term— the postmodern era— we are met with yet more confusion because of the interchange of the terms postmodernity and postmodernism. In the social sciences they make use of the term postmodernity but in the arts and humanities they prefer the term postmodernism. "Postmodernity refers more to a cultural condition or state of being while postmodernism focuses more on a cultural movement or a plurality of movements within culture." The concept of postmodernism itself grew out of the works of men such as Lyortard,

Derrida, Foucault, Habermas, Baudrillard, and Jameson, who in the 1970's and the early 1980's insisted that there was a need for a shift in our understanding of modern life.[29]

These men took their ques from the revolutionary changes (such as in art and architecture) that were impacting society back in the 1960s and the 1970s. The basic idea of deconstruction of meta-narrative was central to their understanding of what was taking shape, and they sought to apply this new understanding to every area of every day life. "Their thesis" says Van Gelder, "is that any particular expression of narrative is relative, and that it is preferable to experience life in terms of eclecticism or as a collage of narratives." This shift to a relativistic world view was inspired somewhat by a number of movements effecting social change in the decade of the 1960s. Such movements as the civil rights movement challenged society to be consistent in balancing equality with freedom. The counterculture movement was yet another that unseated the shoulds and oughts of Christian culture as the basis for guiding social change. Other forces that helped to influence the growing spirit of relativism during that time was the Vietnam War and the antiwar movement (social and political forces) that forced us to rethink our reliance on the reliability of technology to render final solutions to social and moral Complexities. And the Watergate scandal worked to demythologize the intrinsic authority of institutions over our lives. Social and political changes such as the foregoing, were wide spread in the wider culture, and led inevitably toward fragmentation and relativism.[30]

Defining postmodernism within this context and in the simplest terms would mean that postmodernism is as some suggest a dislocating of the human condition characterized by two things: a disbelief in any claim to objective truth and a deep seated belief that morality is relative. Coming as a reaction to modernism, postmodernism is therefore characterized by the idea of the deconstruction of the meta-narrative or the dismantling of absolute constructs on reality. As David S. Dockery has suggested "people are unlikely to believe that there are universal ideals or truths. Students in high school and institutions of higher education are likely to have been bombarded with conflicting truth claims and have thus concluded that all ideals or truths are relative."[31]

A recent experience that I had while attending the NJEA Convention for teachers bears out the fact that individuals today hold to the idea that truth is relative. I happened to stop by the table of a school teacher from the Northern Jersey area who had authored a set of teaching-guide manuals for grade teachers. As I conversed with this teacher on the nature and content of her teaching manuals, our conversation entailed a brief mention of the postmodern ideas on truth claims. Where upon this teacher asserted that she considered herself to be a postmodern person because she believed and shared the view that no one has or knows whether or not there is any one truth that is above or central to any other. She stated that truth was not the sole possession of any one, or group, or community. Truth in her opinion was relative and conditional on the situation or persons making such claims. In her own admition, and from a religious point of view, she had been "tired of people" (those that shared their religious convictions with her) "trying to cram their religion down my throat." This attitude is common among people in today's world, as such people are encountered on all levels and in most areas of our society. People have adopted an eclectic approach to life in which they decide what is true or not true according to their own taste. "Claims to truth, proclamation of that truth, and sharing one's faith are viewed as improper behavior or bad manners. Thus, we say postmodernism is dislocating because it tends to throw people out of worldviews they have traditionally held."[32] Postmodernism goes a step further in that it presents a sense of incoherence and defines human experience as lacking a normative or logical explanation of any observable reality. In this respect it is more than just mere relativism. "It impacts our literature, fashion, art, architecture, music, morality, and theology." James Sire has outlined five characteristics of postmodernism: (1) Things and events do not have intrinsic meaning. There is only continuous interpretation of the world. (2) Continuous examination of the world requires a contextual examination. We ourselves are a part of the context. (3) Interpretation depends not on the external text or its author but on the relative view point and particular values of the interpreter. (4) Language is not neutral but relative and value laden. (5) Language conveys ideology.[33]

Postmodernism is also characterized as having nostalgia for the past. This is in keeping with one of its characteristics as being eclectic. A recent article "Boomers on Broadway" featured in *Readers Digest* discusses the nostalgic way Baby Boomers in our day are bringing together today's music with the music of the past. This eclectic production of Broadway musical productions, such as *Jersey Boys,* is intentional for the purposes of bringing the Baby Boomer generation nostalgically into the past. "You're 40 something (okay, maybe 50), and you know you shouldn't, but before you can stop yourself, you're on your feet. Your hips are swaying and you are swinging with the melody. You're back in time, on the dance floor at the high school sock hop. You're home." This is precisely where Marshall Brickman, co-writer of *Jersey Boys*, wants you to be. "His musical, featuring The Four Seasons' infectious blend of doo-wop, R&B and pop, is the latest in a slew of shows celebrating the music of the 60s and 70s."[34]

Baby Boomers are flocking to theaters every where these musical productions are shown, "chasing the music, trying to get home." In this respect the production of Jersey Boys and other Broadway shows such as *Mamma Mia!*, featuring the music of *ABBA,* All Shook Up (Elvis Presely), and Lennon, have been extremely successful. *Mamma Mia!* Which opened in London six years ago and on Broadway in 2001 is said to be the No.1 show in the world, with 11 global productions. The show takes in more than $8 million a week, bringing in more than 18,000 international ticket holders each night. More than 23 million people have seen it. The cast album is reported to have gone platinum in this country. Most of these sales are from Baby Boomers who are said to account for half of the discretionary spending of this country. This nostalgia for the past which is characteristic of the postmodern period has been exhibited by the Baby Boomer generation- a generation that is characterized as "the first mass media generation, and their common bond music....there's an impulse toward nostalgia, when things were a little more coherent, a little more solid, a little simpler."[35]

This nostalgia for the past that allows for the postmodern eclectic approach to life, not only finds expression in the entertainment world of art forms such as music and Broadway Theater, but is also evident in the new approach to spirituality and religion.

The return to religion is yet another aspect of postmodernism that is truly eclectic in nature. Traditional religions are experiencing revival and renewal, and this new interest in religion and spirituality is given the pejorative label of fundamentalism. Social scientists are calling this the "unsecularization of the world."[36]

It is to be noted however that this so-called unsecularization of the world needs to be taken with a great deal of caution. This postmodern reaction against what is perceived as the decline and failure of the "false gods" (quasi-religious movements as communism, secular humanism, and the western belief in the inevitability of progress) carries with it eclecticism. This return to what could be considered "traditional religion," incorporates a multiplicity of choices on religious themes that could be labeled pastiche spirituality. This has very significant implications for our understanding of secularization as it is pushed forward by postmodernism, for "it is obvious that religion lies at the very heart of the postmodern condition." Some observers express the need for caution in jumping to conclusions about this return to religion by postmodern people. This return to "the old gods along with the rise of the New Age" is considered to be "a step backward rather than forward."[37]

This step backward is a step into eclecticism, a characteristic of the postmodern condition that celebrates the relativism of all view points and the freedom of individual choices. While we maybe hopeful, because of the return to religion in the traditional sense by the secular- postmodern people of our day, we must recognize that it does not represent a substantive approach to faith as fundamentally understood. Rather this return is characterized by a radicalized form of modernism.[38]

In the modern period the emphasis was on the self-sufficiency of reason and the scientific approach to life, thus sidelining God and faith-pushing both to the margins of public domain. In the postmodern era, on the other hand, it could be argued that religious experience and spirituality are central to human life. That religious experience and that spirituality that is experienced by the postmodernist however, is nothing more than a radicalized modernism. The postmodern person sees all truth claims as relative and all such claims are equally valid.

Thus all religions and all religious experiences are deserving of equal status. What's more, since there is no universal objective truth or any grand overarching story, or any absolute standard to which one is to subscribe, the individual determines his or her own truth by exercising individual choices from a collage of meanings. William Lane Craig puts it this way, "the postmodernist is not merely saying that we cannot know with certainty which religious worldview is true and we therefore must be open-minded; rather he maintains that none can be excluded in deference to the allegedly one true religion." What does this say for the unsecularization of the world?[39]

Indeed what does this say about the challenge the church now faces in advancing the uncompromising claims of Divine revelation embodied in Scripture as truth with a capital T? Humberto M. Rasi maintains that postmodernism, although understood as a reaction to the progressive and rationalistic claims of modernism, has nonetheless pushed forward secularization by maintaining that human beings cannot have access to reality and, therefore, have no way of perceiving truth. This has led Rasi to conclude that such secularizing influences as that already discussed, has seriously curtailed the church's ability to mold society and to convey truth as God's revelation. "Indeed" says Rasi, "the process of secularization has reached a point where the church's claim as the preserver and proclaimer of truth is largely disregarded, if not rejected, in Western societies."[40]

The task of reaching a secular-postmodern society doesn't seem to be getting any easier, although the playing fields are changing in significant ways. The position of the church and Christian truth claims that were accorded a favorable hearing in certain contexts is now in the decline. As will be observed in chapter three of this book, Christians are now experiencing a status as the new beleaguer minority in particular societal institutions and cultural environments. This is all characteristic of the post-modern element of pervasive pluralism. This characteristic (pluralism) is a further development in our attempt to understand the post-modern condition.

Pluralism, discussed as a characteristic of postmodernism, does not necessarily exhaust any attempt at defining such a difficult concept. It is however critical to our understanding the secularization process in the postmodern context. For this reason we must focus on pluralism as an element that gives us added insight into a very difficult cultural ethos of our time. The basic driving force behind the pluralism that flourishes in the postmodern context has been the shift in the intellectual clime from the modern era into what is styled post-*the-modern*. This developing postmodern mind has sometimes been prone to a dogmatic relativism and a compulsively fragmenting skepticism. According to Richard Tarnas the cultural ethos that has accompanied it has at times deteriorated into cynical detachment and spiritless pastiche. It is evident, says Tarnas, that along with complexity, and ambiguity, one of the most significant characteristics of the larger postmodern intellectual situation is pluralism. This referent characteristic is among the necessary characteristics of ambiguity and complexity that allows for an emergence of a fundamentally new form of intellectual vision— an intellectual vision that will both preserve and transcend the current state of extraordinary differentiation.[41]

Defining the postmodern era in the context of a pluralism that pushes forward the secularization process is necessary to our understanding of the major shift in the intellectual climate of our day. This intellectual shift from the modern period to that of the contemporary scene allows for no one perspective, according to Tarnar, "religious, scientific, or philosophical," to have "the upper hand, yet that situation has encouraged an almost unprecedented intellectual flexibility and cross-fertilization, reflected in the widespread call for, and practice of, open conversation between different understandings, different vocabularies, different cultural paradigms." Considered as a whole, the extreme fluidity and multiplicity of the current intellectual scene can hardly be over emphasized. Tarnar maintains that the postmodern mind as it presently stands is not only a maelstrom of unresolved diversity, but just about every element of the Western intellectual past is currently active in one form or another, contributing to the vitality and confusion of the present situation.[42]

Many of postmodernism's predecessors have reemerged to play new roles in the current intellectual scene. Because of this, any generalizations about the postmodern mind have to be qualified by a recognition of the presence of such major predecessors as the "various still-vital forms of the modern sensibility, of the scientific mind, of Romanticism and Enlightenment, of Renaissance syncretism, of Protestantism, Catholicism, and Judaism-all of these, at various stages of development and ecumenical interpretation, continue today to be influential factors."[43]

There are still yet other elements, says Tarnas, that have reemerged to play new roles in the current intellectual scene. Certain elements of the Western cultural tradition going as far back as the Hellenistic era and classical Greece-Platonic and Pre-Socratic philosophy, Hermeticism, mythology, the mystery religions—all have reentered the stage on the new postmodern intellectual front. These in turn have been impacted and affected by still other non-western cultural traditions such as the Buddhist and Hindu mystical traditions; "by underground cultural streams from within the West itself, such as Gnosticism and the major esoteric traditions; and by indigenous and archaic perspectives antedating Western civilization altogether, such as Neolithic European and Native American spiritual traditions-all gathering now on the intellectual stage as if for some kind of climatic synthesis."[44]

The present climate that fosters open conversation, and embraces various traditions, and cultural and intellectual understandings, continues to affect the cultural and intellectual role of religion in the present secularizing and pluralistic developments in the postmodern era. While it can be substantiated that the influence of institutionalized religion has been on the decline, religious sensibility itself has been revitalized by the newly ambiguous intellectual circumstances of the postmodern era. Contemporary religion, says Tarner has been revitalized by its own plurality, finding new forms of expression and new sources of inspiration and illumination that include Eastern mysticism and psychedelic self- exploration to liberation theology and ecofeminist spirituality.[45]

How does such religious interest, and such an intellectual openness, characterized by a pluralism in our postmodern times, demonstrate the secularizing influence of the present intellectual climate that allows for no traditional and or orthodox Christian understanding and Biblical truth claims? The answer to this question is embedded in the aforementioned discussion on the epistemological understanding in the postmodern view. With all previous social constructs on reality, and any meta-narrative or absolute claims on truth having been met with greater skepticism and delegitamizing collapse on meaning, it is not surprising that a professed openness to all views and particular truth claims that is supposedly found in the pluralism of today, is still discriminatory toward any view that claims to be exclusive or normative. It is in this way that postmodernism with its variant relativism and incredulity toward any absolute claims on reality, relegates any substantive Christian faith and truth claims to the margins, and confine them "to a sort of cultural red light district,"[46] to the same extent and more radically so, as was the case in the modern take. A very recent and familiar case in point, is the ABC Barbara Walters Special on the topic, "Heaven, where is it, and how do we get there?" It is considered to be one of the most interesting TV specials ever done by Barbara Walters. The point of major intrigue was the obvious inclusiveness of all major religions, and their views of Heaven and how we get there. The conversation was wide open to any belief system including atheists who had a definite say about the matter. This particular special took two hours, a considerable time slot for any such topic, one that presented all of the options— "the long cafeteria line of religious opinions that characterize American pluralism."[47]

But of course such openness is but a reflection of the pervasive pluralism in the postmodern intellectual climate that says one view is as good as another, in particular, when it is in reference to humanity's quest to find God and secure a place in the after life. Gregory Tomlin writing for the *Baptist Press* online, in an article titled "FIRST PERSON: Do all roads lead to heaven?" makes the point that from the outset the goal is clear: "present what you can in two hours about humanity's millennia of struggle in every corner of the globe to find peace with God and enter into His presence. In the process, all things are to be presented equally...supposedly."[48]

What is to be noted however is the obvious lack of journalistic objectivity on two very important counts. The first is what Tomlin refers to as Barbara Walters' obvious lack of journalistic objectivity in that she "fawns over the Dalai Lama in a remote mountain village in India, even going so far as to offer him a kiss on the cheek, which the reincarnated Buddha accepts with gratitude." Tomlin goes on to report that Rob Wallace, the program's producer, told him that "Walters was feeling much more compassionate after her brief meeting with his holiness in the Himalayas."[49]

Contrasted with this is the second point on the obvious lack of journalistic objectivity when it came time to interview Pastor Ted Haggard, former pastor of the New Life Church in Colorado Springs, Colo., and former president of the National Association of Evangelicals. Tomlin observes that "Haggard walked into the interview with a mammoth bulls-eye tattooed on his forehead, figuratively speaking. He was, after all, the only person in the program, save a member of Islamic Jihad, who preached an exclusive message of salvation through his God."[50]

Keeping in mind that this particular interview is supposedly inclusive and all embracing of the major points of view in the pluralist conversation, makes the comments that follow during the interview with Pastor Haggard much more enlightening.

The following comments made by the interviewer Barbara Walters and the interviewee Pastor Haggard highlights very well this second point of concern. Haggard was one of the leaders of the modern evangelical movement, of which Walters is said to have commented that they (modern evangelicals) "see themselves as the purist version of the faith, with a God-given mission to save the world." Walters also pointed out the fact of evangelicalism's support of George W. Bush and the fact that so many red-state voters voted for "43" in the November 2004 election. Added to this are the comments made on the social emphases of the conservatives. Such "social issues like abortion, stem cell research, euthanasia and same-sex marriages" which says Walters "critics say the evangelicals and other conservative groups inappropriately apply the Bible's lessons to fit their agendas." Keep in mind that all this was said during the documentary on heaven.[51]

"Yes," says Tomlin, "this is the agenda of those nasty evangelicals, those born again." Tomlin is quick to point out that Haggard describes evangelicals as people who hold to the belief that you must be born again, that Jesus is the Son of God and that the Bible is God's word.[52]

Further Haggard himself commented during the interview that "there is only one guaranteed way to go to heaven according to the scriptures, and that is through Jesus Christ...when asked by Walters if a homosexual could go to heaven, he replied, Homosexuals, lesbians, Republicans, Democrats...everybody must choose to respond to the love of God in Jesus Christ on the cross and have a guarantee of eternal life."[53]

What is most interesting is the way this former evangelical Christian representative's comments were singled out as being "judgmental."[54] Certainly these are exclusive claims made by a Christian in an open dialogue in the pluralist conversation. But then this is exactly the point I have been making as concerns exclusive or absolute truth claims in the traditional Christian sense. Within the postmodern context of a new sensibility toward inclusiveness and open tolerance of all points of view there is still the unwritten code that says no one making claims to having the only way to truth, or as in this case the way to heaven, is allowed in. Such claims are seen as narrow minded, bigoted and at best down right judgmental. So, where does that leave us? What does all this say in response to the proposition that the wide spread interest in religion in the postmodern world is evidence of the unsecularization of the world? Indeed as a Seventh—day Adventist minister I must ask, where does that leave us who make bold claims of being the one true church, with God's last warning message to a perishing world, whether religious and/or otherwise? What does this say to you and me who make the unapologetic claim that the "Three Angels Messages" is the present truth for this time and that we as a church have the truth as sure as God Himself lives? Viewing these questions within the context of what is being discussed on the subject of postmodernism, leads one to understand that instead of an unsecularization of the world, the postmodern condition pushes forward the secularization process in more radical ways than we ever realized. We are challenged more than ever before to preach the gospel and live the Christian faith with more intentionality and in ways that must exceed the traditions of the past. It is very evident that we do not live in an unsecularized world or culture, but rather in a secular-postmodern world and culture, that disavows any absolute truth claims, any grand overarching story to life, any meta-narrative, or any centralized construct to claims on reality.

The church is now the odd man out, the dissident voice in a pluralist world.

Although there is undeniable interest and widespread return to spirituality and religion in the postmodern context (to the point of asserting an unsecularization of the world, as opposed to what was considered its secularization in the modern era), I still maintain that the secularization process is pushed forward in more radical ways even amidst the present religious and spiritual interests that characterize this postmodern era. I hold to this position for two basic reasons. The first is in reference to what I have previously hinted at in describing both the modern and postmodern eras as it relates to the secularization process. While one must be wary of any oversimplification of the subject under discussion, it is to be noted that the term "secularization" in its historical development within western society, is related to its effect on the function and role of religion within society. Of equal importance are the historical and cultural movements that have largely contributed to the shape of the undeniable phenomenon that is still a force in the postmodern world, namely, secularization. Some of these forces can be identified as the period of Romanticism, the Renaissance, the period of the Enlightenment and Scientific Revolution, the Protestant Reformation, and the Catholic Church itself. Out of these movements and institutions came the modern project with many of its institutional realities and social constructs that exerted their secularizing influences that are still with us, even within the postmodern context. As Craig M. Gay has so ably put it, "although modernity may well be passé in many intellectual circles, typically modern ideas and assumptions are still quite effectively communicated within contemporary culture by many of the institutional realities that surround us and by many of the ways we do things today. A number of these institutional realities and ways of doing things continue to underwrite the plausibility of practical atheism, in spite of post-modernity's purported openness to 'spirituality.'"[55]

It is also to be noted that many of the essential features of postmodernism are held to be demonstrably modern in nature. Thus it can be said that we are moving into a period "in which the consequences of modernity are becoming more radicalized and universalized than before."[56]

The second reason why I hold to the idea that secularization is pushed forward in more radical ways within the postmodern context, is not only on the examples and arguments previously cited, but also on my understanding and definition of the term "secularization," and also the question of how and in what frame of reference I define religion or religious experience in relation to my understanding of secularization. It is my position that secularization must be defined based on ones definition of the role and function of religion as understood within the traditional Christian concept. In this respect, I define and refer to religion and the religious experience on the substantive level as opposed to a functional level. On the functional level, religion is understood to be more of a epiphenomenon reflecting certain more basic requirements of social life, and in terms of how religious beliefs function socially and/or psychologically.[57]

Despite the fact that belief in God, and even more so the practice of religion, as central to the whole of life both public and private is in the decline from a substantive point of view, there is still a spiritual quest in the postmodern context- a religious interest that is more on the individual level, with the individual determining what is true or not true on his or her own terms, in radically private ways. Individuals engage in spiritual concerns as religious consumers, feasting on an unending serial of religious options that has no substantive claims on life or behavior. In addition, all roads lead to heaven—all truth claims are valid and have equal plausibility status because every thing is relative. To define secularization on the basis of the functional definition of religion would make secularization an impossibility.[58]

Hence the resurgence of current spiritual experience in its various varieties in our contemporary society is hailed by some as a return to the sacred cosmos as in the premodern understanding, and hence the belief that we are experiencing the unsecularization of the world in the postmodern condition. On the substantive level however, religion and the religious experience is defined as a "sui generis human phenomenon,"[59] and in terms of its actual beliefs and the effects those beliefs have in the individual's life and the individual's faith experience in the transcendent Other. Religion and religious beliefs defined on the substantive level also underscores the absolute truth claims and exclusive demands of a central reality—that of the Divine Being who is above and apart from the finite and is to be worshiped as such. It is on this basis that I define secularization, resting it upon a substantive definition of religion as per the traditional Christian concept. Such an understanding of secularization resting on a substantive definition of religion, makes it easier to understand why in a postmodern world where there is a professed openness to the pluralist conversation, there is still an aversion to any truth claims or any ideas that are exclusive or held to be normative. It was not surprising therefore, that Pastor Haggard's exclusive claims to salvation through Christ as the only guaranteed way to heaven was singled out as being judgmental. The religious sensibility that characterizes the postmodern condition functions with the same underlying intellectual claims that there is no objective or absolute reality, no absolute truth, no central overarching story to life, but rather every thing is open to and subject to individual interpretation and determination. There is no one vantage point, no absolute norm. Any expression of religious truth claims that goes counter to this postmodern understanding is suspect and even avoided. The ultimate challenge for the church therefore is the proclamation of God's word as the authoritative source of inspiration—the source of truth with a capital T, in a secular-postmodern world. Realizing that secularization and secularism has posed a serious challenge to the mission of the church in the modern era, and an even greater challenge in the postmodern context, leads one to appreciate the necessity of understanding secularization, and the secular-postmodern mind. The following definitions are an attempt to present a difficult subject with considerable disagreement on its meaning, especially as we have a resurgence of religious interest in the postmodern context. Secularization as addressed in this book from the point of view of its development in the modern and postmodern periods is basically understood to mean "a largely inadvertent process in which religion-at least as it has traditionally been understood-forfeits its place in society..... a process in which religious ideas, values, and institutions lose their public status and influence and eventually even their plausibility in modern societies."[60] The various definitions offered below is presented in support of this basic concept, and helps to set the stage for what follows in this book.

Various Definitions of Secularization

Staples states that secularization is the result of a long conflict between science and religion in which the concepts of the scientific method, with rigorous criteria of rational objectivity, have increasingly become the standard mode of Western thought. The swift expansion of the influence of "modern scientific epistemology, grounded in the objective description of empirically demonstrable fact," has not allowed very much space for the more subjective and intuitive bases of religious knowledge. Western thought has so been influenced by this scientific method of comprehending reality that even the terms of religious discussion "are dictated by the norms of scientific rationality."[61]

George G. Hunter III defines secularization as "the withdrawal of whole areas of life, thought, and activity from the control or influence of the church." There is a lost influence in all areas of Western society's life, including everything from education to government, economics, art, architecture, literature, music, personal morality and community life.[62]

The *Oxford Encyclopedic English Dictionary* defines the word *secular* as (1) that emphasis which is concerned with the affairs of this world; not spiritual or sacred, (2) (of education, etc.) not concerned with religion or religious belief, (3a) not ecclesiastical or monastic, (b) (of clergy) not bound by a religious rule, (4) occurring once in an age or century, (5) lasting for or occurring over an indefinitely long time.[63]

In keeping with the *Oxford Dictionary*, L. Rush Bush defines secularism as the doctrine that morality should be based solely in regard for the well-being of mankind in the present life to the exclusion of all consideration drawn from belief in God or in a future state.[64]

For Bush, it also means lay as opposed to clerical. It also means profane, of the world, not sacred or religious. Its root meaning is "generation" or "age." Thus to be secular is to be given to the concerns of the present age, to lack a transcendent perception of reality, to belong to the present world as distinguished from the spiritual or eternal reality of God.[65]

A more recent definition of secularization by Craig M. Gay approximates L. Rush Bush's earlier view. Gay states that the word "secular" comes from the Latin *saeculum*, which meant "age" or "century" and signified the temporal as opposed to the eternal. The word *secularization* was supposedly first used in Europe during the seventeenth century in negotiating the peace of Westphalia to indicate the transfer of properties from ecclesiastical to "secular" political authorities. The term is now used in Roman Catholic canon law to describe the return to the "world" of an individual formerly under monastic or clerical orders.[66]

Craig further argues that in a sociological sense the concept of "secularization" does not refer to the explicit promotion of secularity over against religion. For Craig it describes a subtle and largely inadvertent process in which religion—at least as it has traditionally been understood—forfeits its place in society. Craig suggests that "secularization describes a process in which religious ideas, values, and institutions lose their public status and influence and eventually even their plausibility in modern societies."[67]

Christopher B. Kaiser defines secularization in the tradition of Thomas Luckmann and Peter Berger, in which case secularization is not seen as the decline of religion but as a redefinition of its role in such a way that religious beliefs are dissociated from the secular processes of world-structuring, and secular values are separated from the area of religion (both a functional and substantive approach).[68]

Thomas Luckmann holds that there has been an important, even radical, change in the relation of the individual to the social order and that this transformation resulted in associated changes in religious consciousness.[69]

Luckmann states that

> "the change from archaic, primitive, traditional and, less radically, from pre-industrial, modern times to our contemporary situation in which industrial bureaucratic and capitalist principles of social organization (in its several

36

varieties from West to East) are dominant, is characterized by the emergence of what may be parsimoniously called privatization of personal existence. Accompanying this is the privatization of the sacred cosmos. . . . Religion could be and was increasingly perceived as the ideology of an institutional system. Its jurisdiction over matters of "ultimate" concern was restricted to matters that could be of "ultimate" concern to the "private individual" only. The most important link of the sacred universe to the world of everyday life was broken. Religious institutions maintained their massive presence in society as highly visible institutions but suffered a sharp restriction in the jurisdiction of their norms. The "secular" segments of the social structure developed pragmatic norms whose actual (or assumed) tendency toward "functional rationality" justified the liberation of the institutional domains from the values embodied in the traditional sacred cosmos."[70]

For Peter Berger secularization is the dissolution of a "sacred canopy" and the emergence of a radical plurality of spheres of life—public and private, secular and spiritual. For Berger, secularization is also a

"process by which sectors of society and culture are removed from the domination of religious institutions and symbols. When we speak of society and institutions in modern Western history, of course, secularization manifests itself in the evacuation by the Christian churches of areas previously under their control or influence—as in the separation of church and state, or in the expropriation of church lands, or in the emancipation of education from ecclesiastical authority. When we speak of culture and symbols, however, we imply that secularization is more than a social-structural process. It affects the totality of cultural life and of ideation, and may be observed in the decline of religious contents in the arts, in philosophy, in literature and, most important of all, in the rise of science as an autonomous, thoroughly secular perspective on the world. Moreover, it is implied here that the process of secularization has a subjective side as well. As there is a secularization of society and culture, so is there a secularization of consciousness. Put simply, this means that the modern West has produced an increasing number of individuals who look upon the world and their own lives without the benefit of religious interpretations."[71]

Gottfried Oosterwal has given a meaning to secularization that accentuates it as a multidimensional phenomenon when he listed its characteristics as (1) the decline of religion as a factor shaping human life and thought and behavior; (2) the desacralization of life; (3) the loss of faith; (4) the change from a community-oriented way of life to one which is based on a societal system, with its pluralism and privatism, its specialization and differentiation, its impersonal technical order, its rational planning and institutionalism; (5) the development of a particular way of thinking and relativism, pragmatism and positivism, empiricism and existentialism; and (6) conformity with the world, expressed in religious peoples' and organizations' acceptance of and adaptation to contemporary social and cultural values.[72]

This particular definition brings together a multiplicity of forms, some of which overlap. Out of this variety comes an attempt to see the whole. This suggests that no one aspect or definition given here holds the key to our understanding of this process, and that secularization cannot and should not be measured by one or two of these offerings only.[73]

A Personal Definition

With this in mind and for the purpose of this study, I would suggest that secularization is a phenomenon in our modern world that is characterized by a *desacrilization* of the "sacred cosmos." With the rise of the rational, scientific, and industrial order came a privatization in society, resulting in the separation and alienation of religious practice and function from cultural and societal institutions, both public and private. This has resulted in a major reduction in faith and belief in God as a thought-shaping worldview of our universe and earthly existence. God and the sacred are marginalized, and the rational, scientific, and a pragmatic knowledge of life and the world dominates the thinking and lives of most men and women. Life is lived in a pluralistic, privatized, relativistic way, with competing social and cultural values in modern society, lacking the benefit of a transcendent perception of reality, or a divine and religious interpretation of life.[74]

Defining the Secular Mind

The following definition of the secular mind necessitates an understanding of what the secular mind is not. Jon Paulien, in his book *Present Truth in the Real World: The Adventist Struggle to Keep and Share Faith in a Secular Society*, asserts that a secular person is by no means an atheist. He or she has not consciously rejected God and religion in the ultimate sense. A secular person may believe in God, yet not always be aware of God's involvement in the practical matters of everyday life.[75]

George G. Hunter III makes a similar point when he argues that it is not the case that secularization has erased all religious consciousness from people's minds, leaving no more religious a priori within human personality, resulting in an age of "no religion." To the contrary, Hunter compares Western culture to ancient Athens, where in Acts 17 Paul gave witness to people influenced by a range of religions and philosophies "from Epicurianism and Stoicism, to various Gnostic and mystery religions to the cult of the Emperor."[76]

While most secular-minded people are not professedly "Christian" or have rejected what is termed "hypocritical Christianity," Ronald S. Sider suggests that their monistic gods are marketed under a modern, New Age label.[77]

People who do not explicitly reject religion sometimes exhibit a syncretism that sociologists label "pastiche spirituality." This is attributed in part to our consumer culture, which has an impact on all forms of religion in America. This pastiche spirituality appropriates familiar themes from a variety of different sources, Christianity included, but there is particular interest in Eastern religions, especially in some of the techniques for achieving spiritual awareness that those religions espouse, such as zen, yoga, tai chi, and even the mysteries of kabbalah.[78]

A good example of this pastiche spirituality is Phil Jackson's *Sacred Hoops*. Jackson has intentionally integrated elements of Zen Buddhism, Lakota Sioux religion, and his parents' Pentecostal Christianity into his own personal spiritual system.[79]

Hunter suggests that people follow other forms of religion which include: the deification of the State—as in Nazi Germany; the deification of political ideologies—as in Communism; and the deification of specific cultures—as in Japanese Shinto or "the American way of life." Secularization has not made people less "religious."… People are incurably "religious," though some people feast, serially, from a growing menu of religious options that the church no longer controls.[80]

Steve Bruce's explanation of the decline of the popularity and importance of religion in today's modern world does not suggest that "patently false superstitions will be replaced by patently obvious truth" as people become more educated, or that modern people will become converted to an atheistic and materialistic understanding of themselves and the universe. They have not become committed rationalists; belief in the supernatural has not disappeared. Rather it has become idiosyncratic and is expressed through piecemeal and consumerist involvement in elements of a cultic world.[81]

This is what Reginald W. Bibby, in his book *Fragmented Gods*, calls "religion à la carte."[82] Secular people seem to fit this profile. Instead of being absolute conscious rejecters of God and religion, they are drawing upon religion as consumers, picking and choosing a belief here and a practice there.[83]

Further, secular people are not just immoral. There is still a moral consciousness in this highly secularized age. "Secular people participate in many moral struggles and make an unprecedented number of moral choices."[84]

The philosopher Michael Polanyi has characterized secular society, viewing it by a "moral inversion," with two features:

1. Many people dread "hypocrisy" and cherish "honesty"; they adopt a "unholier-than-thou" lifestyle, concluding that it is better to live honestly from low motives than from high motives one may not always reach.

2. At a deeper level, modern secular society has experienced "the outbreak of a moral fervor which has achieved numberless humanitarian reforms and has improved modern society beyond the boldest thoughts of earlier centuries."[85]

There is a sense of moral obligation, or at least an awareness of the need for some kind of agreement on morality.[86]

Secular people demonstrate personalized moral choices. James Peterson and Peter Kim, in *The Day America Told the Truth*, predicted that the 1990s would be characterized by personalized moral crusades, with the environmental movement as one such example.[87]

No longer "programmed by Christian 'enculturation'" they see people influenced for moral choices more likely from parents, peers, or pop-culture than from the church or its Scriptures. The twentieth century saw a proliferation of moral causes "from civil rights, human rights, women's rights, and animal rights, to pro-life and pro-choice, to antinuclear and antiapartheid crusades, to humanitarianism movements for refugees, feminine victims, prisoners of conscience, and endangered species."[88]

Finally, it is not the case that all secular people are "philosophically sophisticated geniuses who have read Christian literature from Augustine to Zwingli and rejected the Christian case in toto on rational grounds."[89]

The majority of secular people are not epistemologically sophisticated. Gerhard Szczesny, in *The Future of Unbelief*, states that "unbelief" is no longer the prerogative of an especially enlightened minority. It is the fate of a contemporary type of Western person who may actually be in the majority, or who at any rate is very frequently encountered.[90]

Hunter also asserts that while secular people are not strongly literate, many of them have a religious agenda, and they ask important religious questions.[91]

Szczesny says they are concerned with the "old basic questions: Who am I? What is the nature of the world? What can I believe in and what must I do about it?"[92]

How many people are secularist? No one knows, but the number probably is great in North America and Europe. Secularism has found its way into the lives of many—perhaps most—people. Many people who still believe in God and even go to church are practical secularists. In the final analysis, they rely on human solutions rather than on God.[93]

What, then, are the characteristics of the secular mind? How does the secular mind think? Since secular people are not for the most part atheists or a-religious, immoral, or sophisticates, how then can the secular mind be described?

Several experts have outlined what is considered a characterization of the way secular-minded people think. Among them is one who is considered to be a leading authority in this area, Langdon Gilkey. In his book, *Naming the Whirlwind*, he advances an extensive description of secularity in four distinctive traits.[94]

According to Gilkey, the secular mind entertains a world view whose presuppositions are radically this-worldly.[95]

There is a tendency to view life and existence within the immediate, physical, temporal world with no reference to an eternal order beyond this existence. Life is not dependent on a transcendent being who rules time and history. "Modern man feels he has 'come of age' in a contingent, faceless world." The "secular spirit" that dominates our age believes that no one but people themselves should direct their own destinies. There is "a fundamental attitude towards reality, truth, and value, . . . expressed not only by our own most fundamental reactions to life, but also objectively in the dominant philosophies, the creative arts, and the most profound literature of our day."[96]

Gilkey has given the following four general characteristics to describe this secular spirit or mind set:

1. <u>Contingency</u>: This carries the meaning that what is—the world and its inhabitants—is the result of causes that are neither necessary, rational, nor purposive.[97] Everything that is was

caused by some other natural event that preceded it.[98] Nothing that has evolved in time and space is necessary or intended. They are mere accidents and do not call for an explanation as to how or why they are, because they are a mystery beyond our capacity to comprehend. This understanding of finite reality as contingent, arising as an end result of seventeenth-century science, has since been extended and further radicalized, especially through Darwin's influence. It is central to and dominates most modern philosophy as perhaps its pivotal concept.[99]

Accordingly, the underlying implication of contingency is that the basic elements of the physical universe must have always existed, and our galaxy, solar system, and planet all developed from them. Out of inorganic matter, amino acids were somehow formed, and from amino acids came organic matter. Through a process of evolution and natural selection, homo sapiens emerged and man took his place in this universe.[100]

Campolo sees in this an implication that by a contingent creation, the world and all its inhabitants were accidents. The assumption is that the process can be discerned through research. Through empirical research a series of causes could be followed leading to the rise of humanity. Such research, however, would ultimately give no plausible reasons to why humanity should have come into existence.[101] "The essence of this modern sense of contingency is that the given is ultimately arbitrary, and consequently beyond the given there lies nothing, no ground, no ultimate order, no explanation, no reason."[102] There is no purpose to being, and absurdity rules.[103]

Paulien points out that another term for this way of thinking is naturalism.[104] In this instance, secular people make decisions about life on a scientific basis, without any benefit of a supernatural, divine Being who rules over time and space. God is crowded out of their experience, and by living out their lives within the boundaries of reality as their five senses experience it, they have no inherent purpose or meaning to life.[105]

This idea of contingency thus leads to the belief that people take charge and order their own lives. This leads to a second characteristic given by Gilkey (not necessarily in this order): autonomy.

2. <u>Autonomy</u>: This second characteristic of the secular mind refers to the autonomy and freedom of the individual, his or her inalienable right, and one's innate ability to know one's own truth, to decide about one's own existence, to create one's own meaning, and to establish one's own values.[106] This way of thinking follows on the heels of the contingent. By limiting the boundaries of reality to the five senses, people exempt the supernatural transcendent order from life, and God has no room for providing direction in their lives. They take charge of their own lives, becoming a law unto themselves. "They retain for themselves all the rights and privileges in decision making that they once assigned to God."[107]Where once the theological perspective pinpointed the way for people and specific meaning for their lives, the autonomous secular person now sees life as having a variety of meanings. People now choose and decide what meaning will be attached to their own lives.[108] Thus Gilkey succinctly states that

> "the modern spirit holds that a man must, in some essential regard, live his life in autonomy if that life is to be creative and human, and insofar as it is optimistic in mood, this spirit believes that man can increasingly exercise his freedom over the blind forces of destiny and so be 'master of his own fate'. Thus the modern spirit . . . is dedicated to the proposition that any external social authority— whether of church, of state, of local community, or of family—will in the end only crush man's humanity if his own personal being does not participate fully and voluntarily in whatever help that authority represents and in whatever creative forms his life may take."[109]

3. <u>Relativism</u>: The third general characteristic of the secular mind and related to autonomy is relativity or relativism. All things are considered relative to each other in the passage of time—all forms of the cosmos, of natural life, of the human race itself, of political and social structures, the important events of history, the noblest of ideas, even of the most sacred Scriptures, institutions, or creeds. Nothing anywhere in experience is absolute. All is relevant to all else and is conditioned by its relevant environment.[110]

In this secular way of thinking, since there is no supernatural being and since people are autonomous (deciding their own destinies, being a law unto themselves), it naturally follows that meaning, values, and truth become situational.[111]

Nothing holds permanency or absoluteness, it all becomes a question of perspective. There is no universal privileged vantage point that allows anyone to decide what is right and what is wrong. Everything depends on the situation. What is right for you may not be right for me. What is wrong in my context may be right and even preferable in your context. "Morality," says Paulien, "becomes a social contract." The group decides what is right and wrong based on agreement.[112]Relativity denies that there are objective morals and principles that should control the development of society. There are no absolutes. All values are relative, and any moral system is viable only for the group that creates it. Rather than speaking about "truth" or right and wrong, secular people like to talk about whatever is "right for you."[113]

For the secular mind, therefore, everything has become relative and all belief systems are to be regarded as equally plausible.

4. <u>Temporality</u>: The fourth and final general characteristic of the secular mind is temporality. Temporality is understood as transience, the becomingness and thus the mortality of all the things there are. "All is in time, and time being in all things, each has its appointed terminus."[114]

Human life is saturated in time, time that is pushing life towards finality. According to Nathan A. Scott, Jr., in *The Broken Center*, "Everything . . . is bracketed within the consecutive flow of temporality and death is the form that finality takes for all living things, whether they be vegetable, or animal or man."[115]

This secular way of thinking has heightened the consciousness of mortality. Many secular people are therefore time-bound in their thinking. Eternity and the afterlife, heaven or hell, have no significance. We "arrive on this earth . . . live for a short time, then . . . pass on."[116] They do not think in terms of rewards and punishments in the afterlife, since it cannot be verified by logic or scientific evidence. Life is real this side of death, and meaning and significance must be attained before one dies. Temporality thus places the emphasis on the here and now with no ultimate significance to what one becomes or achieves. This life is all that there is; all else is wishful thinking.[117]

These four essential traits of the secular mind are the main elements of the mood and spirit of our age. This is an age where the secular mind is set within a contingent, relative, and temporal context. However, there are a variety of lifestyles among secular people that are the result of autonomy and relativity. The four basic traits discussed thus far do not necessarily exhaust the possibilities. Paulien observes that secular people are as diverse as snowflakes, despite the fact that there are some common patterns in their way of thinking. Another observation is that, while these four categories are descriptive of the way secular people face the issues of life, the average person on the street does not use these terms to describe them.[118]

There are some more general characteristics which give more added detail into the way secular people view their existence in this life. These I have found in Hunter's *How to Reach Secular People* and Wright's *Unfinished Evangelism*. I have brought these together to form Appendix B. This appendix will accentuate the four basic characteristics already discussed for a broader picture of secular people and how they think. This, I believe, will give a sufficient insight into the traits and characteristics of secular people for the purposes of this study.

Secular Mind Grouping

This section suggests that secular people do not exist as a single, homogeneous group; there are many distinct audiences—with differences in ethnicity, culture, age, needs, education, and socioeconomic class.[119] As Paulien has observed, not all secular people think alike, and although there might be some common patterns in their thinking, they are nonetheless as diverse as snowflakes.[120] This diversity is a result of the "inevitable consequences of autonomy and relativity," each person appropriating meaning and values on their own terms, with great diversity of belief and lifestyle among secular people.[121]

Russell Halle's interview with unchurched people in the United States surfaced ten distinct groups of unchurched people, seven of whom Hunter considers to be substantially secular. Hunter further observes that there are probably 120,000,000 secular people in the United States alone (14 or older), who vary in their consciousness of Christianity. He divides these into three groups: (1) "ignostics"—they have no Christian memory; they do not know what Christians are talking about; (2) "notional" Christians—they have a distant Christian memory; they think of themselves as more or less Christian because they assume their culture is more or less Christian; (3) "nominal" Christians—these are somewhat active in churches, but their religion is civil religion (which they mistake for Christianity) and most gospel washes past them. Mark Finley also categorizes four types of secularists, with some general characteristics found in both Halle and Hunter's groups: the secular materialist, the religious dropout, the secular hard hat, and the secular philosopher.[122]

All the above subgroups are considered to be secular, owing to the fact that their lives are not significantly influenced by the Christian faith. "Their assumptions, vocabularies, decision making, and life-styles reflect no Christian agenda."[123] They may have some mental or distant notion of a belief in the existence of God, but they live without the benefit or intervention of a divine, transcendent reality in their personal everyday lives. They make choices and live by values that are more reflective of the cultural milieu than by any religiously informed biblical point of view.

Summary

In this chapter I have looked at some generally held definitions of secularization. While it does not summarily dismiss all religious and spiritual activity, it does suggest that a traditionally religious society comes increasingly under the influence of rationality and modernity. As a result, religion is relegated from the public realm to private life, and becomes increasingly marginalized and denuded of power and influence.[124]

I have also looked at a general description of the secular mind. The description given does not exhaust the possibilities, but shows what obtains when the secularization process continues apace in the wider society. This is further developed in secular-mind groupings, showing a religious-secular mentality. It is typical of a laissez-faire attitude of a large number of people who for one reason or another neglect to nurture their spiritual beliefs.

Chapter 2 Notes:

1. Steve Bruce, *Religion in the Modern World: From Cathedrals to Cults* (New York: Oxford University Press, 1996), 37.

2. Christopher B. Kaiser, "From Biblical Secularity to Modern Secularism: Historical Aspects and Stages," in *The Church Between Gospel and Culture: The Emerging Mission in North America,* ed. George R. Hunsberger and Craig Van Gelder (Grand Rapids, MI: William B. Eerdmans Publishing Co., 1996), 81.

3. Ibid. See also Dr. Rob Frost, "The Process of Secularization," in *Evangelical Forum for Theology* (accessed 16 August 1999); available from www.ox-west.ac.uk/wmsc/ eft/secular/html; Internet.

4. Russell Lynn Staples, *Transmission of the Faith in a Secular Age* (New Orleans, LA: Andrews Society for Religious Studies, 1990), 3.

5. Rodney Stark and Lawrence R. Iannaccone, "A Supply-Side Reinterpretation of the 'Secularization' of Europe," *Journal for the Scientific Study of Religion* 33 (1994): 230-232.

6. Bruce, 37.

7. Kaiser, 81. I have read the case in Christopher B. Kaiser, *Creation and the History of Science* (Grand Rapids, MI: Wm. B. Eerdmans Publishing Co., 1991), 1-309. See also Richard Tarnas, *The Passion of the Western Mind: Understanding the Ideas That Have Shaped Our World View* (New York: Ballantine Books, 1993), 223-323.

8. Staples, 3.

9. Ibid.

10. Peter L. Berger, "Some Second Thoughts on Substantive Versus Functional Definitions of Religion," *Journal for the Scientific Study of Religion* 13 (June 1974): 132, 133.

11. Kenneth D. Boa & Robert M. Bowman Jr., *An Unchanging Faith in A Changing World: Understanding and Responding to Critical Issues that Christians Face Today* (Nashville: Thomas Nelson Publishers, 1997), 88.

12. Ibid.86-88.

13. Graham Johnson, *Preaching to a Postmodern World: A Guide to Reaching Twenty-First Century Listeners* (Grand Rapids, Michigan: Baker Books, 2001), 24.

14. James W. Sire, The Universe Next Door: A Basic Worldview Catalog (Downers Grove, Illinois: InterVarsity Press, 1997), 176.

15. Stanley J. Grentz, *A Primer on PostModernism* (Grand Rapids, Michigan: William B. Eerdmans Publishing Company, 1996), 3.

16. Sire.177.

17. Humberto M. Rasi, "The Challenge of Secularism," in *Adventist Missions in the 21st Century* (Hagerstown, MD: Review and Herald, 1999), 62,63.

18. Oden in Gene Edward Veith Jr., *PostModern Times: A Christian Guide to Contemporary Thought and Culture* (Wheaton: Crossway, 1994), 27. See also, Johnson, *Preaching to a PostModern World,* 24.

19. Craig Van Gelder, "Defining the Center-Finding the Boundaries: The challenge of Re- Visioning the Church in North America for the Twenty-First Century"in *The Church Between Gospel and Culture: The emerging Mission in North America* (Grand Rapids, Michigan: William B. Eerdmans Publishing Company, 1996), 27.

20. Ibid.30.

21. Daniel J. Adams, "Toward a Theological Understanding of Postmodernism," in *Cross Currents,* taken from htt://www.aril.org/adams.htm, Internet, Feburary 3, 2004, p.3.

22. David F. Wells, *God in the Wasteland: The Reality of Truth in a World of Fading Dreams* (Grand Rapids, Michigan: William B. Eerdmans Publishing Company, 1994), 12.

23. Ibid.12,13.

24. Ibid.13.

25. Ibid.

26. R. Albert Mohler, Jr., "The Integrity of the Evangelical Tradition and the challenge of the Postmodern Paradigm"in *The Challenge*

of Postmodernism, ed. David S. Dockery (Grand Rapids, MI: Baker Academic, 2001) 69.

27. Wells, 15.

28. Mohler, 70.

29. Gelder, "Defining the Center...," 30.

30. Ibid; Van Gelder, "A Great New Fact of Our Day: America as Mission Field" in *The Church Between Gospel and Culture*, 61.

31. David S. Dockery, "The Challenge of Postmodernism" in *The Challenge of Postmodernism,* 12.

32. Ibid.

33. James Sire, "Logocentricity and Post Modern Apologetic: On Being a Fool for Christ and an Idiot for Nobody" (Unpublished paper presented at the Wheaton Theology Conference, 7-8 April 1994): Quoted in "The challenge of Postmodernism" in *The Challenge of Postmodernism,*12.

34. Alanna Nash, "Boomers on Broadway" in *Readers Digest*, Nov. 2005, 104.

35. Ibid.104-107.

36. Adams, "Towards a Theological Understanding of Postmodernism," 2.

37. Ibid. 2. See also, Gabriel Moran, "Response to William B. Kennedy," *Religious Education* 87, no. 4 (1994):517-18.

38. See, Van Gelder, "Defining the Center..." 31-34.

39. William Lane Craig, "Politically Incorrect Salvation," in *Christian Apologetics in the Postmodern* World, ed. Timothy R. Phillips and Dennis R. Ockholm (Downers Grove, IL: Intervasity Press, 1995), 77. Quoted in Boa and Bowman Jr., An Unchanging Faith In A Changing World. 50.

40. Rasi, "The challenge of Secularism," 64.

41. Tarnas, *The Passion of the Western Mind.* 402.

42. Ibid.402,403.

43. Ibid.

44. Ibid.

45. Ibid.

46. William M. McClay, "Two Concepts of Secularism," in *Religion Returns to the Public Square*, eds. Hugh Helco and Wilfred M. McClay (Washington, D.C.: Woodrow Wilson Center Press, 2003), 33.

47. Gregory Tomlin, "FIRST PERSON: Do all roads really lead to heaven?", in *BPNews*, from http://www.bpnews.net/bpnews. asp?ID=22320, internet, January 16, 2006, p.1.

48. Ibid.

49. Ibid. 2.

50. Ibid.

51. Ibid.

52. Ibid.

53. Ibid.

54. Ibid.

55. Craig M. Gay, *The Way of the (Modern) World: Or, Why It's Tempting to Live as if God Doesn't Exist* (Grand Rapids, Mi: Wm. B. Eerdmans Publishing Co., 1998), 17,18.

56. Ibid. 18.

57. Ibid. 19.

58. Ibid.

59. Ibid.

60. Gay, p. 19.

61. Staples, 3.

62. George G. Hunter III, *How to Reach Secular People* (Nashville: Abingdon Press, 1992), 521.

63. *The Oxford Encyclopedic English Dictionary*, ed. Joyce M. Hawkins and Robert Allen (Oxford: Clarendon Press, 1991), s.v. "secularism."

64. L. Rush Bush, "What Is Secularism?" *Southwestern Journal of Theology* 26, no. 2 (Spring 1984): 6.

65. Ibid.

66. Craig M. Gay, *The Way of the (Modern) World.* 18, 19.

67. Ibid., 19.

68. Kaiser, 82. On the changed role of religion alluded to here by Kaiser in Luckmann and Berger, see, e.g., Thomas Luckmann, *The Invisible Religion: The Problem of Religion in Modern Society* (New York: MacMillan, 1967), 35-39; Peter Berger, *The Sacred Canopy: Elements of a Sociologic Theory of Religion* (New York: Doubleday, 1990), 107, 132-134; see also Peter Berger, Briggette Berger, and Hansfield Kellner, *The Homeless Mind: Modernization and Consciousness* (New York: Random House, 1973), 79-81, 156-157. For further understanding and analysis of Berger's treatment on the role of religion, see Robert C. Fuller, "Religion and Empiricism in the Works of Peter Berger," *Zygon* 22 (1987): 497-510. A helpful overview of the treatment of secularization as "Segmentation," as found in Luckmann and Berger is given by Peter E. Glasner, *The Sociology of Secularization: A Critique of a Concept* (London: Routledge and Kegan Paul, 1977), 50-56. Also, for an understanding of "functional and substantive" approaches to define secularization, see Roy Wallis, "Secularization," *The International*

Encyclopedia of Sociology, ed. Michael Man (New York: Continuum, 1984), 346, 347.

69. Thomas Luckmann, "The Structural Conditions of Religious Consciousness in Modern Societies," *Japanese Journal of Religious Studies* 6 (March-June 1979): 123.

70. Ibid., 123, 133.

71. Berger, *The Sacred Canopy*, 107, 108. See also Peter Berger, Brigitte Bugh, Hansfield Kellner, *The Homeless Mind* (New York: Random House, 1973), 4-65, 79-80, 156-157.

72. Gottfried Oosterwal, "The Process of Secularization," in *Meeting the Secular Mind: Some Adventist Perspectives*, ed. Humberto M. Rasi and Fritz Guy (Berrien Springs, MI: Andrews University Press, 1985), 42.

73. Ibid., 42, 43.

74. See the following definitions already given on secularization: Luckmann, "Structural Conditions of Religious Consciousness," 123, 133; Berger, *The Sacred Canopy*, 107, 108, 110, 161; Kaiser, "On the Changing Role of Religion," 82, 83; Staples, "Transmission of the Faith in a Secular Age," 3; Bush, "What Is Secularism?" 6; Oosterwal, "The Process of Secularization," 42, 43; *The Oxford Encyclopedic English Dictionary*, s.v. "secular."

75. Jon Paulien, *Present Truth in the Real World: The Adventist Struggle to Keep and Share Faith in a Secular Society* (Boise, ID: Pacific Press Pub. Assn., 1993), 47.

76. Hunter, 42.

77. Ronald J. Sider, *One-Sided Christianity? Uniting the Church to Heal a Lost and Broken World* (Grand Rapids, MI: Zondervan Publishing House, 1993), 194, 195.

78. Cynthia A. Jurisson, "Pop Spirituality: An Evangelical Response," *Word and World* 28, no. 1 (winter 1998): 16, 17.

79. Phil Jackson, *Sacred Hoops: Spiritual Reflections of a Hardwood Warrior* (New York: Hyperion, 1995), 4.

80. Hunter, 42.

81. Bruce, 234.

82. Reginald W. Bibby, *Fragmented Gods: The Poverty and Potential of Religion in Canada* (Toronto: Irwin Publishing, 1990), 80.

83. Ibid., 80-82.

84. Hunter, 43.

85. Drusilla Scott, *Everyman Revived: The Common Sense of Michael Polanyi* (Chippenham, England: Antony Rowe, 1995), 98.

86. Alister E. McGrath, *Intellectuals Don't Need God and Other Modern Myths* (Grand Rapids, MI: Zondervan, 1993), 39.

87. James Patterson and Peter Kim, *The Day America Told the Truth* (New York: Prentice Hall, 1991), 230.

88. Hunter, 43.

89. Ibid., 43.

90. Gerhard Szczesny, *The Future of Unbelief* (New York: George Braziller, 1961), 14.

91. Hunter, 43.

92. Szczesny, 14.

93. See "Meeting the Secular Mind: Some Adventist Perspectives," Selected working papers of the Committee on Secularism of the General Conference of Seventh-day Adventists 1981-1985, 16, 17; Paulien, chapter 4, "Defining the Secular" and chapter 5, "Becoming Secular," 53-68. In 1996 George Hunter stated that by the turn of the century "a third of all teenage and adult Americans will have no religious training in their background. . . . Add to that . . . people who did once experience some 'religious training', but they did not 'get it', it did

not 'take', they cannot now recall it, and there is no sense in which it informs their life, we see that a majority of the people of the U.S. are functionally 'secular'." *Church for the Unchurched* (Nashville: Abingdon Press, 1996), 20.

94. Later authors such as Anthony Campolo and Jon Paulien have corroborated and accepted these four characteristics by incorporating them into their own understanding of the secular mind. See Anthony Campolo, *A Reasonable Faith: Responding to Secularism* (Waco, TX: Word Books, 1983), 43-45; Paulien, 43-47.

95. Langdon Gilkey, *Naming the Whirlwind: The Renewal of God-Language* (Indianapolis: Bobbs- Merrill Company, 1969), 39.

96. Ibid.

97. Ibid., 40.

98. Campolo, 43.

99. Gilkey, 40.

100. Campolo, 43.

101. Ibid.

102. Gilkey, 40, 41.

103. Campolo, 43.

104. Paulien, 43.

105. Ibid., 4.

106. Gilkey, 58.

107. Paulien, 4.

108. Campolo, 44.

109. Gilkey, 59.

110. Ibid., 48.

111. Paulien, 45.

112. Ibid.

113. Ibid., 45, 46.

114. Gilkey, 53.

115. Nathan A. Scott, Jr., *The Broken Center: Studies in the Theological Horizon of Modern Literature* (New Haven, CT: Yale University Press, 1966), 25.

116. Paulien, 46.

117. See Campolo, 45; Hunter, 45, 46; Paulien, 46, 47.

118. Paulien, 47.

119. Hunter, 41.

120. Paulien, 47.

121. Ibid., 47, 48.

122. For a fuller discussion of these groups mentioned in Halle's findings, and also the groups suggested by Hunter and Finley, please refer to Appendix A. See also J. Russell Halle, *The Unchurched: Who Are They and Why They Stay Away* (San Francisco: Harper and Row Publishing, 1980), 99-108. See also George Hunter, *How to Reach Secular People*, 40-54, and Mark Finley, "Targets and Tactics," in *Meeting the Secular Mind*, 101, 102.

123. Hunter, 41.

124. Michael Pearson, "The Problem of Secularism," in *Cast the Net on the Right Side . . . : Seventh-day Adventists Face the "Isms,"* ed. Richard Lehmann, Jack Mahon, and Borge Schantz (Bracknell, England: European Institute of World Missions, 1993), 90, 91.

CHAPTER 3

SECULARIZATION IN AMERICA

In chapter 2 I looked at secularization and some definitions as given by theologians and sociologists. I also gave some definitions on the secular mind with a section on secular mind groupings. In this chapter I will discuss the impact of secularization in America by looking at the secularization of the "Academy" or the educational system, and the religious experience of America as illustrative of the way secularization has impacted individuals and churches.

Is America the Exception?

The question can be asked, Has America become or is America becoming a more secular society? Is what is happening in America a reflection of the secularization model? Due to the scientific revolution and the rise of the enlightenment of the eighteenth century, many Western intellectuals expected that there would be an eventual demise and disappearance of religion. They expected the advance of scientific knowledge to be accompanied by a corresponding disbelief in the supernatural. They were optimistic that one day reason would triumph over superstition. In light of these expectations one must ask the question, Does American society look anything like the "God is Dead" claim of Friedrich Nietzsche—that faith in the Judeo-Christian God is no longer tenable? Has America spawned the dawn of a new era in which "the infantile illusions of religion would be outgrown"?[1]

At first glance it would appear that the United States is the exception to the secularization model. Here we have a modern industrial and urban society heavily dependent on advanced technology, which apparently shows little or no evidence of long-term decline in religion and church involvement.[2] On any given Sunday it is estimated that there are more people in churches than the number that attends sporting events in an entire year.[3] There were approximately 310,000 Protestant churches in the U.S. with a reported average attendance of 92 adults (per church) in 1995. This average attendance by adults at the worship services of Protestant churches has varied in the past decades. For example, in 1987 the average attendance was 97 adults. The attendance went up to 102 adults attending services in 1992 and dropped again in 1995.[4] As regards the "Mega-Churches" (representing less than 2 percent of the 310,000 Protestant churches), they are said to have 2,000 or more adults attending every weekend.[5]

In a Gallup poll taken in 1993, 59 percent of Americans considered religion "very important" in their lives. Another 29 percent said that religion was "fairly important," while a mere 12 percent indicated that it was "not very important."[6]

Despite this apparent health of religion in America, and while one cannot deny the fact that religion plays a significant part in the development and life of American society, the process of secularization is nonetheless thought by many to be advancing in America.[7] There is a seeming contradiction, where in America religious institutions are thriving amidst a highly technological and secularized society. Secularization in America in this respect manifests itself differently from that in Europe. Whereas in Europe secularization meant wholesale defection from the Church, in the United States it means that, although churches and religious institutions tend to thrive, "their specifically religious character has become steadily attenuated."[8] Dale Hurd, commenting on the state of religion in Europe as compared to the United States, Says that whereas Christianity is still very relevant in the United States, "Europe...has sunk below unbelief, and is now labeled 'Christophobic' and 'anti-religious.'" Whereas in America people might still look favorably on a church building, in certain parts of Europe that would rarely be the case. In France for example, "religion is more likely to be associated with oppression, irrelevance, or simply the past." It is also the observation of some that in the United States, people would more quickly turn toward at least Christ-in general-and Christianity because it is considered to be somewhat a part of the culture-in general. In Europe however, the people have gone beyond that point and expect nothing from religion-apart from some very abstract hope that there is something after this life.[9]

Bryan Wilson makes this observation however, that,

> "superficially, . . . and in contrast to the evidence from Europe, the United States manifests a high degree of religious activity. And yet, on this evidence, no one is prepared to suggest that America is other than a secularized country. By all sorts of other indicators it might be argued that the United States is a country in which instrumental values, rational procedures and technical methods have gone furthest, and the country in which the sense of the sacred, the sense of the sanctity of life, and deep religiosity are most conspicuously absent. The travelers of the past who commented on the apparent extensiveness of church membership, rarely omitted to say that they found religion in America to be very superficial."[10]

Two areas of American culture and society will be examined as symptomatic of the growth of secularization in the United States: (1) the growth of secularization in the educational system and institutions, referred to as the "secularization of the academy," and (2) the quality of religious experience and commitment.

"Secularization of the Academy"[11]

It is noted that large numbers of Protestants in the United States support almost no distinctively Christian program in higher education except that of the theological seminaries.[12] Despite the fact that over

60 percent of Americans are church members and more than half of them are Protestants, and over 55 percent of the population generally say that religion is "very important" in their lives, almost no one seems to think that religion is "very important" for higher education.[13]

George M. Marsden has observed that, in America, evangelicals and moderate liberals are about evenly divided. Neither of them, however, support, to any degree, major universities that are Protestant.[14] A fair number of small liberal arts colleges are controlled by Protestants, and schools that are connected to the mainline denominations tend to be very little influenced by Christianity. More than a hundred of the evangelical colleges are strongly Protestant, some being fairly good schools. However, it is pointed out that their total number of students is about the same as that of two state universities. There is practically no Protestant graduate education outside of seminaries.[15]

This particular situation is very interesting in light of the long tradition of Protestant higher education in the U.S. Marsden points out that in this country higher education was a primary function of the church well into the nineteenth century.[16]

While the Catholic experience presents a significant alternative, Protestants and their heirs were, nevertheless, heavily in control of setting the standards for American universities during this period. Thus, by the time of the Revolution, there were nine Protestant colleges in America. According to Warren A. Nord, these colleges had denominational origins: Harvard, Yale, and Dartmouth were Congregationalist; William and Mary and King's College (later Columbia) were Anglican; the College of New Jersey (later Princeton) was Presbyterian; the College of Rhode Island (later Brown) was Baptist; and Queen's College (later Rutgers) was Dutch Reformed. Only the College of Philadelphia (later the University of Pennsylvania) was nonsectarian.[17]

According to Richard Hofstadter, the education of the clergy served as "the most urgent and immediate reason" for founding seven of the nine colleges, but he adds that "it is equally true and equally important that their curricula were not those of divinity schools but of liberal arts schools."[18]

Until the Civil War, most American colleges were founded by churches, with state or community tax support. These Protestant colleges were not only church colleges but also public institutions. State colleges and universities that were founded after the American Revolution became broadly Protestant institutions. They required chapel and church attendance on Sunday. Many of the faculty were church members and were free to express their Christian perspectives in the classroom.[19]

Up until a century or so ago Christianity played a leading role in shaping the educational enterprise in America. It has now become entirely "peripheral to higher education" and is considered "absolutely alien" to that which is considered important to the enterprise.[20] Vestiges of the older informal religious establishment continued during the time following the Second World War, but in vague and peripheral ways. Then in the cultural pressures mounted in the 1960s, most of what was substantial subsided, almost without a trace or a protest.[21]

Marsden posits that it was obvious that university education must be secular to be free from religiously informed ideas. Academics see it as a matter of academic freedom. Education and the intellectual probing that are associated with it, they believe, by its very nature "excludes religiously informed points of view."[22] There were some weaknesses and flaws in the older system that needed to be improved upon. Although these institutions had many good features as well, they needed to be disestablished and to be improved upon academically. They needed to be changed in ways that would survive the twentieth-century settings.[23]

Marsden proposes three major categories of forces to which the leadership of the emerging universities of the late nineteenth and early twentieth centuries were responding: (1) the demands of a technological society, (2) ideological conflicts, and (3) pluralism and related cultural change.[24]

An underlying force behind this secularization trend in education was the vigorous demands of an industrialized, technological society. What helped to change the smaller colleges and universities into what they had now become was funding from industry and government for technical research and development. By serving the technological economy, training its experts, and supporting professionals, and carrying out much of its research, the universities became important in American life. Thus, while claiming to be free of religious controls, the universities nonetheless came under outside financial control from business and government, which bought their technical benefits and therefore dictated their agenda. These technological forces affected areas of higher education where Christianity would have very little impact, and even some Americans saw it as having almost no relevance.[25]

Other factors that affected the secularization of education in America are the cognitive and demographic. Cognitively, refinement of the enlightenment (the enlightenment is usually applied in an arena outside the bounds of twentieth-century America, but it nonetheless applies there, too) created structures of credibility within which many of Christianity's truth-claims were brought into question. This sharpening of the Enlightenment critique was visible in its contention of four areas: (1) the historical study of the Bible, (2) the Darwinian revolution in natural history, (3) the development of materialist analysis of the human self and of society, and (4) in a multitude of efforts to substitute "science" for other authorities in a variety of specific contexts.[26]

By the end of the nineteenth century many Americans were commenting on the growing impact of the emerging secular worldview. Americans were questioning long-held "fundamental moral presuppositions" about the world, the origin and significance of humanity, and the course of human history. Traditional religious assumptions about such matters promised to be almost unintelligible to high-school and college students.[27]

Smith asserts that naturalistic patterns of thought, based on physical and social evolution and reductionism, strongly affected American life between 1865 and 1930. Smith further states that those holding naturalistic views were always a numerical minority. Nonetheless, this naturalistic philosophy exerted a powerful influence because its chief advocates were scientists, professors, lawyers, business leaders, and journalists.[28]

Hollinger indicates that by the turn of the nineteenth century many of the leading intellectuals whose professional work was not associated with the defense of a religious sensibility—Josiah Royce and William James, for example—knew better than to lean on biblical evidence as among the reasons for accepting a given idea as true. Such careers as those of Margaret Mead, David Riesman, and Daniel Bell indicate the extent to which social scientists replaced the clergy as the most authoritative public moralists for educated Americans.[29]

This "cognitive demystification" (a product of the enlightenment) or secular modes of thought helped to weaken the place of Christianity in the West, and along with a demographic diversification helped to weaken the Protestant hegemony, leading to more diversity and pluralism.[30]

Demographically, the immigration of large numbers of people between 1880 and 1924, and again after 1965, brought to the United States those who lacked the Protestant past that church goers shared, as well as those who were also non-Protestant. There were a number of non-Protestants in these historic migrations, such as Catholics from Europe in the first instance and also from Latin America and the Philippines in the second. In the earlier migrations there were many Jews, Muslims, Hindus, and Buddhists in the more recent one.[31] Religious variety represented as important a dimension of migration as did the variety of ethnic strains.[32] Indeed, the increasing numbers of Catholic and Jewish immigrants were beginning to threaten Protestant dominance.[33]

The cognitive and demographic pressures on Protestant hegemony were not altogether unrelated. "One leitmotif of the Enlightenment commentaries on Christianity . . . had been the diversity of the world's religions, and the extent to which some of the most esoteric of these actually contained myths similar to those basic to Judaism and Christianity."[34] This diversity of religious witness was part of the nineteenth-century free thought and was brought to the consciousness of American Protestants by such men as Col. Robert Ingersoll in his scandalous public lectures, and later by William James in Varieties of Religious Experience.[35]

Another representative ideology of the turn of the century insisted that "the scientific method is cosmopolitan," because it is truly "world wide" and endeavors to take everyone's reports into account.[36] Immigration brought to the United States a small portion of the world that the ideologies of science believed they could eventually encompass, but in the wake of even this measure of ethnic and religious diversity immigration joined science as an influence for the destabilization of a public culture grounded in Protestantism.[37] Belief (as in a belief in God and His word as a religious thought-shaping view) has become sub-cultural. Opinion surveys show from time to time that most Americans believe in God, representing most of the whole culture, yet that believing no longer functions as the unifying and defining element of the entire culture; it no longer provides a common heritage that underlies our diverse worldviews.[38]

While wrangling over prayer in public schools is one minor eruption—pointing to the major shift of a once Protestant hegemony[39] to a now pluralistic culture—the impact of pluralism and cultural change in the secularization of higher education is nonetheless a good example of this revolution.

One development of the transition from a Protestant hegemony to a pluralistic culture has been the privatization of religion.[40] Already since 1867 religion had become for Charles Eliot Norton "the most private and personal part of the life of every man."[41] Since that time and to the present, religion has moved from near the center a century or so ago to an incidental periphery. There is also a definite bias against any "perceptible religiously informed perspectives getting a hearing in the university classroom."[42] Besides other forces, concerns for pluralism and justice supply a rationale for this course of action.[43] Any proposal about openness on religious perspective is seen as having potential for reversals of some hard-won gains for diversity and tolerance. "Conservative Christians" are looked upon as the "oppressors and the quieting of their voices could only be viewed as a gain."[44] This multiculturalist's reaction to the appeal for a more open Christian scholarship is viewed as trivializing religious commitment, since one is not allowed to voice these commitments abroad, and "threatens evangelical notions of religious authenticity."[45]

Another development that has come about as a result of the change from a Protestant hegemony to a pluralistic culture is that Christians are now presented as victims, thus appropriating for Christianity— in its newly adopted role as a beleaguered minority—the arguments developed by feminists, gays, and ethno-racial minorities seeking full participation in the society and its polity. The complaint is that

Christians are discriminated against and that their opinions are not taken seriously.[46] Marsden observes on this point that whereas Christianity was the dominant religion in the Western world and dominant in the nineteenth century in a more informal cultural establishment, in twentieth-century America this informal establishment was largely dismantled in the interest of promoting diversity and equality in public life. "This second disestablishment," says Marsden, "has involved an overreaction against religious viewpoints in public life so that we are now at a point where in the name of multi-culturalism we have silenced some of our major sub-cultures."[47]

One reason for discriminating against religious viewpoints within the universities is that many advocates of such viewpoints are prone to be

FIGURE 1. Multiculturalist Controversy. From David A. Hollinger, Science, Jews and Secular Culture: Studies in Mid-Twentieth Century American Intellectual History (Princeton, NJ: Princeton University Press, 2000), 11 (originally published in the Colorado Springs Gazette Telegraph, n.d.).

conservative politically. They hold views regarding lifestyle, the family, or sexuality that may be offensive to powerful groups on campuses. Hence in the name of tolerance, pluralism, and diversity, intellectual expressions of such religious perspectives could be discriminated against. Pluralism, as it stands in that context, seems to be almost a code word for its opposite, a new expression of the melting-pot ideal. Persons are welcomed into the university from a wide variety of races and cultures (as for example the African-American community) but only on condition that they conform to the more liberal way of thinking. Religious views that do not accord with the multicultural milieu are excluded.[48]

The accompanying cartoon (figure 1) displays a cultural pluralism that is typical of academia in America today and shows some of the categories among which religious viewpoints are situated. This manifest pluralism in the "academy" is perhaps one of the greatest evidences of secularism in America. Alan R. Crippen has pointed out that in the interest of maintaining "neutrality" toward religion, the schools have become channels of a secularist understanding of life, "religious free zones."[49] Students feel marginalized in the classroom, not because they are African-American, Asian-American, or international students, but primarily because they are Christian believers.[50]

In this cartoon a Bible-carrying and cross-wearing family (presumably evangelical) is positioned alongside an Orthodox Jewish family and in front of a Muslim couple. Religious categories are thus at the center of this multicultural scene, but the cartoonist understandably situates religious identity within a panorama of dress-coded identities defined by race, sexual orientation, and "lifestyles" ranging from straights and gypsies through deadheads and bikers.

Religious Experience

With respect to the religious experience in the United States, there seems to be an anomaly. Though the United States is secular in many ways, religious participation and affiliation remain relatively high, more so than other Western industrialized nations.[51] Rates of religious activity, self-reporting of church attendance, and surveys on the importance of faith and religion in individuals' lives, coming from Gallup polls and other religious and social surveys, yield somewhat high percentages. These percentages are often cited by sociologists and others to bolster attacks against the "secularization hypothesis."[52]

It is generally agreed upon, however, that secularization has indeed taken place in Western civilization during the last few centuries. To what extent, then, is the religious experience of America reflective of the secularization of this country?

Certain poll data taken over the years reflect fairly constant levels of religious experience and profession.

Church Attendance

In a survey taken in 1981, George Gallup, Jr., who is president of the Gallup Poll and Executive Director of the Princeton Religion Research Center, observed that church going in America has remained constant. Attendance, says Gallup, has varied only by two percentage points since 1969, after having suffered a decline from the high points of 49 percent recorded in 1955 and 1958. Four adults in every 10 (41 percent) attended church or synagogue in a typical week in 1981. The comparable figure in 1980 was 40 percent.[53] Between both Protestants and Catholics, decline in church attendance has been sharpest among Catholics. Judging 1958 as the peak year for church attendance, Gallup noted that attendance at mass fell 22 points—from 74 and 52 percent—between 1958 and 1978, and stood at 53 percent in 1981. Since 1973, Catholic church-going has remained fairly stable. In contrast, among Protestants church-going has remained fairly constant up until the same time period since 1958.[54]

Another more recent report by the Princeton Religion Research Center maintains that attendance at church services has remained fairly constant between 1959 and 1991. In 1959, 49 percent of Americans claimed to have attended a church or synagogue during the previous seven days. In 1991 this figure stood at 42 percent.[55] Hadaway, Marler, and Chaves show, however, that many more Americans claim to attend church services than actually do. Their observation is that the characterization of American religious participation as strong and stable is not totally accepted. According to them, "many social scientists, as well as church leaders, are skeptical about consistently high rates of church attendance." Membership losses among "old line" Protestant denominations and declining growth rates among large conservative denominations raise serious questions about such claims.[56] George Barna has pointed out, for example, that although "megachurches" and "super churches" bask in the media spotlight, the reality is that most churches in America have fewer than 100 people in attendance on any single day of worship.[57]

Hadaway, Marler, and Chaves have drawn together evidence that church attendance rates, based on respondents' self-reports, are actually overstated. Their empirical strategy was to compare church attendance rates based on counts of actual attendees to rates based on random samples of respondents who were asked to report their own attendance. They made use of various data sources and data-collection strategies (they relied on survey data and church statistics) for three types of data: (1) poll-based estimates of religious preferences for residents of the area, (2) poll-based estimates of church attendance for Protestants, and (3) actual counts of church attendance for all Protestant churches in the area surveyed. They estimated count-based church attendance rates among Protestants in a rural Ohio county and among Catholics in 18 dioceses.[58]

The results showed that church attendance rates for Protestants and Catholics are approximately one-half the generally accepted levels. The Episcopal Church became one such example. Whereas this denomination should have grown by more than 13 percent from 1967 to 1990 (according to the percentage of Americans who claimed to be Episcopalians and/or church members), instead the membership declined by 28 percent. Contrary to what self-defined Episcopalians claimed, attendance among Episcopal parishes was down. Gallup surveys and other poll data reported 35 percent of Episcopalians saying they attended church during the last seven days.[59] On this point, Hadaway, Marler, and Chaves pointed out that if 2.5 percent of Americans claim to be Episcopalians and 35 percent of Episcopalians attend worship, total attendance during an average week should exceed two million. Instead, average weekly attendance was less than 900,000 in 1991. Rather than the 35 percent reported, approximately 16 percent of self-defined Episcopalians attended worship at an Episcopal church during a typical week. The point that Hadaway, Marler, and Chaves are making is that if Episcopalians over-reported their church attendance (based on claims by those reporting they attended church when, in fact, they did not), then it is quite natural to assume that other denominations also over-report their church attendance.[60]

This assumption is what led Hadaway, Marler, and Chaves to their hypothesis. According to this hypothesis, the percentage of Americans who attend church worship during an average week is considerably lower than the 40 percent or so that is accepted as a "social fact" in the United States.

To confirm their hypothesis, Hadaway and his associates went to painstaking lengths to estimate accurately attendance at all known Protestant churches in one county in Ohio. They took lists of churches from registers and church yearbooks; they also traveled every paved road (and some unpaved) in order to find unlisted churches. Where they could not get estimates of attendance from clergymen, they counted cars in the parking lots during services and adjusted the figure for the probable number of passengers. Other methods included a standard telephone survey of reported church attendance. The researchers discovered that the attendance claimed by their respondents was 83 percent higher than their best estimates of actual attendance. Using a slightly different technique, they compared claimed and actual Catholic attendance and came to a very similar conclusion.[61] Hadaway and his colleagues in concluding their report were cautious to recognize that "although the evidence is compelling because it is so uniform, the fact remains that our data pertains to fewer than 20 Catholic dioceses and to Protestants in only one Ohio county."[62]

While this observation is taken in good faith, it is still to be noted that Hadaway and his colleagues made a very important point. Their finding suggests that the constantly cited survey data of high church involvement are at odds with what is known to the churches themselves. Steve Bruce has found, for example, that survey church data in England and Australia have similar discrepancies.[63]

Recent research validates and supports Hadaway, Marler, and Chaves's 1993 survey. In 1998, for example, studies done by Tom W. Smith of the University of Chicago (General Social Survey) and Stanley Presser of the University of Maryland, along with Linda Stinson of the Bureau of Labor Statistics, found that there is indeed over reporting by respondents who are asked about their church attendance. Time and space will not allow for an involved discussion and analysis of their findings. Suffice it to say that the use of questions that shifts the focus from church attendance to events occurring during the week (including doctor visits, eating out, going to movies, etc.) minimized the problems of backward and forward telescoping, social desirability, and identity consistency (that is, behavior consistent with self-perceptions as religious, church-going people). The surveys found that using these questions, along with adjustments for "church attendance" at non-worship events, reduced self-reported attendance from 40 percent to around 30 percent.[64]

Presser and Stinson also suggest that their survey findings reveal that misreporting of church attendance has increased in the last 30 years, thus distorting trends in religious attendance. They contend that there has been a continuous decline since the mid-1960s, "providing support for the hypothesis that America has become more secular."[65]

Religion, however, has been and remains an important part of the American culture and experience, more so than in most other Western societies. While survey data and poll taking reveal this to be true, the work of Hadaway, Marler, and Chaves is important in that it presents for us the difference in the scales of actual and self-reporting poll data concerning church attendance.

Belief in God

Not only have more than 40 percent of Americans claimed to have gone to church in a given week, but an impressive 90 percent of Americans say they believe in God.[66] When asked, "Do you believe in God?" 94 to 95 percent respond, "Yes."[67] This is in keeping with yet another survey, which shows remarkably high levels of Americans who express belief in God or a Universal Spirit during nearly four decades of polling. See Table 1 for the trend.

TABLE 1:
BELIEF IN GOD OR A UNIVERSAL SPIRIT

YEAR	PERCENTAGE
1999	86
1981	95
1976	94
1975	94
1969	98
1967	97
1965	97
1959	97
1954	96
1953	98
1952	99
1944	96

Source: Religion in America—50 Years: 1935-1985 (Princeton, NJ: [Gallup Organization], 1985), 50; "Gallup Poll Topics: A-Z," The Gallup Organization: available from www.gallup.com/poll/indicators/indreligion4.asp accessed 17 January 2001. Internet. See also George Gallup and D. Michael Lindsay, Surveying the Religious Landscape: Trends in U.S. Beliefs (Harrisburg, PA: Moorehouse Publishing, 1999), 25.

Gallup reports that, while the vast majority of Americans believe in some unifying and organizing power behind the universe, only about 66 percent actually believe in a personal God, the God who watches over and judges people—the God of biblical revelation—to whom people are answerable.[68]

There are also subtle differences in these findings both of conceptions of God and in conviction. One study indicates that levels of doubt and disbelief are often greater than the polls would suggest. Among the more educated especially, doubt is fairly common.[69] Roof suggests that much depends on how the questions are worded when people are interviewed: If individuals are given a chance to express doubt, often they will do so, and if allowed to draw distinctions in belief, they are likely to do so.[70] Roof found in his survey that in the young adult generation, levels of doubt and uncertainty, as well as alternative ways of believing, are higher than for the population as a whole. Boomers who were interviewed, for example (almost one-half), said they "never" doubt the existence of God; doubt increased with levels of education, from 50 percent among high-school graduates up to 65 percent among the post-graduates. Among Boomers and Americans generally only 1 percent of those surveyed are classified as atheists. Agnostics or those who say it is impossible to know if there is a God, are in greater numbers, but only 3 percent. Neither atheism nor agnosticism was found to be as common as secular portrayals of the generation might suggest. Uncertainty is much more likely. Sixteen percent are uncertain but lean toward believing. Doubt, or lack of firm conviction, is said to be more common than hardened disbelief or skepticism about the unknowable. Eight percent said they believed in a higher power, and both uncertainty and belief in a higher power were found to be more common among the better educated. That left 72 percent who said they definitely believe in a personal God. Among Boomers, this traditional image of God is held somewhat less so than for Americans as a whole. This is so primarily, says Roof, because of the large number in this generation—almost one fourth—who are either "uncertain about their belief or who hold to a more abstract, non-personal conception."[71]

This concept of religious imagination, how the divine is envisioned symbolically, has some significance and touches on spiritual changes among Boomers. Young Americans and older ones alike (with some slightly differing versions among Protestants, Catholics, Jews, Muslims, etc.) share a rather general view of God: God is thought of in terms of a personal, supernatural being who hears prayers, watches over them, and often responds to their supplications. God is close and approachable, typically held as a loving Father, reigning over the world as an omnipotent and righteous being active in people's affairs.[72] This combination of attributes, both personal and powerful, is what David R. Griffin calls the generic idea of God.

According to this generic idea or definition, the word God refers to a personal, purposive being, perfect in goodness and supreme in power, who created the world, acts providentially in it, is sometimes experienced by human beings, especially as the source of moral norms and religious experiences, is the ultimate ground of meaning and hope, and is thereby alone worthy of worship.[73]

Roof suggests that such a generic view of God was partly shaped out of a defensive posture against contemporary religious pluralism, trends in science, rationality, and secularity.[74]

In this modern era, however, growing numbers have come to find this generic view of God as rather "bland and uninspiring."[75] Looking at the negatives in our world, such as death and destruction, tragedy and evil, some have difficulty in maintaining a notion of an all-good, omnipotent deity.[76]

> "We may believe that God was present in and understood a society where people rode on donkeys and camels, but not the world of high speed freeway travel and air travel and even space travel by rocket ships. Our image of Him is of an old man in a flowing white robe with a long white beard. Such a God does not fit into our present, so we tend to exclude Him in favor of modern science as the means of dealing with contemporary complex issues, and we certainly tend not to expect Him in the future in a post-Christian or postmodern or post-theistic time."[77]

Paulien makes a similar point when he says that many function from day to day as if God did not make a significant difference in their lives. "Theologically", says Paulien, "we may say otherwise, but in practice most decisions are made more on a scientific basis than on what we perceive scripture to say. . . . The blessings of science have their dark side for faith. When a person's view of truth is in practice limited to the reality of the five senses, God is crowded out of that person's existence."[78]

Paulien extends his observations when he states that "science cannot deal with the supernatural." It operates in the sphere of our "natural senses—with a natural bias toward explaining what happens in life as though God either doesn't exist or is uninvolved in the natural processes of life."[79] Many phenomena that were once understood as the action of God are now explained by science in natural terms. With the increase in the credibility of science, says Paulien, has come a corresponding decline in the credibility of religion.[80]

There are other historical and social phenomena that many Americans in general and a generation of Boomers have experienced. Such experiences as the Holocaust, assassination of national leaders, the threat of nuclear warfare, the malicious attack of "911," and environmental destruction have added significance as to how belief in and conceptions of God have been affected. The older patriarchal view of God, for example, appears in contradiction with the liberating forces bringing new life to minorities, women, and the Third World. These are sectors that have long been denied freedom and justice enmeshed in structures often legitimated by religious leaders in the name of God. Old notions of God are also out of step with the modern world. Reason and experience are privileged over revelation and authority, and much in life can be explained naturally, without any reference to divine intervention.[81]

Belief in God has become many things to many people, and God is "not perceived the same as He was by past generations of Americans."[82] Despite the statistics on such things as church attendance and belief in God, it is quite evident that secularization has made a deep impact on American lives. Not only may the statistics overstate the religious reality (people may be telling pollsters what they think makes a good impression) but statistics say nothing of the quality or depth of American religious beliefs. Many who claim a belief in God cannot truthfully say that such belief has substantively impacted their lives and changed their behavior.[83]

The Importance of the Bible in Religious Experience

How important a role does the Bible play in the religious experience of Americans? This is a very important question, the answer to which can help us understand the quality of religious experience in America and the role the Bible plays in shaping that experience.

A Gallup survey reveals that 40 percent of Americans said they would turn first to the Bible to test their own religious beliefs. Another 27 percent said they would seek the guidance of the Holy Spirit, followed by 11 percent who said the church, and 22 percent gave other responses.[84]

A 1993-1994 Barna survey revealed that reading from the Bible, other than during a service, was engaged in by one-third of the adult population (34%). The same segments who attend church (just under half of all adults, 45%) are the ones most likely to engage in Bible reading.[85]

George Gallup, Jr., and Jim Castelli note that Americans revere the Bible, but by and large they do not read it. Despite the large percentage of Americans who believe the Bible is the Word of God, only one-third read it daily and only another 18 percent read it one or more times a week. Another 12 percent read the Bible less than weekly, but at least once a month. More than half of all Americans read the Bible less than once a month, including 24 percent who say they never read it, and 6 percent who cannot recall the last time they read the Bible. This minimal reading of the Bible explains why America knows so little of the Bible.[86] Gallup, in his survey quoted in Christianity Today, says that "professing believers remain woefully ignorant about basic facts of Christianity, and that the U.S. is 'really a nation of Biblical illiterates'."[87] While, for example, virtually every home in America has at least one Bible, and eight in ten Americans say they are Christians, only four in ten know that Jesus, according to the Bible, delivered the Sermon on the Mount. Fewer than half of all adults can name Matthew, Mark, Luke, and John as the four Gospels of the New Testament, while many do not know that Jesus had twelve disciples or that He was born in Bethlehem. In addition, a vast majority of Americans believe that the Ten Commandments are still valid rules for living today, but they have a tough time recalling exactly what those rules are.[88]

Another shocker is the lack of knowledge of the Bible among college graduates. Only four in ten, for example, know that Jesus delivered the Sermon on the Mount. Gallup and Castelli quote sociologist Miriam Murphy as saying "that there are many people in America today with 'a Ph.D. in aerodynamics, but only a third-grade knowledge of the Bible'."[89]

The cycle of biblical illiteracy, says Gallup, is likely to continue—today's teenagers know even less about the Bible than do adults. The celebration of Easter, which Christians believe marks the resurrection of Christ, is central to the faith, yet three in ten teenagers—and 20 percent of those teenagers who attend religious services regularly—do not know why Easter is celebrated.[90] The decline in Bible reading is said to be attributed to several factors: (1) the feeling that the Bible is inaccessible, (2) the belief that it has little to say to today's world, (3) a decline in reading in general and less emphasis on religious training.[91]

Other Observations

According to George Barna, the most quoted "Bible verse" in America is, "God helps those who help themselves." Eighty-two percent believe that is a direct quote from Scripture. Actually this passage was originally penned by Benjamin Franklin—and when carefully examined, reflects, to a great extent, American theology. In essence, says Barna, "it teaches that we must make things happen on the strength of our own abilities and efforts, and when we prove ourselves capable or succeed in achieving our goals, then God is obligated to bless us."[92]

Barna further observes that, even though the majority of Americans believe they already know the fundamental truths of the Scriptures, fewer than 10 percent of them actually possess a biblical worldview;

"a perceptual filter through which they see life and its opportunities." Without the filter, says Barna, "most Christians make important decisions on the basis of instinct, emotion, assumptions, past experience, external pressure, or chance."[93] In essence, while millions of Americans possess beliefs that qualify them as Christian, assert that the Scriptures contain practical lessons and principles for life, and claim that they believe God wants to bless their efforts, they ignore their spiritual resources when the tire meets the road. This has led Barna to conclude that

> "the spirituality of Americans is Christian in name only. We desire experience more than knowledge. We prefer choices to absolutes. We embrace preferences rather than truths. We seek comfort rather than growth. Faith must come on our terms or we reject it. We have enthroned ourselves as the final arbiters of righteousness, the ultimate rulers of our own experience and destiny. We are the Pharisees of the new millennium."[94]

While this may seem a strong and caustic observation on the part of Barna, it probably reflects what he sees as the actual as opposed to that which might otherwise be indicated by surveys and poll data, his own included. This is not to say, however, that all American- professed Christian experience is on this level. There are, it would seem, some genuinely, seriously committed Christians who enjoy a daily prayerful walk with God. In one particular survey, it was estimated that one-tenth of Americans (10 percent) fall into the category of "highly spiritually committed."[95] Generally speaking, however, survey data cannot always be interpreted at face value. It would seem that what should be an all-pervasive experience of religiousness in American society is fairly superficial and lacks serious life-changing impact. Barna points out that only God truly knows the nature of the human condition. "Our best efforts," says Barna, "are riddled with error. Such survey results are simply an attempt to help us estimate what is happening regarding the spiritual condition of America."[96]

These findings, therefore, should be held tentatively and not dogmatically. Wade Clarke Roof has pointed out, for example, that since mid-century, the images and symbols of religion have undergone a quiet transformation. Popular discourses about "religion" and "spirituality," about the "self" and "experience," about "God" and "faith" all point to subtle—but crucially important—shifts in the meaning of everyday religious life. While beyond our full grasp, these symbolic and subjective aspects of religion are most crucial since they influence our interpretations of our lives and experiences.[97]

Observing the religious scene today, one is struck by a distinct change of mood since two decades ago. Activated more at the inner level, Americans are asking questions such as, "does religion relate to my life?" "How can I find spiritual meaning and depth?" And "what might faith mean for me?"[98] This inward search for greater spiritual depth was revealed in a poll taken in 1994 which reported that 65 percent of Americans believed that religion was losing its influence in public life, yet almost equal numbers, 62 percent, claimed that the influence of religion was increasing in their personal lives.[99]

Martin E. Marty has also noted this turning inward on the part of Americans. He suggests that religious channels now flow in channels very different from those in the mid-seventies.[100] A great variety of terms now in vogue signal a shift in the center of religious energy: inwardness, subjectivity, the experiential, the expressive, and the spiritual. Inherited forms of religion persist and still influence people, but as Marty says, "the individual seeker and chooser has come increasingly to be in control."[101]

Roof points out that nowhere is this emphasis on the seeker more apparent than in large chain bookstores.

> "The old 'religion' section is gone and in its place is a growing set of more specific rubrics catering to popular topics such as angels, Sufism, journey, recovery, meditation, magic, inspiration, Judaica, astrology, gurus, Bible, prophecy, evangelicalism, Mary, Buddhism, Catholicism, esoterica, and the like. Words like soul, sacred, and spiritual resonate to a curious public. The discourse in spiritual 'journeys' and 'growth' is now a province not just of theologians and

journalists, but of ordinary people in cafes, coffee bars, and bookstores across the country."[102]

All this is going on at a time when the United States and other countries are going through massive social and cultural changes. There is the emergence of the global world, the influx of new immigrants and cultures, widespread change in values and beliefs, and the powerful role of the media and visual imagery in shaping contemporary life. Add to that the expanding consumer-oriented culture targeting the self as an arena for marketing, and the erosion of many traditional forms of community, all of which point to major realignments in religion and culture.[103]

While probably much more could be said, and other factors looked at, the first impressions of survey data show that there is enough change to indicate the impact of secularization in the lives of American people. This is evident in the lives of both Christians and non-Christians alike and on society as a whole.

Summary

In this chapter I have discussed to some degree the secularization process in America. I have looked at two areas: (1) the "secularization of the Academy" or of higher education and (2) the religious experience of America. No attempt has been made to be exhaustive, and therefore the findings are to be held tentatively.

It is evident, however, that while America can be characterized as a religious nation, it has nonetheless been impacted by the process of secularization. In general, the present spiritual quest is anything but orthodox. To a large extent, people's religious experience has become very subjective and lacks traditional biblical values. The impact of secularization is reflected in what Americans think they do and what they actually do.

Chapter 3 Notes

1. Guenter Lewg, *Why America Needs Religion: Secular Modernity and Its Discontents* (Grand Rapids, MI: William B. Eerdmans Publishing Company, 1996), 65. See also Rodney Stark and William Sims Bainbridge, *The Future of Religion: Secularization, Revival and Cult Formation* (Berkeley and Los Angeles: University of California Press, 1985), 1.

2. Bruce, 129. See also *Rethinking Secularization, Revival and Cult Formation* (Berkeley and Los Angeles: University of California Press, 1985), 1.

3. Lewg, 65.

4. George Barna, *The Index of Leading Spiritual Indicators* (Dallas: Word Publishing, 1996), 109.

5. Ibid.

6. George Gallup, Jr., and Robert Besilla, "More Find Religion Important," *Washington Post*, January 22, 1994. See also Gustav Niebuhr, "American Religion at the Millennium's End," *Word and World* 28 (Winter 1998): 9.

7. Bryan Wilson, *Religion in Secular Society: A Sociological Comment* (Middlesex, England: Penguin Books, 1969), 112. See also Steve Bruce, *Religion in the Modern World*, 129-164.

8. Bruce, *Religion in the Modern World*, 129-164.

9. Dale Hurd, "Faithless Europe: The Continent is no longer a bastion of Christianity," in *Christian World News,* (accessed from) http://www.cbn.com/CBNnews/CWN/021006europe.asp, internet, February 11, 2006, p.1.

10. Bruce, 129-164.

11. See the title work, George M. Marsden and Bradley G. Longfield, eds., *The Secularization of the Academy* (New York: ²Oxford University Press, 1992).

12. Ibid., 9.

13. From Gallup Surveys of 1980-1984, appendix, *Unsecular America*, ed. Richard J. Neuhaus (Grand Rapids, MI: Eerdmans, 1986), 131.

14. Marsden, 9.

15. Ibid., 9, 10.

16. Ibid., 10.

17. Warren A. Nord, *Religion and American Education: Rethinking a National Dilemma* (Chapel Hill, NC: University of North Carolina, 1995), 66.

18. Richard Hofstadter, *Academic Freedom in the Age of the College* (New York: Columbia University Press, 1955), 116.

19. Longfield, 10.

20. Ibid., 11. See also John H. Roberts and James Turner, *The Sacred and the Secular University* (Princeton, NJ: Princeton University Press, 2000), 19.

21. Longfield, 11.

22. Ibid., 11, 12.

23. Ibid., 12, 13.

24. Ibid.

25. Ibid., 18-21.

26. David A. Hollinger, *Science, Jews and Secular Culture: Studies in Mid-Twentieth Century American Intellectual History* (Princeton, NJ: Princeton University Press, 1996), 20.

27. Gary Scott Smith, *The Seeds of Secularization: Calvinism, Culture, and Pluralism in America, 1870-1915* (Grand Rapids, MI: Wm. B. Eerdmans, 1985), 36, 37.

28. Ibid., 38, 39.

29. Hollinger, 22.

30. Hollinger, 23, 24. Note that "cognitive demystification" as used here by Hollinger has reference to secular modes of thought descending from the enlightenment.

31. Ibid., 22.

32. *A History of the World Volume II: The Modern World*, ed. John A. Garraty and Peter Gay (New York: Harper & Row, 1972), 193.

33. Smith, 38.

34. Hollinger, 23.

35. Ibid.

36. Conway MacMillan, "The Scientific Method and Modern Intellectual Life," *Science*, n.s., 1 (1895): 541.

37. Hollinger, 22, 23.

38. Turner, *Without God, Without Creed*, 263.

39. Ibid.

40. Ibid., 30, 31.

41. Charles Eliot Norton, "Religious Liberty," *North American Review* 104 (1867): 588.

42. Marsden and Longfield, *The Secularization of the Academy*, 33.

43. Ibid., 34.

44. George Marsden, *The Outrageous Idea of Christian Scholarship* (New York: Oxford University Press, 1998), 31.

45. Hollinger, 31.

46. Ibid., 32.

47. Marsden, *The Outrageous Idea of Christian Scholarship*, 32.

48. George Marsden, *The Soul of the American University: From Protestant Establishment to Established Nonbelief* (New York: Oxford University Press, 1994), 432.

49. Alan Crippen, ed., *Reclaiming the Culture: How You Can Protect Your Family's Future* (Colorado Springs, CO: Focus on the Family Publishing, 1996), 41.

50. Kelly Monroe, *Finding God at Harvard* (Grand Rapids, MI: Zondervan Publishing House, 1996), 14, 15, 16.

51. C. Kirk Hadaway, Penny Long Marler, and Mark Chaves, "What the Polls Don't Show: A Closer Look at U.S. Church Attendance," *American Sociological Review* 58 (December 1993): 741.

52. Ibid.

53. George Gallup, Jr., "Church Going in United States Has Remained Remarkably Constant Since 1971," in *Religion in America: Who Are the "Truly Devout" Among Us* (Princeton, NJ: Princeton Religion Research Center, 1982), 842.

54. Ibid., 44, 45.

55. Ibid., 42-43.

56. Hadaway, Marler, and Chaves, 742.

57. George Barna, *The Frog in the Kettle: What Christians Need to Know About Life in the 21st Century* (Ventura, CA: Regal Books, 1990), 137.

58. Hadaway, Marler, and Chaves, 742.

59. Ibid.

60. Ibid. See also Benton Johnson, "The Denominations: The Changing Map of Religious America," *The Public Perspective: A Roper Center Review of Public Opinion and Polling* 4 (March/April 1993): 3-6.

61. Hadaway, Marler, and Chaves, 743-748.

62. Ibid., 748.

63. Bruce, 131.

64. Stanley Presser and Linda Stinson, "Data Collection Mode and Social Desirability Bias Self-Reported Religious Attendance," *American Sociological Review* 63 (1998): 137-145. See also Tom W. Smith, "A Review of Church Attendance Measures," *American Sociological Review* 63 (1998): 131-136. Other articles that discuss surveys of similar findings are: Penny Long Marler and C. Kirk Hadaway, "Testing the Attendance Gap in a Conservative Church," *Sociology of Religion* 60 (1999): 175-176; idem, "Did You Really Go to Church This Week? Behind the Polldata," *Christian Century* 115 (1998): 472-475. See also C Kirk Hadaway, Penny Long Marler, and Mark Chaves, "Overreporting Church Attendance That Demands the Same Verdict," *American Sociological Review* 63 (1998):122-130. Last but not least, John P. Marcum, "Measuring Church Attendance: A Further Look," *Review of Religious Research* (1999-2000): 122-130.

65. Presser and Stinson, 145.

66. Robert H. Bork, *Slouching Towards Gomorrah: Modern Liberalism and American Decline* (New York: Regan Books/Harper Collins Publishers, 1996), 279.

67. Wade Clark Roof, *A Generation of Seekers: The Spiritual Journeys of the Baby Boom Generation* (New York: Harper Collins Publishers, 1993), 72.

68. Ibid.

69. Roof, 73.

70. Ibid.

71. Ibid., 73, 74.

72. Ibid., 74.

73. David Ray Griffin, *God and Religion in the Postmodern World* (Albany, NY: State University of New York Press, 1989), 52.

74. Roof, 74.

75. Ibid.

76. Ibid.

77. Millard J. Erickson, *Does It Matter if God Exists? Understanding Who God Is and What He Does for Us* (Grand Rapids, MI: Baker Books, 1996), 33, 34.

78. Paulien, 44.

79. Ibid., 54.

80. Ibid.

81. Roof, 74.

82. George Barna, "Absolute Confusion: How Our Moral and Spiritual Foundations Are Eroding in This Age of Change," in *The Barna Report*, vol. 3 (Ventura, CA: Regal Books, 1993), 75.

83. Bork, 279, 280.

84. *50 Years of Gallup Surveys on Religion*, 47.

85. Barna Report, 3:61, 62.

86. George Gallup, Jr., and Jim Castelli, *The People's Religion: American Faith in the 90s* (New York: Macmillan Publishing Company, 1989), 60.

87. Richard Walker, "Trends: More Christians Saying No to Church," *Christianity Today* 32 (September 2, 1988), 57.

88. Gallup and Castelli, 60.

89. Ibid.

90. Ibid.

91. Ibid.

92. George Barna, *The Second Coming of the Church* (Nashville: Word Publishing, 1998), 22.

93. Ibid., 23.

94. Ibid.

95. George H. Gallup, Jr., and Timothy Jones, *The Saints Among Us: How the Spiritually Committed Are Changing Our World* (Harrisburg, PA: Morehouse Publishing, 1993), 31, 32.

96. Barna, *Absolute Confusion*, 91.

97. Wade Clarke Roof, *Spiritual Marketplace: Baby Boomers and the Remaking of American Religion* (Princeton, NJ: Princeton University Press, 1999), 3, 4.

98. Ibid., 7.

99. Eve Arnold-Magnum, "Spiritual America," *U.S. News and World Report* 4 April 1994, 48-59.

100. Martin E. Marty, "Where the Energies Go," *Annals of the American Academy of Political and Social Science* 527 (May 1993): 11-26.

101. Ibid., 15.

102. Roof, 7. See also Cynthia A. Jurisson, "Pop Spirituality: An Evangelical Response," 14-23.

103. Roof, 8.

CHAPTER 4

A BIBLICAL AND THEOLOGICAL RATIONALE FOR REACHING SECULAR PEOPLE

With the impact of secularization in America, individuals, without and even within churches, are becoming increasingly secular. These individuals are abandoning traditional ways of thinking and perceiving reality. As the traditional modes and structures of evangelization are largely maintained in a highly secular age, it has been more difficult to reach and influence a growing audience of modern and postmodern men and women with the gospel. This results in an increasing harvest field that must be reached according to the inclusive nature of the Great Commission in Matt 28:18-20.

According to the harvest metaphor found in Luke 10:2,[1] there are at least three things that lend themselves to an urgent need for reaching secular people:

1. Secular people, though unimpressed with what they perceive as traditional, boring, and irrelevant church programming, and even though resistant to any exclusive claims to truth or moral absolutes, are still open to and are seeking for a satisfying world

view and spiritual fulfillment.

2. One reason for the failure to gather the harvest is that the churches have trouble perceiving the harvest—people-blindness, so to speak.

3. There are too few laborers for gathering the harvest. Many who are asked to invite and bring their neighbors and friends to meetings do not do it.[2]

In light of these crucial circumstances surrounding mission to secular people, it is critical to establish a biblical and theological rationale for reaching this particular group. This chapter seeks to root this rationale in five areas: (1) the *Missio Dei*, (2) the ministry of Christ, (3) examples of how God speaks to people in their own language and reaches them where they are, (4) the ministry of Paul the Apostle to the Gentiles, and (5) the teachings of Ellen White.

The Missio Dei

The *Missio Dei* (Mission of God) is expressive of God's eternal and infinite love in seeking and saving a lost world. The promise in Gen 3:15 come within the context of the fall in Eden and the subsequent alienation of God's earthly creation. It was on the heels of this broken and lost condition (of Adam and Eve) that God promised (Gen 3:15) that He would put enmity between the serpent and the woman, and between her seed and his seed. In the marvelous story of the Fall, we see God's love unfolded in His word. God took the initiative in seeking Adam and Eve's attention and redemption. Because of the separation sin brought, Adam and Eve hid from God in fear, guilt, and shame. God later approached them with the searching love call, "Where are you?" (Gen 3:9). No one in this world (not even secular people) could possibly escape from this question.[3]

The idea that mission is primarily a divine initiative begun slowly in Europe in the 1930s. Karl Barth, as far back as 1932, is said to have been one of the first to write of mission as an activity of God.[4] It was not until the International Missionary Council of 1952 that the idea of the *Missio Dei*, according to Bosch, first emerged as that which derived from the very nature of God.[5] The idea is that mission has its origin in the heart of God. "God is the fountain of sending love... there is mission because God loves people."[6]

The recognition that mission is God's mission (*Missio Dei*) has crucial implications in developing a biblical and theological rationale for reaching secular people. It will help us get rid of any narrow views of mission and help us to realize that God loves all people (including secular people).

The *Missio Dei*, therefore, is inclusive of all men, in every age, in every culture, and certainly this includes our mission in reaching secular people. When Jesus finally "came to seek and save the lost" (Luke 19:10), God was in Christ reconciling the world unto Himself (2 Cor 5:19).

Christ's Ministry

In the actual ministry of Christ we see the expanding nature of the *Missio Dei*. In His inaugural address of Luke 4:16 we are confronted with the sine qua non of the gospel's centrifugal dimensions. Jesus made clear that the gospel was to be preached to the poor, the oppressed, the disenfranchised, the refugee, the homeless, the lame, the maimed, and the blind. This is not a special selection, provincialistic gospel. Jesus intends that the gospel be taken to the palace as well as to the hovel, the rich and the poor, the literate and the illiterate. It is universal in scope (Rom 8:15-21)[7] and is not to be stymied by walls and barriers, cultural, religious, or otherwise.

While carrying out His ministry on earth, Christ demonstrated in no uncertain terms that none of the barriers (cultural, political, social, or religious) that were in existence in His day were to impede in anyway the saving knowledge of His grace for sinners.

There are at least two examples in the ministry of Christ that are instructive of how He dealt with this:

1. His encounter with the Canaanite woman (hereafter also known as the Syrophonecian woman)

2. His encounter with the Woman of Samaria (hereafter also referred

to as the woman at the well).

In Matt 15:21-28 and Mark 7:24-30 we have Jesus' encounter with the Canaanite woman who was a member of a despised race and who did not share in the advantages the Jews daily enjoyed. In His response to this woman (who was beseeching and imploring Him to heal her sick child), Jesus' words could be considered rather harsh: "I am not sent but unto the lost sheep of the house of Israel." At her continued beseeching, Jesus added insult to injury when He said to her, "It is not meet to take the children's bread and to cast it to dogs." Jesus was reflecting the attitude of the Jews of His day. Ironically, however, Jesus did the unthinkable by granting her request and commending her faith (Matt 15:28). Ellen White states that even though Jesus' response to the Canaanite woman appeared to be in accordance with the attitude of the Jews, it actually veiled an implied rebuke intended for the benefit of the disciples. By reason of this incident, the disciples were to be later benefited with the understanding that "He came to the world to save all who would accept Him."[8]

Ellen White mentions that Jesus wished to lead His disciples from their Jewish exclusiveness to be interested in working for others besides their own people." This exclusiveness represented a wall of separation. In our day there are barriers that separate us from people. "Pride and prejudice have built strong walls of separation between different classes of men. Christ and His mission have been misrepresented, and multitudes feel that they are virtually shut away from the ministry of the gospel."[9]

This particular incident demonstrates that there is universality to the gospel and that *all* must be inclusive of our missionary endeavors, and that *all* will include secular people. Christ's dealing with the Phoenician woman has far-reaching implications. One such implication is the need to break down the barriers that exist in our day by developing strategies for reaching secular people, strategies that are intentional and inclusive of this group of people. With reference to this point, Bert B. Beach observes that traditional approaches to evangelism have shown either a lack of awareness or intentionality toward the secular-unchurched population.[10] He observes that there has been little success in dealing with secularism and attracting people with a secular mind-set.[11]

One of the reasons for this lack of success among secular people is due to a predominant feature of evangelism and mission outreach, known as the "fortress model."[12] It is compared to a lighted city or a beacon on a hill that guides those fishing on the sea at night. In this way, the Christian church functions as a prophetic beacon to society. The image given here is also of a fortress-city with walls around it for the purpose of protecting those who are inside from the dangers outside. "Every so often," says Paulien, "the inhabitants of such a city may send out the army to conduct a 'crusade.' They open the gates quickly, rush out to snatch up a few captives, bring them back through the gate, and slam the door. That is the fortress model of ministry."[13] Most Seventh-day Adventists perceive the nature and mission of the church in these terms—"'God's fortress in a revolted world.' (Ellen G. White, The Acts of the Apostles, page 11; Testimonies to Ministers and Gospel Workers, page 16). It is thoroughly Biblical and rooted in such images as **Jerusalem, the city on a hill**, and **the tower** with Christ as its chief cornerstone. Mission and evangelism are understood as calling people out of the world, away from evil, secular associations and into the safety of the city of God. Church growth is primarily seen as increasing the number of those safely behind the walls of the city, expanding its institutions, strengthening its administration, keeping the walls secure and perfecting the citizens."[14]

This particular paradigm tends to maintain constancy in traditional ways of doing outreach ministry and in-house breathing. Evangelism is done by a few specialists supported by the troops as their long suit and is mainly an event-"the crusade." Very few, and sometimes none at all, of the postmodern-secular world are reached effectively by this approach. Herein lies the reason for our lack of growth in our secular context. This fortress model is inflexible in terms of innovative and intentional ways of reaching postmodern-secular people.

In order, however, to be more successful at reaching secular people other methods should be followed as taught and exemplified by Christ. For example, Jesus speaks in Matt 5:13-16 not only of being a light or a city on a hill, but of also being the salt of the earth (vs.

13). How does salt function in this symbolism? "It mingles with the food and disappears. It becomes part of the crowd, so to speak."[15] It takes one outside the walls of protection, outside the cultural and religious boundaries that tend to separate us from people outside the church. Functioning as salt, we are scattered out there, mingling with the people where they are. This particular paradigm is foundational in understanding the nature and mission of the church "described by such Biblical images as **salt, yeast, servants** and **ambassadors**, and **pilgrims**. Mission and evangelism are the task of every believer and accomplished as a way of life rather than as a sideline or a part-time activity, more through spontaneous sharing than through programs, by participating in secular affairs; involvement in the world rather than isolation from the world. Believers mingle with the people of the world, identify their needs and witness through deeds and words. Church growth is seen as a work of healing and restoration. 'This was Christ's method. We should do as Christ did,' (Ellen G. White, Christian Service, pages 117, 119)."[16]

Such a model of ministry is by nature innovative and intentional in relating the gospel in relevant ways to a vast unchurched and postmodern-secular population. Evangelism and mission outreach is carried on in unconventional ways, understood as process and not just event. The church is intensely intentional in its formulation of ministry and service to the community. The church mingles with, the church befriends, and the church seeks to understand and relate to secular people, with a view towards influencing them for Christ.

Another example that demonstrates the intended scope of Christ's mission is His encounter with the Samaritan woman. In John 4:1-42 we have the account of Jesus tactfully and skillfully leading a Samaritan woman to a realization of her need of salvation. At the same time He also taught His disciples an important lesson that was to benefit them in their future mission endeavors: His salvation is intended for all. Jesus wanted His disciples to understand that His work of salvation was for the world, to the intent that all who believes in Him should be saved from their sins. The Samaritan woman was among the "all" that needed salvation:

"The Savior is still carrying forward the same work as when He proffered the water of life to the woman of Samaria. Those who call themselves His followers may despise and shun the outcast ones; but no circumstance of birth or nationality, no condition of life, can turn away His love from the children of men. *To every soul, however sinful,* Jesus says, If thou hadst asked of me, I would have given thee living water. *The gospel invitation is not to be narrowed down, and presented only to a select few who we suppose will do us honor if they accept it. The message is to be given to all.*"[17]

Jesus' encounter with the woman at the well was not only modeling for the disciples, but also for us. God's will, therefore, is that we take the gospel to all men and this includes secular people. Many secular people may be living in sin, so to speak, and if we are not careful we could erect barriers (such as the attitude of the disciples) between us and them.

Two thousand years ago Jesus entered into a world of barriers—barriers erected by the religious leaders of His day. These barriers kept people out. The rules, liturgy, language, and piety made God inaccessible to all but the religiously trained. The religious leaders essentially closed the doors to "sinners and tax collectors"—to anyone who was not like them (see Matt 23:13). The attitude of the religious leaders was, "Come to us on our terms or don't come at all." Tim Wright has ably summed it up when he said that Jesus

"came to remove barriers that keep people from a relationship with God. Driven by his passion to reach lost people, he came to open the door so that all might enter. He did so by laying aside His rights and privileges as God in order to take the form of a servant (Philippians 2:5-11). He met people at their level. He put their needs ahead of his own. He treated people with respect. To the horror of the religious, He befriended the nonreligious. He didn't demand that they act or believe a certain way, before he would speak with them. He didn't expect them to understand certain religious rites before he accepted them. Instead, He loved and accepted them unconditionally. He connected with them. He spoke in their language. He told stories that dealt with their lives. He met their needs. He made the Kingdom of God accessible to them. He invited them into a relationship with Himself, a relationship of forgiveness and grace."[18]

God's strategy for reaching people was to become incarnate in the person of Jesus. In a very real sense, God—in order to understand us, identify with us, and reach us—became the "us" He wanted to reach (Heb 2:14-18). The word became flesh (John 1:14).[19]

That strategy is as true today as it was in Jesus' day. Jesus is still impassioned about reaching lost people. And He calls for us to be the vehicles through which He will find them. He invites us to understand and identify with lost people. He calls us to reach out to the unchurched on their terms and build a relationship with them, a relationship that will point them to God. In other words, He encourages us to follow His strategy: to remove the barriers that keep people from hearing about God's love, and to create a warm, friendly, uncritical, and non-judgmental attitude of acceptance. We need an attitude that encourages anyone and everyone, regardless of their *sitz im leben*, to enter God's kingdom through a saving relationship with Jesus Christ.[20]

We must keep the unbelievers' view of salvation uncluttered by cultural and other biases, just as Jesus did with the woman at the well.[21] The primary issue for Jesus was that this woman needed salvation, and in giving her the opportunity to obtain that salvation, He effectively tore down a communication barrier by a tactful and courteous request for a drink of water. There are two important lessons taught here:

1. <u>Envisioning the Harvest Field - Getting Rid of People Blindness</u>. Jesus wanted His disciples to envision the harvest that was very close to them. They had seen "nothing in Samaria to indicate it was an encouraging field. . . . They did not see that right around them is a harvest to be gathered."[22] John 4:35 is an invitation by

Jesus to take off the blinders. Even though there were many souls among the Samaritans who were spiritually hungry and ready to accept the gospel, the disciples did not see them as such.

Jesus' example is intended to help us get rid of people blindness. In regard to this point, Hunter states that many churches have not, within memory, reached and discipled any really secular people. Many of them, he says, do not even intend to reach lost people outside their church's present circle of influence. Their main concern is to take care of their own members. Many church leaders, says Hunter, are in virtual denial regarding the growing number of secular people in their community. "In many cases, a church's leaders do not know many secular unchurched people, so they assume there aren't many."[23] People, however, have become more secular and many, says Hunter, "need, and seek for, a satisfying world view and spiritual fulfillment."[24]

2. <u>Get Close to the People</u>. Jesus' approach to the Samaritan woman, and His subsequent acceptance of an invitation to stay with the Samaritans for a couple of days suggest the need to get involved in the field (John 4:39-42). In coming close to the Samaritan Jesus began the process of breaking down the partition between Jew and Gentile. He indicated that the gospel was not limited to only Jews, but was to include others also. He slept under their roofs, had table fellowship with them, ate food prepared by their hands, taught in their streets, and treated them with the utmost kindness and courtesy.[25]

There are lessons also for us to learn from the principles laid out in Jesus' example. Jesus demonstrated that fishing for people means going where they are, in the real world, and secular people live in the real world. There can be no impact without contact. Jesus' example of touching the life of the Samaritan woman and the lives of her fellow Samaritans illustrates the importance of contact with people.

Not only did Jesus relate openly to Samaritans, but He also shared table fellowship with outcast public "sinners" and tax collectors (Matt 9:10; 11:19; Mark 2:18-19; Luke 7:31-35). Even though He did not inaugurate a systematic mission to the Gentiles, there are several incidents in the gospels that illustrate a basically open attitude toward the foreigner who was feared and avoided by most of Jesus' contemporaries (Matt 8:5-13; Mark 7:24-30; and Jesus' favorable comments regarding the Gentile towns in Matt 11:20-24). Jesus betrayed the fact that He saw some goodness in those people whom the religious society of His day presumed to be spiritually bankrupt.[26] Obviously those people mattered to Him. This provocative style that characterized Jesus' ministry is inevitably linked with the nature of the *Missio Dei*.

One aspect of the nature of the *Missio Dei* is that "people matter to God." This can be a hard one to fully absorb into our value system.[27] We may readily agree with this statement and cite such texts as John 3:16, 2 Pet 3:9, and Rev 14:6. But do we actually accept and believe it to the very core of our being? How we relate to the concept of the need to reach secular people will directly depend on the degree to which we own and apply this important value.[28]

Jesus owned and applied this particular value. In ministering to the Syrophonecian woman and the woman at Jacob's well, Jesus crossed the bounds of Jewish custom and tradition. In today's lingua we would say He ignored the rule of political correctness. Jesus demonstrated the lengths He was willing to go in order to reach those outside the family of God. Jesus demonstrated that these two women, who were readily avoided and scorned even by His own apostles, mattered to Himself and to God.

Jesus took it to yet another level when He spent some time in the hometown of the woman at the well; a Samaritan village if you please! He slept under their roofs, ate food prepared by their hands, taught publicly in their streets, and treated them with heaven's kindness and courtesy.[29] This involvement of Jesus with the Samaritans was unheard of and unthinkable among the Jewish leaders and people of His day. Not only did He ignore the rules of political correctness, but He also walked through the barriers and obstacles that would have prevented Him from sharing the love of God with the Samaritans.

There were other occasions where Jesus demonstrated that no barrier (whether political, religious, social, or otherwise) would keep Him from ministering to the sinners of His day. Take for example the revealing accusation of the Pharisees and scribes, "This man receives sinners and eats with them" (Luke 15:2). One example of this is found in Matt 9:10-13. In this passage we find Jesus having table fellowship with tax-collectors and sinners. Jesus obviously spared no pains, and missed no opportunity of getting close to such as these. Jesus did not minister in isolation. He was a people's person. People mattered to Him. As a result His ministry transcended all artificial distinctions and social barriers. His purpose was to reach sinners outside of the fold.

Here in Matthew chap. 9, Jesus opened His arms for an uncritical acceptance of all who came. One can imagine that the atmosphere was warm and positive - that is, until the Pharisees arrived, the carriers of the religious shell, the custodians of the inflexible wineskins of tradition. Immediately they mounted their assault by posing the question to the disciples: "Why does your teacher eat with tax-collectors and sinners?" In answer to that question, Jesus cited an ancient proverb, followed by a statement of purpose: "Those who are well have no need of a physician, but those who are sick. But go and learn what this means: 'I desire mercy and not sacrifice.' For I did not come to call the righteous, but sinners to repentance" (Matt 9:12-13).

Jesus took the necessary risks: He forgot about His own reputation (even though He did not sin [1 Pet 2:2]) in order to reach the sinner of His day. He mingled with the people. He entered their world, and reached out to them on their turf. Ellen White's statement on Christ's method bears repeating here. She states that *"Christ's method alone will give success in reaching people* [Italics mine*]. The Savior mingled with men as one who desired their good. He showed His sympathy for them, ministered to their needs, and won their confidence. Then He bade them, 'Follow Me.'"[30]

Jesus has set us an example that we should follow. If we are going to reach secular post-modern people, we have to be willing to take the risks, to go outside the fortress, and employ the unconventional. We have to set in motion forms of ministry that will allow us to get close to secular people, overcome the obstacles, and set aside the barriers that will prevent us from ministering to them in relevant ways. Bert B. Beach has rightly said that "Christianity needs to be relevant and be seen to be relevant. While we are not 'of the world,' we have a need to join the human race. We need to communicate the gospel persuasively and powerfully. But we also need to talk to people about the world they know, or we will talk ourselves out of the world into irrelevance."[31]

As we look at Jesus, we see that He had experienced, and then made the heart of His mission, a renewed appreciation of the free and gracious nature of the God of Israel, a God whose mission is not controlled and limited to carefully structured boundaries, but a God to whom people matter. This prophetic insight of Jesus not only explains many of the features of His mission, but provides a crucial link to the wider mission of the church. It also furnishes a good rationale (from a biblical and theological standpoint) for reaching all peoples, multitudes, and tongues, and that includes secular people (see Rev 14:6).

Other Examples: Logos, Hekate, Revelation 1: 17, 18, Koine Greek and Daniel 2 and 7

There are other examples in Scripture that help to furnish a biblical and theological rationale for reaching secular people. These examples come to us in a more contextualized fashion and include the following: John's use of the word *logos* in the prologue to his Gospel, the Greek goddess Hekate, in references to Rev 1:17, 18, the use of the *Koine* Greek in the writing of the New Testament, and Dan 2 and 7.

Logos

John 1:1 states, "In the beginning was the word and the word was with God, and the word was God." John begins his Gospel very profoundly, by introducing the idea of the "Word." Why did John use the "Word" to introduce Christ in this prologue?

In the original language (Greek), the "word" is *logos*.[32] Why the "word?" In using this term John was trying to reach his audience where they were. To develop this idea, an understanding of how the word *logos* was used and understood in John's day is necessary.

Beginning with the Greek Old Testament, the word (*logos*) of God creates, but is not a person: "By the word of the Lord were the heavens made. . . . He spoke, and it came to be (Ps 33:6, 9). Paulien explains that in this passage, the "word of the Lord" is to be taken literally as the powerful and creative expression of God's speech; not as a person who assisted in creation.[33]

In Prov 8:22-31, there is one that stood by God's side from the beginning as an active agent in creation, but that one is called "Wisdom" (Greek *sophia*, a female expression), not "word."[34]

The Old Testament contains concepts that seem to relate to John's use of the "word" but such usage is not identical to it.[35] It is in the area of Greek philosophy that John's use of the term the "word" finds its explanation.[36]

It was the Greek philosopher Plato (400 BC) who introduced a personality called the "word." The "Word" was great enough to commune with God as an equal and humble enough to get involved in the messiness of material things.[37]

It was Plato's idea that God was pure in mind, while matter was considered to be basically evil. Since God Himself could not "dirty His hands" in the process of creating and sustaining matter, Plato introduced "the Word," an intermediate God between the great God and His creation.[38] Later Greek philosophers such as Heraclitus and the Stoics expanded on Plato's ideas by identifying the Word as eternal, the Creator and Sustainer of the Universe, and the Source of all human reason and intelligence.[39]

At the time of Christ, the great Jewish philosopher Philo "sought to make Greek philosophy palatable to the Jews and the Old Testament palatable to the Greeks," thus he served as a bridge figure between Judaism and Greek philosophy. It was Philo who discerned the parallel between the Jewish concept of wisdom and the Greek concept of God.[40] "The result was a Jewish word-personality, which provided the essential background for John's use of the term 'Word.'"[41]

For Philo the Word was a "'second God,' the High Priest in the heavenly sanctuary, an Intercessor with God, the Law giver, the Mediator of revelation, the Sustainer of the universe, and the God of the Old Testament. Philo also called Him God's first born, His eldest Son, the image of God, and the Second Adam."[42]

Philo's descriptions of the *Logos* and those found in the New Testament bear striking parallels. One can only assume that God used Philo to prepare the world of his day for a personality just like Jesus.[43]

It is no wonder that both the gospel and Christ who is its subject are called "the Word." John's use of the word *logos* as understood in the contemporary Hellenistic world was for him a useful "bridge" word. People who read the gospel would have recognized the term as expressing everything they knew about Jesus.[44]

The essence of all this is that God always meets people where they are and communicates with them in language they can understand. John, as an inspired writer, employed a strategy similar to that of Acts 17. In Acts 17 Paul established common ground in "the unknown God." John in his Gospel employs a useful bridge word, *logos*, and uses it in such a way as to say, "the Word, whom you worship, is the subject of my book. Reading this book will help you understand Him and serve Him better."[45] By connecting with the Greeks and the Jews through the use of the *logos*, John introduced them to the Jesus of his Gospel,[46] whom to know is life eternal: "And this is eternal life, that they may know You, the only true God, and Jesus Christ whom you have sent" (John 17:3).

The lesson to be learned here is that we cannot expect people to appreciate the gospel we preach unless we communicate with them in language they can understand. In order to do this, we must first seek to understand the people we are trying to reach. This will require careful thought and hard work.[47]

It is in the area of language that perhaps more than anywhere else the mission principle of contextualization becomes critical. In our attempts to reach secular people, we need to put biblical truths into language that would be understood by them.[48] Secular people, for example, may not understand the phrase "washed in the blood of the Lamb," or the saying "Jesus is the answer," or the statement, "you must be born again." Statements and phrases such as these will not resonate with secular people. Secular people are, for the most part, ignostic, or biblically illiterate.[49] That is why John's "word" strategy is so instructive to us. We must communicate with secular people within their frame of reference, in order to be successful in reaching them in the twenty-first century.[50] What is the frame of reference that confronts the witness of the Christian Church today? It is the frame of reference in which secular post-modern men and women dismiss out of hand any presentation of the gospel that is cold and rational. The mindset of post-moderns are basically relational and by implication will not be influenced by any presentation of the gospel that is merely propositional. Certainly we "can no longer rely on didactic, cognitive approaches, as if Christianity were a case that could be proven in a court of law or demonstrated by methods suited to the laboratory."[51] Within this frame of reference the gospel must be "storied," presented as narrative, "set in aesthetic, poetic, or dramatic fashion and lived out in relationships and concrete ways." Post-moderns not only need to *know* about the gospel, they also want to *feel* it.[52] We must be story tellers, we must be relational, and we must be community oriented in our communication of the gospel. Cerebral, cold, unimpassioned presentations of the Biblical message must give way to narrative that has feeling and passion.

Hekate, Rev.1:17,18 and Koine Greek

Two other examples of how God reaches people where they are by speaking to them in language they can understand are John's use of a phrase in Rev 1:17, 18 and the apostles' use of the *Koine* Greek in the writing of the New Testament. In Rev 1:17, 18 John states that Christ has the "keys of Death and of Hades," a phrase used to describe the Greek goddess Hekate. Hekate was a popular heathen deity in and around Asia Minor at about the time John wrote the Apocalypse in the first century A.D. The apostle was using the same strategy as in John 1:1, when he introduced Christ as the Logos.

Similarly, the use of the *Koine* Greek in the writing of the New Testament demonstrates how God speaks to humans in the language of humans. The New Testament was not written in a supernatural heavenly language, but in common everyday language of the common folk. The Bible was the people's Book. This demonstrates that God meets us where we are and speaks to us in language we can understand and appreciate.[53]

Hekate, Rev 1:17, 18

This text reads as follows: "And when I saw Him, I fell at His feet as dead. But He laid His right hand on me, saying to me, "Do not be afraid; I am the first and the last. I am He who lives and was dead, and behold, I am alive forevermore. Amen. And I have the keys of Hades and of Death." Here John has a christophany[54] of the post-resurrected Christ. The description given by John in verses 12-16 is nothing short of Christ in His glorified state, a glorified state Jesus anticipated in John 17:5. John said that the One he saw was "like the Son of Man" (verse 13).[55]

David Aune sees this phrase, "one like the son of man" as an apparent allusion to the phrase found in Daniel 7:13.[56] LaRondelle agrees with this in his commentary on Matt 24:30. He states that Jesus referred to His return in terms borrowed from the judgment vision in Daniel 7.[57] For example, Jesus described Himself as the "Son of Man," who came from heaven (See John 3:13, 31, 32; 6:50, 51, 62) and who will return "on the clouds of heaven," meaning on the clouds of angels (See Dan 7:13, 9, 10). Jesus also said He would come as the Son of Man "with His power and great glory" (Matt 24:30), referring to His celestial glory spoken of in Daniel 7:14, 27.[58]

John also describes Jesus as saying, "I am He who lives, and was dead, and behold, I am alive forevermore. Amen. . . ." Here John gives us the *ego-eimi* or "I am" self-predication formula, which occurs five times in Rev (1:8, 17; 2:23; 21:6). This I AM formula is of interest in the Gospel of John.[59] More than any other Gospel, John deals explicitly with Christ's deity. John upholds his worthiness to be not only respected as a great teacher, but also worshiped as God.[60] John gives emphasis to several of these "I AM" statements found in his Gospel. For example, "I AM the bread of life" (John 6:35, 48); "I AM the living bread, descended from heaven" (6:51); "I AM the door" (10:7, 9); "I AM the good shepherd" (10:11, 14); "I AM the resurrection and the life" (11:25); "I AM the way, the truth, and the life" (14:6), and "I AM the true vine (15:1, 5).[61]

These passages allude to the Old Testament formula "I am He," meaning "I am Yahweh." Likewise in Revelation, John uses the "I AM" predications which are uttered exclusively by God (Rev 1:8; 21:6) and Christ (1:17; 2:23; 22:16) and are used to make divine predictions of the speakers (see Rev 1:8; 1:17; 2:23; 21:6, and 22:16).[62]

The idea being presented here is that John as evangelist and revelator, faithfully pursues his objective to present Jesus as God, so that others might "believe that Jesus is the Christ, the Son of God," and that believing they "might have life through His name" (John 20:30; 31). We saw earlier that John introduced Christ as the *logos*. Jesus is very God, who "declared" the Father. Christ is presented as the incarnate expression of the will of the Father that all men should be saved (see 1 Tim 2:4), "God's thought made audible."[63]

In the Book of Revelation, John again introduces Jesus in terms of His divinity. He is presented as the glorified post-resurrected Christ. John also goes a step further and seems to borrow terminology used to characterize Hellenistic deities. That terminology is found in Rev 1:18, where it says, "I am He who lives, and was dead, and behold, I am alive forevermore, Amen. And I have the keys of Hades and of Death." Aune states that the image of Jesus as Keybearer in this passage appears to have been derived from the popular Hellenistic conception of the goddess Hekate as Keybearer.[64] This Greek goddess originated in Asia Minor and was very popular there during the Hellenistic and Roman periods. Aune describes her as "the primary mythological figure associated with the possession of the keys to the gates of Hades."[65] Hekate was also considered *trimorphos*,

> "having three forms or shapes," suggesting cosmic significance connected with her threefold identity as Juno Licina, Trivia, and Luna. Each of these designates has reference to Moon, Earth, and Hades, respectively. Hekate is also said to be one who has "beginning and end . . . you alone rule all. For all things are from you, and in you do all things, eternal one, come to their end."[66]

The language used to describe this popular goddess of the Greco-Roman world, John took, and applied it to the risen Christ. This was an ingenious use of the language familiar to worshipers of this heathen deity. John utilized a "key phrase," so to speak, to communicate persuasively the good news about the risen Christ.

This illustrates how an inspired writer such as John was able to adapt the message about Christ, to the language and culture of the time. The word for this is contextualization.

When John made use of the "I AM" designates to speak about the glorified Christ, he articulated the fact that Christ is Deity, and that this glorified being is the One who came to earth, lived, died, and was resurrected according to the Scriptures (1 Cor 15:3, 3). It is He (by virtue of His death, burial, and resurrection) that holds the keys over Hades and Death.

Because John established common ground with the worshipers of heathen deities, he could invite his audience to read further about Him in his Gospel and in the Revelation. There they would discover that He lives, with life unborrowded and underived.[67] That He alone holds the keys, the symbols of power and jurisdiction,[68] and that by beholding Him they would be drawn to Him and find life everlasting.

Today as in John's day, there is need to dialogue with secular minds by finding the key phrases or key terms that would be a means of establishing common ground. The challenge is no less difficult. Many today have false conceptions of God and even worship false deities of their own. False ideas of God abound in our postmodern world. Many no longer embrace the biblical God but instead a higher consciousness or a sense of the divine from Eastern religions or simply many gods.[69] Ellen White states that "though in a different form, idolatry exists in the Christian world today as keenly as it existed among ancient Israel in the days of Elijah."[70] What is needed is the kind of language that would close the gap, and make the gospel simple for them to understand. This may seem unfamiliar territory, and may be for some a cause for apprehension, but we need to remember that it is the content of our message that is inspired and not the form.[71] It is somewhat regrettable that few if any of the traditional forms of communicating the gospel are still relevant. Here is an area that could be very troubling for us as Seventh-day Adventist. Our in-house lingua is all too familiar to us and provides the basis of our self-understanding and religious identity. We know no other and are comfortable with no other. We therefore need to keep two very important things in mind as we consider our challenge in communicating the gospel in a vastly different world than our forbearers. The first is that our postmodern-secular society is for the most part biblically illiterate and is somewhat if not entirely unfamiliar with traditional Christian liturgical practices and symbols, not to mention the nomenclature. They will not readily connect with the language and the phraseology that the faithful understand and readily embrace. The second thing we need to be conscious of is that mentioned earlier- our added in-house Adventist coded phraseology. Such phrases as "The Message," "The Third Angel," "The Spirit of Prophecy," "The Remnant," "The Loud Cry," "The Health Message," "1844 and The Investigative Judgment," are unintelligible to the "outsider." Add to these some theological phrases such as "Righteousness by Faith," "The Blood of the Lamb," "The Atoning Blood," "Our Great High Priest," etc., etc., terminology that we learned from childhood in kindergarten, and some of us through indoctrination at a latter stage. Such language however, is unintelligible to a secular person who is unschooled in the traditional Christian sense, and in particular the Adventist sense. It is therefore imperative that we learn the principle of contextualizing our "message" in such a way as to communicate with effectiveness, the way God intended that we should, as we endeavor to reach this generation- our postmodern society.

Koine Greek

Another important example of how God speaks to people in the language of people is how the inspired writers used the lingua franca or the *Koine* Greek, to write the New Testament. The Scriptures make mention that God sent forth His Son in the fullness of time (Gal 4:4). The *Seventh-day Adventist Commentary* states that "not only did the Messiah come at the most favorable time in all history. . . there was a universal language, Greek."[72]

The Greek spoken in the time of Christ is recognized as the *koine* Greek.[73] Koine was an evolution from the classic or attic Greek.[74] Attic Greek flourished at the height of Greek culture around the fourth and fifth centuries BC, and was the standard form of classical Greek. It was the chief literary language. Its influence was enhanced through its use by the greatest contemporary intellects, including the playwrights

Aeschylus, Euripides, and Sophocles, the orator Demosthenes, Plato, and the historians Thucydides and Xenophon.[75]

After the conquests of Alexandria the Great (c. 336-323 BC), Attic Greek underwent far-reaching changes. Alexander carried the Attic form of the language along with Greek culture more generally, far into the Near East where it became the standard language of commerce and government, existing alongside many local languages. Greek was adopted as a second language by the native people of these regions and was ultimately transformed into what has been called the *koine* or common Greek.[76] Koine became the universal language of the then known world. It became the common language of the common folk. It was into this environment that the Holy Spirit inspired the Gospels as Greek texts.

The records in Greek of Jesus' teaching and accomplishments prepared the way for the gospel to spread throughout a Greek-speaking culture.[77] "It is," as notes Nikolakopoulos, "an undisputed and remarkable fact, that the writers of the Christian message have made known Jesus' life, doctrine, and work by using the Greek language, which, in spite of Roman rule, dominated in all the known Mediterranean world of that time."[78]

This Koine or common language in which the New Testament was written, and was widely spread, "constituted no extreme philological form of the generally used language; it was the simple, daily, spoken and also written language of the people."[79] By using the colloquial tongue, the Bible became a people's book, and not merely a literary work in which the highly educated of the era would alone be interested.[80]

The language of the 27 books of the New Testament is not some phenomenon of supernatural dimensions descended from heaven. The inspired apostles wrote in the Greek Koine, which was spoken by almost all nations of the then-known world.[81]

Applying this great principle today will require that we present the gospel in language a secular audience can understand and appreciate. We have to learn how to rap (to use a colloquial expression) to the secular people we are trying to reach. Secular people for the most part do not possess a Christian vocabulary. The typical presentation of the gospel that characterizes most of our evangelistic efforts has no appeal for them. We are not scratching where it itches.

What I am suggesting is that we become intentional in seeking to understand the things that secular people value. Efforts should be made to understand their world view. It is also critical that we understand their language in order to communicate with relevance.

New methods and new approaches will have to be developed, where our secular audiences are concerned. This may not be as easy as it sounds. But the same God of the apostles, who inspired and guided their minds in the writing of the New Testament, is the same God who will grant us the wisdom we need in our efforts to reach secular people today.

Dan 2 and 7

In Dan 2 and 7 we have a good example of how God gave the same prophetic message to two different individuals, using different imagery and symbols due to their *Sitz im Leben*.

In Dan 2, God gave Nebuchadnezzar a dream of a great statue that was composed of different metals, listed in order of descending value.[82] The dream given to Nebuchadnezzar was an intended lesson for his realm.[83] The dream was intended to reveal to Nebuchadnezzar that the course of history was ordained by the Most High and subject to His will.[84]

The *Seventh-day Adventist Bible Commentary* states that "God approached King Nebuchadnezzar through a dream because, evidently, that was the most effective means by which to impress his mind with the importance of the message thus imparted, win his confidence, and secure his cooperation."[85]

Nebuchadnezzar, like other ancient peoples, believed that the gods revealed their will to men by means of dreams.[86] It is said for example that the Egyptian Pharaoh Meneptah (thirteenth century BC) reported seeing a huge image of the god Ptah in a dream. The god gave him permission to go to war against the Libyans. In another dream reported during the reign of Ashurbanipal, an inscription on the base of a statue of the god Sin forecast the failure of the rebellion in Babylon.[87]

Other ancient Mesopotamian records tell of royal dreams. In one of these Gudea saw a man with a kingly crown upon his head whose statue reached from earth to heaven. Such dreams were regarded with awe and treated as revelations from deities. The ancients also sought to discover their true interpretation.[88] Statues of mixed elements were also not uncommon. Walton, Matthews, and Chavalas mention, for example, that in a mid-second- millennium Hittite prayer a promise is made to supply a life-sized statue of the king with head, hands and feet of gold, and the rest of silver. Numerous second-millennium divine images have been uncovered that are made of bronze and covered with gold or silver.[89] It is not surprising to see why God would reveal future events to the heathen monarch by means of an immense and dazzling statue. "Divine wisdom always meets men where they are."[90]

In chap. 7 Daniel is also given a dream by God that concerns the same future events depicted by the mixed metal statue of Nebuchadnezzar's dream in chap. 2.[91] Chap. 7 has addressed details that expand on chap. 2. In chap. 7, however, God adjusted the content and symbols. Instead of a statue, we have four beasts. When one considers the fact that the content of both dreams represents the rise and fall of the same four world empires (Babylon, Medo-Persia, Greece, and Rome), then the question arises: Why did God communicate the same message, to two different individuals, with different figures and symbols? The answer to that is that God reaches people where they are by adapting His modes of working with people to the capacity of each individual, and to the environment in which each lives.[92]

On this point William Shea makes an observation. He states that the use of animals to represent kings is known especially from prophets who were contemporary with Daniel in the sixth century BC.[93] For example, Ezekiel referred to Nebuchadnezzar as an eagle (17:1-6). He also referred to Pharaoh of Egypt as an eagle, a lion, and a dragon (17:7-10; 32:2). Jeremiah applied the metaphors of a lion to Nebuchadnezzar twice (4:7; 50:17) and to the King of Assyria once (50:17).[94] Why were these shown to Daniel and not to Nebuchadnezzar?

Shea points out that since Nebuchadnezzar's religious convictions undoubtedly were those of a pagan polytheist, a fair amount of information in chap. 7 would not have been meaningful to him.

Shea observes, for example, that in order for the king to have grasped the significance of the "blasphemy" uttered by the little horn, he would have had to understand the monotheistic religion of Yahweh. "Nebuchadnezzar would have had considerable difficulty understanding much about the 'saints of the Most High' who were designated as the recipients of the final kingdom in chapter 7."[95]

In Dan. chap. 7 the elements in the dream were more relevant to God's people and would be readily understood by Daniel than by Nebuchadnezzar. But as concerns chap. 2, the king received a more rudimentary depiction of world history which he was better able to comprehend.[96]

It is therefore not only the language but also the very form and mode of communication that becomes critical in reaching people with God's message. This will require considerable effort, brainstorming, and creativity. Nevertheless, we are encouraged by the examples we have studied thus far. "When God presented His word to humanity, He gave it the time, place, language, and culture of specific human beings."[97]

This we have seen in the Gospel of John, the Revelation, and the use of *Koine* in the writing of the New Testament. Perhaps even more significant than the unique language and writing styles of the human authors of Scripture is the fact that God saw fit to adjust the content of dreams and visions to suit the individual he wanted to reach (Dan 2 and 7).

Paul's Ministry

Another important link in the expanding nature of the *Missio Dei* is the ministry of the apostle Paul. Paul's ministry is summed up in Rom 15:15-33. Paul as the apostle to the Gentiles had taken Jerusalem as his starting point out into Gentile territory.

Paul preached to many audiences. He covered three prolonged and extensive tours, the principle cities and provinces of Western Asia, Macedonia, and Greece, culminating in Rome, the renowned capital of the world. In the cities of Iconium, Lystra, and Antioch, Paul spoke in the Jewish synagogues and many Jews and Gentiles believed the gospel (Acts 14:1, 21, 22).[98]

As a result, Paul encountered various groups and classes of men. He used diverse methods and approaches in reaching his many audiences during his ministry. Paul speaks of this experience when he says:

> "For though I am free from all men, I have made myself a slave to all, that I might win the more. To the Jew I become as a Jew, in order to win Jews; to those under the law I become as one under the law—that I might win those under the law. To those outside the law I become as one outside the law—not being without law toward God but under the law of Christ—that I might win those outside the law. To the weak I become weak, that I might win the weak. I have become all things to all men, that I might by all means save some." (1 Cor 9:19-22, RSV)

Paul did not use a one-size-fits-all approach in his missionary endeavors. He adopted his method to suit the particular target audience. He was inclusive of all people, and sensitive to their cultural differences. In our day, many of the tried and tested methods that have been used in reaching evangelistic audiences are losing their appeal. In a contemporary secular society such as we find ourselves, it is necessary to employ new methods that will appeal to the needs of the people.[99]

While Paul refers to his "strategy" indirectly, and while one should be cautious in spelling out any overall plan he may have had, one can still see the apostle's deliberate attempt to reach all classes of people. For example, in his use of the Greek word *pantos* in vs. 22, expressing the meaning "by all means" seems to suggest that he was willing to adjust to the customs, habits, and opinions of all classes of people in order that he might save some.[100]

In summarizing his self-sacrificing concern, Paul declares, "I have become all things to all men, that I might by all means save some" (vs. 22).[101] All this is done "for the sake of the Gospel," "to win all the more"—as many souls as possible. Paulien has accurately summarized this point of view:

Jesus Christ did not remain in the isolation of His comfortable heavenly neighborhood, waiting for us to rescue ourselves. He came down, became one of us, reached out to us in our own world—a world that was hostile to everything He stood for. He thereby did for us what we could never have done for ourselves. When Paul acts "for the sake of the gospel," he seeks to bring to the lost the great blessings that Christ had brought to him. In light of the great salvation he had already received, he is compelled to go. Thus in 1 Corinthians 9 he calls on Christians to follow his example of reaching out to the lost in "radical" ways.[102]

Here we have a powerful rationale for reaching out and strategizing to reach secular people. While it may be radical and at times risky, it is, however, within our mission possibilities. We do well to take a chapter from the life of Paul, who himself said, "Be imitators of me as I am of Christ" (1 Cor 11:1). He ministered with both feet in the real world. Jesus Himself prayed to the Father on our behalf, "My prayer is not that you take them out of the world but that you protect them from the evil one" (John 17:15). We are to reach the lost where they live, work, and play—in the real world. This is radical, and yet not overly radical; it is simply doing what was exemplified by both Christ and Paul.[103] We are admonished to spend time with the people. We cannot effectively communicate God's word in insulation that is marked by temerity and trepidation. Rather, we are to spend time with people in their every-day lives and issues. This sort of mingling with secular-postmodern people prepares us to better minister God's word to them in relevant ways, addressing their felt needs and applying the Divine scratch to their earthly itch. The story is told of John Wesley who took one of his young preachers on a walk through the London fish market. "When the young man recoiled at the colorful, earthly language of the fishmongers and started to flee, Wesley said, 'Stay...and learn to preach!' Preachers" (and/or laity), "cannot be too sanctimonious to hear the people, even when every expression is not sanitized."[104]

Paul's example suggests fishing for people by going where they are. If we approach people with an attitude of acceptance rather than an overly critical attitude that is judgmental, people will feel accepted and respond to us. Some of the most open people, whose hungry hearts are ripe for the gospel, smoke, curse, and tell off-color jokes. The Christian who desires to reach them must be willing to encounter some corruption and adversity. I am not advocating participation in such unholy activity, nor am I promoting total isolation from it. The more moderate track of a critical presence is advised. A mature Christian can survive in such an atmosphere on a limited basis and still not practice or condone any of these questionable activities.[105] It does indeed take a special kind of person to reach out to secular people in a meaningful way without crossing the barriers of social propriety. Paulien refers to such a person as a "two-horizon" person—a person who is not only comfortable in a traditional religious setting, but who can also step out and be comfortable in the secular world.[106]

Such was the apostle Paul. He became all things to all people, without sacrificing principle. He was being under the law to those who were under the law, yet he was not without law to Christ. Paul was not willing to allow non-salvation issues to stand in the way of the salvation of others. We, too, like Paul must refuse to condone, without condemning, the non-Christian for practices that, though unseemly, will not keep him or her out of heaven. This was the problem of the Pharisees in Paul's day. They were content to fish in isolation—in stained-glass aquariums—and came up empty. In our day a major weakness in evangelism is due to this Pharisaic unwillingness to live in the real world. We have become insular, what Hull refers to as "rabbit hole believers," just sticking our head out for a peek at that nasty world every now and then.[107] It is true that God says "Come out from among them and be ye separate" (2 Cor 6:17), but God requires more than insulation from those we are commanded to reach.

The fatal mistake we need to avoid is the tendency to treat the unbeliever as the enemy rather than the victim of the enemy. We need to be careful not to erect unnecessary barriers between ourselves and the very ones we are trying to reach. These barriers are usually cultural and not theological. We should also guard against any legalistic attitude that says, "If you practice certain activities, you are not welcome in the Christian community." Such a legalistic, judgmental attitude repulses the unbeliever, alienating him from the one who should be graciously accepting him or her.

In a recent article entitled "A Sinner among Saints: Is There Room for Me in Your Church?" Cesar Gonzalez tells of an experience involving a young man who lived life on the edge and whose physical appearance told the story all too well. The young man's body was covered with tattoos among which were swastikas and other hate symbols. His appearance testified of a hard and ruthless life.

He was invited to attend a Christian youth convention, "Excite 98," in southern California. No sooner had he arrived than an older woman began to take offense at his appearance. She began to shout from a distance such questions as "Who are you?" "What are you doing here?" "What have you done to yourself? Don't you know that the Bible says that our bodies are temples of God?" She badgered him with other questions such as "Don't you know that you are going to hell if you don't repent?" "What do you have to say for yourself?"

Needless to say, the young man became very tense and was about to lose his temper. Gonzalez stood between the young man and the older lady and demanded that she leave him alone. She left sneering and yelling holy insults.

Later Gonzalez asked the young man what he would say to church members if he could. His answer was, "I would tell them to remember that the church is for sinners. I would tell them that the worse shape someone is in, the more help they need. I would tell them to be more forgiving and less judgmental. There is no need for that in the church, that's what cops and judges are for."[108] Not so was the apostle Paul. He kept the unbeliever's view of salvation uncluttered with cultural biases. He kept the message of salvation simple and pure, by becoming all things to all men in order to obtain their salvation.[109] His purpose was to reach men on their own turf, to rub shoulders with them, to find common ground in order to bring them to higher ground in the gospel.

This strategy we see carried out in Paul's ministry. Everything that Paul did, his ready adaptation to the particular society in which he found himself and his willingness to be tolerant and patient toward all men, had but one objective—the saving of those who would believe in his message. Paul did not say he would save all, because he was aware of the fact that many would not believe (Rom 9:27; 11:5). By his course of adjustment to the customs, habits, and opinions of all classes of men in order that he might save some, Paul followed closely the pattern set by the Savior, of whom the prophet wrote: "A bruised reed shall he not break" (Isa 42:1-3).[110]

Adaptability is one of the most useful qualities that we can cultivate. It will help us to work as Jesus worked: in the homes of the poor and ignorant, in the market place among merchants and financiers, at the feasts and entertainments of the wealthy, and in conversation with the wise. We should be willing to go anywhere and use whatever method is most suitable in order to win men and women for God's eternal kingdom of glory and peace.[111]

Ellen White

Among the many statements found throughout the writings of Ellen White are several on the extent and nature of the gospel commission to reach every class of people in the world. She speaks of getting close to the people, meeting them where they are. Many of her statements are in harmony with the kind of mission outreach it would take to reach secular people. Since some of these statements can be applied within the context of the need to reach secular people, some of them are incorporated here.

Gospel Invitation to All the World

"The gospel invitation is to be given to all the world—'to every nation, and kindred, and tongue, and people' (Rev 14:6). The last message of warning and mercy is to lighten the whole earth with its glory. It is to reach all classes of men, rich and poor, high and low. 'Go out into the highways and hedges,' Christ says, 'and compel them to come in, that my house may be filled'" (Luke 14:23).[112]

Every Soul to Be Reached

In the command to go into the highways and hedges, Christ sets forth the work of all whom He calls to minister in His name. The whole world is the field for Christ's ministers. The whole human family is comprised in their congregation. The Lord desires that His word of grace shall be brought home to every soul.[113]

Highways and Hedges

In commenting on the phase "highways and hedges," Ellen White applies it to the need of reaching different classes of people. The following statements are in support of this.

The message is first to be given in the highways—to men who have an active part in the world's work, to the teachers and leaders of the people.

> 'Let the Lord's messengers bear this in mind. To the shepherds of the flock, the teachers divinely appointed, it should come as a word to be heeded. Those who belong to the higher ranks of society are to be sought out with tender affection and brotherly regard. Men in business life, in high positions of trust, men with large inventive faculties and scientific insight, men of genius, teachers of the gospel whose minds have not been called to the special truths for this time—these should be the first to hear the call. To them the invitation must be given. There is a work to be done for the wealthy.[114]

Those who stand high in the world for their education, wealth, or calling are seldom addressed personally in regard to the interests of the soul. Many Christian workers hesitate to approach these classes. But this should not be. If a man were drowning, we would not stand by and watch him perish because he was a lawyer, a merchant, or a judge. If we saw persons rushing over a precipice, we would not hesitate to urge them back, whatever might be their position or calling. Neither should we hesitate to warn people of the peril of the soul.[115]

Again Ellen White shifts her emphasis in yet another statement that is inclusive of the poorer classes:

> Christ instructs His messengers to go also to those in the byways and hedges, to the poor and lowly of the earth. In the courts and lanes of the great cities, in the lonely byways of the country, are families and individuals—perhaps strangers in a strange land—who are without church relations, and who, in their loneliness, come to feel that God has forgotten them. They do not understand what they must do to be saved. Many are sunken in sin. Many are in distress. They are pressed with suffering, want, unbelief, despondency. Diseases of every type afflict them, both in body and in soul.
>
> God has given a special command that we should regard the stranger, the outcast, and the poor souls who are weak in moral power. Many who appear wholly indifferent to religious things are in heart longing for rest and peace. Although they may have sunken to the very depths of sin, there is a possibility of saving them.[116]

This explanation by Ellen White of the highways and byways as it relates to the gospel commission is all-inclusive. Among every rank and in every place the gospel is to be taken. This all-inclusive emphasis no doubt will include secular people, who will be found among all classes and ranks of people.[117] It is safe to assume, therefore, that when Jesus commanded His servants to go into the highways and byways, ministry to secular people could also be included here.

Jew and Gentile

Before ascending to heaven, Christ gave His disciples their commission. To you, my disciples, I commit this message of mercy. It is to be given to both Jews and Gentiles—to Israel, first, and then to all nations, tongues, and peoples. All who believe are to be gathered into one church."[118]

> The Saviour Himself, during His earthly ministry, foretold the spread of the gospel among the Gentiles. In the parable of the vineyard He declared to the impenitent Jews, "The kingdom of God shall be taken from you, and given to a nation bringing forth the fruits thereof" (Matt 21:43). And after His resurrection He commissioned His disciples to go "into all the world" and "teach all nations." They were to leave none unwarned, but were to "preach the gospel to every creature" (Matt 28:19; Mark 16:15).[119]

> The commission given to the disciples is given also to us. Today as then, a crucified and risen Saviour is to be uplifted before those who are without God and without hope in the world. The Lord calls for pastors, teachers, and evangelists. From door to door His servants are to proclaim the message of salvation. To every nation, kindred, tongue, and people the tidings of pardon through Christ are to be carried.[120]

Ellen White advocates different methods and ways of trying to reach the people.

Different Methods

To preach the gospel means much more than many realize. . . . Some will be attracted by one phase of the gospel, and some by another. We are instructed by our Lord to work in such a way that all classes will be reached. The message must go to the whole world.[121]

> "The gospel invitation is to be given to the rich and the poor, the high and the low, and we must   devise means for carrying the truth into new places, and to all classes of people."[122]

New methods must be introduced. God's people must awake to the necessities of the time in which they are living. God has men whom He will call into His service—men who will not carry forward the work in the lifeless way in which it has been carried in the past.[123]

"Means will be devised to reach hearts. Some of the methods used in the work will be different from the methods used in the work in the past; but let no one, because of this, block the way by criticism."[124]

"Let every worker in the Master's vineyard study, plan, devise methods to reach the people where they are. We must do something out of the common course of things."[125]

"From Christ's methods of labor we may learn many valuable lessons. He did not follow merely one method; in various ways He sought to gain the attention of the multitude; and then He proclaimed to them the truths of the gospel."[126]

Ellen White has said that Christ's method alone will bring success. The question, therefore, is, what was Christ's method?

Christ's Method

"Christ's method alone will give true success in reaching the people. The Savior mingled with men as one who desired their good. He showed His sympathy for them, ministered to their needs, and won their confidence. Then He bade them, 'follow me.'"[127]

Jesus "sought access to the people by the pathway of their most familiar associations."[128]

He taught in such a way as to make people "feel the completeness of His identification with their interests and happiness."[129]

"He passed by no human being as worthless, but sought to apply the healing remedy to every soul. In whatever company He found Himself He presented a lesson appropriate to the time and the circumstances."[130]

Jesus accepted the hospitality of people, He slept under others' roofs, and ate at their tables the food prepared and served by their hands. He taught in their streets and treated them with kindness and courtesy.[131]

> He was not indifferent to the wants of others but was awake to the needs of all.[132]

Thus Ellen White has shown that mission outreach should be adapted to various methods and strategies for reaching different people.

Summary

This biblical and theological rationale has endeavored to show the universal scope of mission, and to show God's intent of reaching every human being with the everlasting gospel. From Matthew to Revelation, the New Testament emphasizes the full extent of the church's task: "This gospel of the kingdom will be preached throughout the whole world" (Matt 24:14); "you shall be my witnesses . . . to the end of the earth" (Acts 1:8); "Then I saw another angel flying in mid heaven, with an eternal gospel to proclaim to those who dwell on earth, to every nation and tribe and tongue and people" (Rev 14:6).

The context in which we must carry out our mission, however, is not essentially different from the one that early Christians faced— people either ignorant of or hostile toward Christianity. We face mission wherever there is unbelief and, of course, this will include the secular. Looking at the nature and scope of the *Missio Dei*, the work and ministry of Christ, the various examples of how God reaches people otesnwhere they are, the ministry of the apostle Paul, and the teachings of Ellen White, we see that we have a good basis for developing and implementing strategies that would be a means of helping us to fulfill our gospel mandate in reaching all groups of men and women and in this case the secular mind.

Chapter 4 Notes

1. The harvest field to which our Lord refers is the whole world, all nations, races, and ethnic and cultural groups, of which secular people are just a part. See Luke 10:2 and Rev 14:6.

2. Hunter, *Church for the Unchurched*, 23, 24.

3. Gerhard F. Hasel, *The Covenant in Blood* (Mountain View, CA: Pacific Press Publishing Assn., 1982), 13.

4. Norman E. Thorne, ed., *Classic Texts in Mission and World Christianity* (Maryknoll, NY: Orbis Books, 1998), 101.

5. David J. Bosch, *Transforming Mission: Paradigm Shifts in Theology of Mission* (Maryknoll, NY: Orbis Books, 1998), 390.

6. Ibid.392.

7. Vimoth Ramachandra, *The Recovery of Mission: Beyond the Pluralist Paradigm* (Grand Rapids, MI: William B. Eerdmans Publishing Company, 1997), 230.

8. Ellen G. White, *The Desire of Ages* (Mountain View, CA: Pacific Press, 1940), 400, 401.

9. Ibid., 403.

10. Bert B. Beach, "Adventism and Secularization," *Ministry*, April 1996, 22.

11. Ibid.

12. Paulien, *Present Truth in the Real World*, 81, 82.

13. Ibid.

14. Harold L. Lee with Monte Sahlin, *BRAD: Visionary Spiritual Leadership,* (Huntsville, Alabama: Bradford-Cleveland Institute, 2005), 70.

15. Pauline, 81, 82.

16. Lee, Sahlin, 71.

17. White, 194; italics supplied.

18. Tim Wright, *Unfinished Evangelism: More Than Getting Them in the Door* (Minneapolis: Augsburg, 1995), 62.

19. Ibid.

20. Ibid.

21. Bill Hull, *Jesus Christ, Disciple Maker: Rediscovering Jesus' Strategy for Building His Church* (Grand Rapids, MI: Fleming H. Revell, 1994), 101.

22. White, *The Desire of Ages*, 195.

23. Hunter, *Church for the Unchurched*, 24, 25.

24. Ibid., 23.

25. White, *The Desire of Ages*, 193.

26. Donald Senior and Carroll Stuhlmueller, *The Biblical Foundations for Mission* (Maryknoll, NY: Orbis Books, 1989), 147.

27. Mark Mittleberg, *Building a Contagious Church: Revolutionizing the Way We View and Do Evangelism* (Grand Rapids, MI: Zondervan Publishing House, 2000), 35.

28. Ibid.

29. White, *The Desire of Ages*, 193.

30. Ellen G. White, *The Ministry of Healing* (Mountain View, CA: Pacific Press Publishing Association, 1942), 143.

31. Beach, 24.

32. "A Study of Christ: the Prologue to John," *A Journal of Exposition* 3, no. 4 (May 1996), [journal on-line]; available from http://www.scripturestudies.com/index.html; Internet; accessed 12 January, 2001.

33. Jon Paulien, *The Abundant Life Bible Amplifier--John* (Boise, ID: Pacific Press Publishing Association, 1995), 39.

34. Ibid., 40.

35. Ibid.

36. See for example Richard B. Hays, *The Moral Vision of the New Testament* (San Francisco: Harper-San Francisco, 1996), 140-142; and Walter A. Elwell, ed., "Logos" *Evangelical Dictionary of Theology* (Grand Rapids, MI: Baker Book House, 1984), 645, 646.

37. Paulien, *Bible Amplifier*, 40.

38. Ibid.

39. Ibid.

40. Ibid.

41. Ibid.

42. Ibid., 41.

43. Ibid.

44. Paulien, *Bible Amplifier*, 41.

45. Ibid.

46. Ibid.

47. Mittleberg, 51.

48. Ibid.

49. For an understanding of the secular mind, please refer back to chapter 2 of this study.

50. Paulien, *Bible Amplifier*, 41; Mittleberg, 51, 52. See also "Secular Mind Grouping" in chapter 2 of this study.

51. Michael Pocock, Gailyn Van Rheenen, Douglas McConnell, *The Changing Face of World Missions: Engaging Contemporary Issues and Trends* (Grand Rapids, MI: Baker Academic, 2005), 104,107.

52. Ibid. 107, 103.

53. See David Aune, "Revelation 1-5," *Word Biblical Commentary* "Revelation 1-5" (Dallas, TX: Word Books, 1997), 52:100. See also Christine Downing, "Hekate," *The Encyclopedia of Religion* (New York: Collier MacMillan Publishers, 1987), 251, 252. See Konstantine Nikolakopoulous, "The Language of the New Testament and an Example for the Historical Unity of the Greek Language," *Greek Orthodox Theological Review* 42 (1997): 259-266. For a fuller discussion of Hekate and the Koine Greek, please refer to Appendix.

54. David Aune, *Word Biblical Commentary* "Revelation 1-5 (Dallas, TX: Word Books, 1997), 52: 100.

55. Ibid., 90.

56. Ibid.

57. Hans K. LaRondelle, *Light for the Last Days: Jesus' End-Time Prophecies Made Plain in the Book of Revelation* (Nampa, ID: Pacific Press Publishing Association, 1999), 17.

58. Ibid.

59. Aune, 100.

60. Ibid. See also *A Study of Christ*, vol. 3, no. 4, 1 of 1.

61. Aune, 101.

62. Ibid.

63. "Word" (Gr. *Logos*) *Seventh-day Adventist Bible Commentary*, ed. F. D. Nichol (Hagerstown, MD: Review and Herald Publishing Association, 1980), 5: 879). See also Ellen G. White, *The Desire of Ages*, 19.

64. Aune, 104. See also Christine Downing, "Hekate," *The Encyclopedia of Religion* (New York: Collier MacMillan Publishers, 1987), 251, 252.

65. Aune, 104.

66. Ibid.

67. See Ellen G. White, *The Desire of Ages,* 530.

68. "Keys," *Seventh-day Adventist Bible Commentary*, ed. F. D. Nichol (Hagerstown, MD: Review and Herald Publishing Association, 1957, 1980), 7: 740.

69. Andrew Walsh, "Church, Lies, and Polling Data," in *Religion in the News* 1 (Fall 1998 no.2), 4.

70. Ellen G. White, *The Great Controversy* (Boise, ID: Pacific Press Publishing Association, 1950), 583.

71. Ellen G. White, *Selected Messages* 2 vols (Washington, DC: Review and Herald Publishing Association, 1958), 1: 21, 22.

72. "Fullness," *Seventh-day Adventist Bible Commentary*, ed. F. D. Nichol (Hagerstown, MD: Review and Herald Publishing Association, 1980), 6: 695.

73. Note that it is also recognized that Jesus and His apostles spoke Aramaic. That does not mean, however, that the Greek language was not spoken in Palestine during the time of the Lord. See

Konstantine Nikolakopoulous, "The Language of the New Testament and an Example for the Historical Unity of the Greek Language," in *Greek Orthodox Theological Review* 42 (1997), 259.

74. It is not the intent of this study to deal with a detailed historical development of the Greek language. For further study on this issue, please refer to: Larry Lee Walker, "Biblical Languages," in *Baker Encyclopedia of the Bible*, ed. Walter A. Elwell (Grand Rapids, MI: Baker Book House, 1988), 337-339. See also Geoffrey Horrocks, *Greek: A History of the Language and Its Speakers* (White Plaines: Longman Publishing Group, 1998).

75. George E. Duckworth, "Greek Language," an Encarta Encyclopedia Article, available from http://encarta.msn.com/index/conciseindex/04/00403000.htm (accessed 9 January, 2001), internet.

76. Ibid.

77. Walker, "Biblical Languages," 338.

78. Nikolakopoulos, "The Language of the New Testament," 259, 260.

79. Ibid., 261.

80. "Greek" (Language), *Seventh-day Adventist Bible Dictionary: Commentary Reference Series*, ed. Siegfried H. Horn (Hagerstown, MD: Review and Herald Publishing Association, 1979), 444.

81. Nikolakopoulos, 266.

82. William H. Shea, "Unity of Daniel," in *Symposium on Daniel*, 3 vols., ed. Frank B. Holbrook (Washington, DC: Biblical Research Institute, General Conference of Seventh-day Adventists, 1986), 174.

83. "Dream Dreams," *Seventh-day Adventist Bible Commentary*, ed. Frank D. Nichol (Hagerstown, MD: Review and Herald Publishing Association, 1977), 4:766.

84. Ibid., 767.

85. Ibid.

86. Ibid.

87. John H. Walton, Victor H. Matthews and Mark W. Chavalas, *The IVP Bible Background Commentary: Old Testament* (Downers Grove, IL: InterVarsity Press, 2000), 733.

88. "Dream Dreams," *SDABC*, 4:766.

89. Walton, Matthews, and Chavalas, 733,

90. C. Mervyn Maxwell, *God Cares* (Nampa, ID: Pacific Press Publishing Association, 1981): 1: 35. See also the "Dream Dreams," *SDABC*, 4:767.

91. For a detailed discussion of the unity of Dan 2 and 7, see William Shea, "Unity of Daniel," 2 and 7, pp. 165-182, and William Shea, *The Abundant Bible Amplifier*, 2 vols. (Boise, ID: Pacific Press Publishing Association, 1996), 1:131-183.

92. "Dream Dreams," *SDABC*, 4:767.

93. Shea, Symposium On Daniel, 174.

94. Ibid.

95. Ibid., 175.

96. Ibid.

97. Paulien, *Scratching Where It Itches*, 1.

98. Earl P. W. Cameron, *Evangelism in Today's World: Attracting Evangelistic Audiences in a Secular Society* (Oshawa, Ontario, Canada: Maracle Press, 1996), 23.

99. Ibid., 24.

100. Ibid., 26.

101. Ibid., 25, 26.

102. Paulien, Present Truth in the Real World, 75.

103. Hull, 104.

104. Lee, Sahlin, 28.

105. Hull, 102.

106. Paulien, Present Truth in the Real World, 137.

107. Hull, 102, 103.

108. Cesar Gonzalez, "A Sinner Among Saints: Is There Room for Me in Your Church?" *View*, Summer 1999, 12-15, 22.

109. Hull, 101.

110. "Save Some" [1 Cor 9:22], *The Seventh-day Adventist Bible Commentary*, ed. F. D. Nichol (Washington, DC: Review & Herald, 1980), 6: 734, 735.

111. Ibid., 735. See also White, *Ministry of Healing*, 23-25; idem, *Gospel Workers*, 118, 119.

112. Ellen G. White, *Positive Christian Living* (Washington, DC: Review & Herald, 1952), 202.

113. Ibid.

114. Ibid., 203.

115. Ellen G. White, *Christian Service* (Hagerstown, MD: Review and Herald, 1983), 202.

116. Ibid., 205-206.

117. Hunter stated that in the United State alone there are at least 120, 000, 000 secular people (14 or older). These are not a single homogeneous group as some would like to think. Hunter states that secular people compose many distinct audiences based on differences in ethnicity, culture, age, needs, education, socioeconomic class, etc. (*How to Reach Secular People*, 41).

118. White, *Acts of the Apostles*, 27, 28.

119. Ibid., 174.

120. Ellen G. White, *Gospel Workers* (Washington, DC: Review & Herald Pub. Assn., 1915), 29.

121. Ellen G. White, *Evangelism* (Washington, DC: Review & Herald, 1974), 536.

122. Ibid., 549.

123. Ibid., 70.

124. Ibid., 105.

125. Ibid., 122, 123.

126. Ibid., 123.

127. E. G. White, *The Ministry of Healing*, 143.

128. White, *Evangelism*, 55.

129. Ibid.

130. White, *The Ministry of Healing*, 25, 26.

131. Ibid., 26.

132. White, *Evangelism*, 636.

CHAPTER 5

THREE MODELS FOR REACHING SECULAR PEOPLE

In the previous chapter, I discussed the biblical and theological rationale for reaching secular people. The concept of the Missio Dei, with emphasis on the ministry of Christ, Paul, and the writings of Ellen White, was the main point of reference in establishing that rationale. The all-inclusive nature of Christ's ministry and method, Paul's strategy to become all things to all men, and Ellen White's observations and statements on the need to devise new plans and strategies out of the ordinary suggest that plans and methods must be used to meet people in their unique contexts.

The intent of this chapter is to survey and analyze three models for reaching secular people: Bill Hybels—Willow Creek Community Church; Greg Taylor and Erin Miller—Foster Seventh-day Adventist Church; and Rick Warren—Saddleback Community Church.

There will be a general survey of each model for the purpose of ascertaining their basic strategy. Following will be a critical analysis that will take into account the strengths and weaknesses of these three models.

Bill Hybels—Willow Creek Community Church

Bill Hybels is founder and pastor of the Willow Creek Community Church in the northwest Chicago suburb of South Barrington, Illinois. Pastor Bill Hybels was influenced by certain individuals as he grew into his ministry and the development of the Willow Creek Community Church. The two individuals who are believed to have had a significant impact on Bill Hybels's life and ministry are Professor Gilbert Bilezikian and Robert Schuller.[1]

Kind of Church

The kind of church that Hybels started in Willow Creek grew out of the Son City days.[2] The Son City youth group that Hybels led was designed to reach unchurched high-school-age young people for Christ. The services were designed for non-believing friends. They used multimedia, contemporary music, skits, and messages that would help high-school students. In three years, attendance had increased to more than a thousand young people.[3] Hybels did not stop there. Haunted by the vision of the church as presented by his mentor Dr. Bilezikian—that the church is God's redemptive tool in the world, that the church can impact the world, and that the church and the church alone can transform the world—Hybels realized that he could not limit his ministry to kids only. "Kids have the zeal and sincerity, but they lack the depth, the leadership skills, the life experience, the resources, the leverage, the power to impact the world."[4] What Hybels had in mind was a church so strong, so biblical, so well-resourced, and so alive with the reality of Christ that it could be a major player in the drama of God's world-wide plan. Thus in 1975 Hybels started Willow Creek Community Church with a clear purpose in mind: "to build a biblical community that could some day carry out God's redemptive purposes in the world."[5]

Hybels began by surveying the South Barrington community. Included in the survey were questions such as, "Are you active in a local church?" If the answer to that question was "yes," Hybels and his team would then move on to the next house. If the answer was "no," the following question would be, "Would you be willing to tell us why you do not attend?" A range of answers were given from, "Pastors talked about issues that had nothing to do with my daily life" to such things as "Church services are lifeless, boring and predictable," and a very frequent response was "The churches were always asking for money."[6]

This survey helped to convince Hybels that traditional and often boring services would not attract the vast majority of adult non-churched people. Drawing cues from what he learned from the survey, from his experience with Son City, and the influence of Dr. Bilezikian and Robert Schuller, Hybels and his staff developed a strategy for reaching and meeting the needs of what became the principal target of the Willow Creek Community Church, namely, unchurched Harry and Mary.[7]

The key to understanding Willow Creek's basic philosophy and why they do what they do to attract seekers is to understand what their profiled target audience is like.[8]

Basic Strategy

Part of Willow Creek's strategy for reaching non-Christians involves gathering information about them, learning all about who they are, their background, their environment, their tastes and beliefs. Mark Mittleberg, who is the evangelism director of Willow Creek, asserts that Willow Creek can only begin to move unchurched Harrys when these elements are known. "That is the nature of persuasion—bringing a person from where they are to where they need to be."[9]

According to Hybels, everything that happens in a weekend service is a direct response to the target audience that Willow Creek has selected.[10]

Profiling Unchurched Harry and Mary[11]

This profiling of unchurched Harry and Mary (heretofore referred to as Harry) is inclusive of more than just age, education, and marital status, etc. It also includes Harry's lifestyle, needs, and attitude toward religion.

Age

Willow Creek's target audience is between 25 and 45 years of age. Thus Harry is found among a range of age groups. Sixty percent of Willow Creek's weekend audience are Baby Boomers, ages 27 to 45. Another 14 percent are Baby Busters, ages 14 to 26. Nearly 75 percent of the Willow Creek weekend audience is between ages 14 and 45. The average age of an attendee is 36.

Marital status

About 60 percent of the Harrys that attend Willow Creek's weekend seeker services are married and most have children. Only 25 percent of the audience are single and 12 percent are divorced.

Education

The majority of the weekend attendees at Willow Creek are well educated. Those who have graduated from college represent about 50 percent. Another 25 percent are either enrolled in college or have attended some college.

Jobs

The majority of Harrys who attend Willow Creek are professionals. According to Pritchard, about 12 percent are self-employed. Only about 3.7 percent are unemployed as compared to the national rate of 7 to 8 percent.

Harry lives in a middle to upper middle-class neighborhood, but is financially stretched. Harry has high credit card bills, is living on the financial edge, and has little excess cash.

Harry's felt needs

What are some of Harry's felt needs?

1. The need for personal fulfillment

2. A need for understanding self and personal identity

3. A need for companionship growing out of frequent feelings of intense loneliness

4. The need for intimacy, which is strained due to the pursuit for personal fulfillment, and is evidenced in high divorce rates

5. The need for moral and spiritual training of Harry's children as evidenced in a statement made by Lee Strobel that says, "Even if Harry is not spiritually sensitive, he wants his children to get quality moral training"

6. A need for relief from stress; stress from job, extended family, kids, and marriage follows on the heels of stress resulting from a desire for intimacy and fulfillment. A survey of the Willow Creek Church revealed that about one-third of those in attendance feel "totally stressed out."

Harry and Mary's attitude toward religion

1. Harry and Mary may have rejected church, but they have not necessarily rejected God. They are "religious" persons with spiritual interests. They are simply turned off by the church. They perceive the church as archaic and irrelevant.

2. Harry and Mary are morally adrift, but secretly want an anchor. They are searching for moral direction for their lives.

3. Harry and Mary are resistant to rules but respond to reason. He or she does not like being told what to do.

4. Harry and Mary do not understand Christianity, and they are also ignorant about what they claim to believe in.

5. Harry and Mary have legitimate questions about spiritual matters, but they do not expect answers from Christians. This is partly due to their perception of the church as a place where no questions are allowed.

6. Harry and Mary are not just asking "Is Christianity true?" they are asking, "Does Christianity work?" Gary Collins and Timothy Clinton, in their book Baby Boomer Blues, suggest that baby busters, for example, expect that their needs should be met, jobs will be provided, money will be available, and problems will be solved. They expect everything right away. Life is to be lived for the present. They are the "now" generation that has little interest in any religion that speaks of "the sweet by and by." Harry and Mary want to hear about a faith that works now and brings immediate results.

7. Harry and Mary not only want to know something; they want to experience it. They want to have a personal encounter with God, not just have information passed on about Him. They want to move beyond philosophical discussions of religion to the actual experience of God in their lives. In this respect they are not expecting church services to be stilted, stale, and stiff; they expect them to be sincere, stimulating, and spirited. Harry and Mary are looking for a climate that is conducive to their quest for a personal experience with God.

8. Harry and Mary do not want to be treated as somebody's project. They want to be somebody's friend—no strings attached. Harry and Mary do not want to feel that the motive behind the friendship is to convert them. They want authenticity.[12]

Seven-Step Strategy

A central feature in the overall strategy of Willow Creek Community Church is the seven-step strategy. This seven-step strategy helps to fulfill the purpose of turning "irreligious" people (such as Harry and Mary) into fully devoted followers of Christ." The members are encouraged to do the following in the seven-step strategy:[13]

Step 1. Build an authentic relationship with a nonbeliever. Willow Creek empowers its members to proactively build relationships with irreligious people through the "Being a Contagious

Christian" training course. The ultimate purpose for building these relationships is to lead irreligious people to Christ.

Step 2.   Share a verbal witness. "It is not enough to merely enter into the world of nonbelievers, build relationships with them, and live out our faith in front of them," says Hybels, but, "as the apostle Peter cautioned, 'always be prepared to give an answer to everyone who asks you to give the reason for the hope that you have' (1 Pet 3:15)." Believers are also taught how to verbalize their testimony about how Christ changed their lives. They are also trained in how to master several techniques of communicating their faith in a graphic and concise way.

Step 3.   Bring the Seeker to a Service designed especially for them. After having built meaningful relationships with irreligious individuals, praying for them, caring for them, and sharing with them how Christ has changed their lives, etc., believers are then encouraged to invite their friends to a seeker service. Those in the church who are gifted as musicians, actors, producers and teachers, dancers, and vocalists knock themselves out to present the basic truths of Christianity in a creative, compelling, and Spirit-anointed way. Believers are encouraged to use this approach as a personal witnessing tool. The end result is "team evangelism."

Step 4.   Regularly attend a service for believers. This service is called the "New Community Worship" and takes place on Wednesday and Thursday nights. In this service new believers come to thank and praise God. They also express their enthusiasm in their new-found faith. In this service new believers are also nurtured and encouraged, challenged and inspired. It is also a "core meeting" of the church, aside from the seekers. It is where Hybels can "exert leadership among the family . . . shore up a sagging value, talk about a new opportunity . . . handling "family matters" without . . . seekers."

Step 5.   Join a small group. The small group is a place where spiritual growth can take place. Hybels says that "small groups provide the optimal environment for incubating the maturing process." Small groups also provide for transparency and for applying biblical truth to real-life situations. Small groups function as little platoons where there is loyalty and compassion, commitment and caring, and prayer and mutual sacrifice. Members of the small group also expose their faith and fears, seek counsel and encouragement, hold each other accountable, grow together spiritually, and give and receive love of another kind.

Step 6. Discover, develop, and deploy your spiritual gifts. At Willow Creek, they start, not with a volunteer and a slot to fill, but with the person. They seek to find out what spiritual gifts God endowed the person with. They seek out their passion, temperament, and personality. Once that is determined, that individual is matched with a position in one of the ninety-four ministries that fit him or her well.

Step 7. Steward your resources in a God-honoring way. At this point, new believers are taught the New Testament value that all they are and all they have belong to God, and that they should honor Him by giving at least the historical 10 percent called the tithe. Financial stewardship is seen as being more than a money issue. It is seen as a heart issue as well. That is why it is the last of seven steps. Willow Creek recognizes that the human heart needs to be transformed before a person's wallet reflects full devotion to God.[14]

Seeker Services

Another aspect of Willow Creek's strategy is the Seeker Service itself. The biblical model that guides the seeker style is the story of Paul's preaching about an "unknown God" in Athens, as recorded in Acts 17:16-34. The passage delineates how Paul accommodated the presentation of his message to his hearers in order to get its content across to them. Cultural accommodation, without gospel compromise, is the goal of the Seeker Service.[15]

The Seeker Services are designed with "good programming that provides an exciting, creative and interesting experience for unchurched Harrys."[16]

What comprises the Seeker Service? Willow Creek uses cutting-edge communication methods: contemporary Christian music, drama, multimedia, video, and dance.[17] The typical Seeker Service is built around two important goals: (1) to influence unchurched Harry and Mary, and (2) to serve as a preparation for the speaker's message.[18] For a synopsis of a Seeker Service see Appendix C.

The Message is the essential core of Willow Creek's Seeker Service. There are seven elements to Willow Creek's messages: credibility, identifying, relevance, Christianity 101, truth, the gospel, and commitment.[19]

Hybels states that he discusses topics that are relevant to the seekers, i.e., "their marriages, their priorities, their emotions, their finances, their parenting, their quest for fulfillment, and their sexuality." Hybels asserts that he addresses these topics from a biblical perspective to help them understand that Christianity is not just true but that it also works in their lives. Throughout the year evangelistic messages are woven in to help bring people across the line into God's family.[20]

Blueprint

In order to get unchurched Harry and Mary to a Seeker Service, believers are encouraged to follow the blueprint. The blueprint spells out how Willow Creek will accomplish its mission. The mission is spelled out in one sentence: "We want to turn irreligious people into fully devoted followers of Christ."[21]

Critical Analysis

In this section I will look at what is considered to be the strengths and weaknesses, the positives and the negatives of this model for reaching unchurched or secular people.

Willow Creek

Positives/strengths

There are important concepts that are commendable and positive in the strategy of Willow Creek. One of these is the idea of a "church" for the unchurched, which is a creative innovation that has great potential for the communication of the gospel.

The new paradigm of Willow Creek Community Church is designed to offer Seeker Services that are considered to be a safe public environment where secularized, modern, and urbanized people can come and have the gospel presented and explained. It is an attempt to meet people where they are, to be relevant.[22]

Paulien states that this effort to meet people where they are is following God's example. "Scripture is an illustration of the fact that God expects us, and is even Himself willing, to reach out to people where they are; to speak their language. This is clearly outlined as a strategy by Paul in 1 Corinthians 9:19-23."[23]

Creative persuasion

By using persuasion, Willow Creek Community Church is identifying with one of Paul's methods. This method of persuasion is central to the Christian gospel. Paul in his evangelistic efforts in different cities did not just use the same rote message and then move on. He sought to preach, defend, proclaim, and explain the gospel in a way that made sense in each separate context. For example, when Paul was at the Areopagus in Athens, he affirmed his pagan audience's belief in an "Unknown God." He also quoted a pagan poet and then began to explain the gospel (Acts 17:16-34). In contrast, when Paul entered the synagogue at Thessolanica, "on three Sabbath days, he reasoned with them from the Scriptures, explaining and proving that Christ had to suffer and rise from the dead" (Acts 17:1-3). Paul sought to persuade each audience, creatively using references and language that they could understand.[24]

We need to remember that "God has placed within human beings a natural barrier against persuasion." When unchurched Harry and Mary enter a Seeker Service, perhaps for the first time, they are probably defensive to any Christianity or gospel that they suspect is being foisted on them. Willow Creek's use of drama and the speaking style of Hybels are creative forms of persuasion. The idea is to get behind their "psychological brick wall" and lower their defenses.[25] The use of "drama, video and music touch people on an emotional level to help thaw the deep pools of spiritual longing that often lay just beneath the surface."[26]

It is to be remembered that the Holy Spirit leads men and women to faith in Christ. The question, therefore, is whether or not the Holy Spirit can use a persuasive process to do this. The answer to that is yes. Thousands of people have come to faith in the Willow Creek Church.

The intended consequences of the Willow Creek Seeker Service are to (1) have an attractive setting to communicate the gospel, and (2) to have a persuasion process to help the unchurched become believers. The church seems to be successful in both of these fundamental goals.[27]

The Willow Creek weekend service attendance has increased from approximately 1,000 in 1975 to 14,326 in 1995 and on up to 16,888 in 1999. Their targeted goal for the year 2,000 was 20,000.

In 1998 Willow Creek averaged an attendance of 16,587 at their weekend services. In the same year, a church-wide survey was taken during a weekend service that yielded 2,785 respondents. The survey included a variety of questions. A specific question was, "Would you say there was an identifiable time or point in your life when you became a follower of Jesus Christ?" Eighty-five percent said yes and 15 said no. Those who said yes responded to another question that asked whether it was before or after attending Willow Creek, and 30 percent said it was after attending Willow Creek. While this does not say much in terms of who they are reaching, it does show that some are coming to faith in Christ as a result of attending Willow Creek.[28]

The assimilation process

I have found the assimilation process in the Willow Creek Church to be purpose driven and intentional. The goal is to bring the new believers along the path to full development and commitment to Christ, and to help them find their unique ministry through the developments of their gifts and talents.

This is methodologically done. For Willow Creek it is their "seven-step strategy." Part of the process generally includes taking certain classes that lead to commitment and maturity, such as Christianity 101, or 201, or 301, etc. Each class brings the person to a new level of commitment. The new believers are also encouraged to join a small group. A small group can be a place where spiritual growth takes place, where people can find mutual caring and sharing in non-threatening ways. It is also where Bible study and prayer are regularly engaged in and a place where one can stay connected with others. The church is automatically the provider and trainer of its new members. Assimilation takes place within the very framework of the proposed strategy.

Communicating through understanding

The goal of seeking to understand unchurched Harry and Mary is correct. The aim is to understand Harry and Mary in order to be able to more effectively communicate the good news of the gospel. It is to help them comprehend the astonishing news that God has broken into history to reveal Himself and has offered them a "forever friendship" with Himself.[29]

There is a very good reason why missionaries study the culture, history, and language of the people they are trying to reach. They realize that effective communication necessitates an empathetic understanding of the people.[30] Preachers also understand this principle. John R. W. Stott mentions that "we have good news to communicate. So if evangelism is to take place, there must be communication—a true communication between ancient revelation and modern culture."[31]

Negatives/Weaknesses

The first weakness or negative that concerns the Willow Creek Community Church is their use of programming, and in particular the arts. I am not against the use of arts, nor do I share in the total rejection of the way Willow Creek uses them (some critics do), nonetheless there are some very legitimate concerns:

1. The first potential problem of the use of the arts is that ultimately the method of how one communicates tends to shape the message. Hybels has himself issued warnings concerning this aspect of his services based on past experience. For example, he states, "We believe that the Word of God is not only totally true but that it is the primary change agent in the lives of individuals and in the church itself. . . . Danger lurks whenever we depend on anything else."[32] He then issues a warning to "watch out for the sizzle of programming talents, and the temptation to make everything produced and slick."[33] The use of the arts, says Hybels, has always been intended to support and lead up to that moment in the Seeker Service when the Bible is opened and taught from. Preaching, says Hybels, should always be the central focus, because ultimately it is the word of God that is capable of changing lives.[34]

   These warnings by Hybels are indicative of lessons learned from the so-called "Train Wreck of '79." It was a time when Willow Creek was shaken to its very foundation and nearly destroyed. Hybels states that this vulnerability is due to "imbalanced teaching. . . . It was my fault," he said. In spite of the fact that the messages presented were biblical, certain themes were stressed to the near exclusion of others. "In that era, I inadvertently emphasized grace but not holiness, and as a result, we adopted a kind of careless Christianity."[35]

   Concerns along these lines are raised on the use of entertainment features as having the potential for compromising the message, watering down Christian worship, etc.[36] Does the method of how one communicates have potential for shaping the message? It is believed that this is the case in modern communication, where it is said that news reporting has been shaped by the medium of television. Robert MacNeil, for example, co-anchor of the MacNeil-Lehrer News Hour, reveals some important assumptions behind news shows: that "complexity must be avoided, that nuances are dispensable, that qualifications impede the simple message, that vital stimulation is a substitute for thought, and that verbal precision is an anachronism."[37]

There is this potential weakness in the use of the arts at Willow Creek. And while it is an honest attempt by Hybels and others to seek to be faithful to the apostolic example of cultural accommodation without gospel compromise, there is always the potential danger to allow the method of how one communicates to shape the message.

2. The second potential weakness is that of going to the extreme with "felt-need" or "helpful" messages. Again it is Hybels himself who sounds the warning. He warns that being involved in seeker ministry can lead to the temptation to go for long periods of time on what he calls "junk-food preaching diets. . . . In other words, giving people biblical wisdom to improve their relationships, smooth their emotions, deal with their daily problems, and put some zip back in their marriage." Hybels further explains that dealing with felt needs demonstrates that biblical truth can indeed improve our day-to-day lives, which is a valuable lesson for seekers to learn. However, Hybels stresses the fact that we are responsible for teaching the whole counsel of God in a balanced, biblical, and mature fashion so that the teaching diet accurately reflects Scripture as a whole. Hybels further states that no one will ever grow up on a diet of spiritual Twinkies.[38]

This potential weakness grows out of the attempt to be relevant. And there is no other aspect of Willow Creek's strategy that is more controversial than the idea of relevance. Part of the problem comes from how some people define the term. This is not the time nor would space allow for a full discussion of the issue. Generally speaking, most evangelical scholars tend to take a dim view of Willow Creek's understanding of what it means to be relevant. Pritchard believes that Willow Creek's understanding of relevance is due to Barna's teachings that relevance necessarily means meeting individuals' felt needs. This overemphasis, says Pritchard, comes from the marketing theory that guides their strategy, resulting in a theology that teaches that Christianity will bring fulfillment. Another critic of Willow Creek, John McArthur, believes that relevance automatically causes compromise.[39]

None of these two emphases are adequate in and of themselves. A more striking balance would be to look at a biblical model in Jesus. Jesus ministered to people where they were in their unique context, where they lived. He did not have rote speeches for each new crowd. Jesus addressed the Pharisees and the scribes many times according to their situation. When they were insincere and stubborn He addressed them in parables: "They knew he had spoken the parable against them" (Mark 12:12).[40]

> "Jesus taught people the truth, rather than the truth to people. The truth did not change, but the particular point of application did depending on the context or person that Jesus was addressing. This style of responsiveness was true for both his teaching and his evangelism."[41]

> Jesus met felt needs, but He was also confrontational. Jesus was relevant in that He understood the individuals whom He was addressing and He communicated with them in a way that spoke to their unique situation. This is neither a sellout to "felt-need" or "helpful" messages, as Hybels put it, nor is it a compromise of truth. There is a place for relevance, and we must be relevant. But we must guard against overpsychologizing the message in an attempt to meet felt needs in order to be relevant.

Charles E. Bradford speaks to this issue when he states,

> "I am not knocking sermons where the thrust is toward
> problem solving. I am against any approach to preaching
> that tends to become man-centered. There is a certain
> attraction in humanism, a subtle appeal in the new
> psychology or behavioral science. It is exciting to discover
> what makes men tick. Over and against the gloomy
> Puritan ethic, with its angry God and helpless man, Freud
> and Jung do have their appeal. But the swing may now
> have gone too far."[42]

Bradford's appeal is for biblical preaching. He believes that under the ministration of the Holy Spirit old truths can flash forth with new relevance. "Skillful biblical preaching releases the dynamic that is in the Word, and Scripture once again becomes profitable for 'teaching the truth and refuting error, or for reformation of manners and discipline in right living' (2 Tim. 3:16 NEB)."[43]

This tendency to go "overboard with 'felt need' or 'helpful' messages" is an unintended consequence of the Willow Creek approach to relevance. It is obvious, however, that Hybels is well aware of the danger and is striving for faithfulness in the right balance. There is need for a critical contextualization. This approach takes the Bible seriously as the rule of faith and life. Contextualized practices, like contextualized theologies, must be biblically based. This means that the message must be at the same time faithful and contemporary. First it must be faithful—faithful, that is, to Scripture. The message first and foremost is not in any existential situation, but in the Bible.[44]

Dr. Visser't Hooft, in an article entitled "Evangelism in the Neo-pagan Situation," wrote:

> "I do not believe that evangelism is adequately described
> as answering the questions which men are asking, however
> deep those questions may be. For evangelism is in the first
> place the transmission of God's question to man. And

that question is and remains whether we are willing to accept Jesus Christ as the one and only Lord of Life."[45]

But he goes on to say that we must "try to relate God's question to the existential situation of men and show that as they answer God's question they find at the same time the answer to their deepest concerns."[46]

Now it is fairly easy to be faithful if we are not concerned about being contemporary, and equally easy to be contemporary if we do not bother to be faithful. It is the search for a combination of truth and relevance which is exacting.[47]

This would suggest two important factors:

1. The message we present to the secular or unchurched person is primarily based on Scripture. The whole Bible, the whole counsel of God, becomes the guiding authority.

2. On the other hand, many of these unchurched, secular people do not really know what the Bible says. If we relate Scripture in an antiquated and outdated fashion to the contemporary person, we stand a risk of losing them.

If the Bible is presented faithfully and relevantly as that which provides the answers to the most important questions in life, many of the unchurched would likely stop and listen.[48]

Thus we strive toward a balance for truth and relevance and avoid the "going overboard emphasis on 'felt-need' or mere 'helpful' messages." This is one of the potential weaknesses or negatives in the search for relevance in relating the gospel to the unchurched.

Greg Taylor and Erin Miller—Foster Seventh-day Adventist Church (SDA)

In a formal letter to me, dated May 6, 1999, Pastor Greg Taylor submitted a brief synopsis on the history of the Foster Seventh-day Adventist Church in Asheville, North Carolina, from 1906 to the present time.

According to Pastor Taylor, Foster Seventh-day Adventist Church was established as a traditional Seventh-day Adventist Church in 1906 and continued as such until 1992. Since 1992 the church has embarked on a transition process to a contemporary model of church ministry. The church from 1906 had grown over the years to a vibrant congregation and then started to decline. "We had nearly 400 members on the books in 1992, but only 120 in weekly attendance."[49] The tried and true methods of evangelism were no longer effective in that area. The church members became discouraged, and people in the surrounding community were turned off to mainstream Adventist evangelism. The church services seemed lifeless and boring to the young people. They were an older, dying church.

Being motivated and influenced by the Willow Creek Community Church in Chicago, Pastor Taylor and the members decided in 1992 to convert to a seeker-targeted model similar to that used in the Willow Creek Community Church. Pastor Taylor stated that Willow Creek

> "had found great success in reaching the unchurched through contemporary services including the use of the arts, drama, contemporary music, and relevant biblical teaching starting from common ground with the unchurched and moving to strong biblical solutions to everyday problems." [50]

After spending significant time in prayer and vision casting, they launched the new approach as an experimental model to prove God's leading. The process of transition proved to be a difficult one.

When it became apparent that the new plan was working, many of the long-term members decided to leave and started a more traditional church nearby. No one was lost to the Adventist church during this transition. The new more traditional church is also growing and is mission-minded.

Meanwhile, says Pastor Taylor, the Foster Seventh-day Adventist Church has grown by leaps and bounds as a result of putting the new evangelistic style into action. They now hold two services each Saturday morning, and over 50 percent of their growth has been from the unchurched population.[51] The attendance in 1999 averaged 120 to 150 in their morning worship and 225 to 275 in their community worship.[0]

Kind of Church

The Foster Seventh-day Adventist Church is trying to be an Acts 2 community within the context of the Seventh-day Adventist message. Their mission statement, "Building a biblical community where secular people become fully devoted to Christ," is indicative of what they are trying to accomplish.

It is a church that is seeking to bring people without assurance of salvation to a confident, active, committed relationship with Christ and a full understanding of the Seventh-day Adventist message (Matt 28:19, 20). They also nurture, support, and encourage the spiritual growth of the members of their congregation. They direct their outward energy toward those who are not attending their church. This includes former or inactive members, dropouts from other churches, and those with no church background. The Foster SDA Church is specifically trying to meet the needs of the segment of the population which is most absent from church circles, but will welcome anyone. Foster's aim is to also become a biblically functioning community (Acts 2:42-47).

The Foster Seventh-day Adventist Church has certain stated beliefs and a set of core values (see Appendix).

Basic Strategy

The Foster Seventh-day Adventist Church has adopted a strategy that was "borrowed from Willow Creek Community Church in Chicago." This strategy has seven evangelistic steps that were discussed in the Willow Creek Strategy.

The Target

By using the seven-step strategy, Foster SDA Church hopes to reach and bring Asheville Andy into a confident, active, committed relationship with Christ.

Who is Asheville Andy? In describing Asheville Andy, the Foster SDA Church recognizes him or her (a composite figure) as being a Baby Buster or Boomer between the twenty-something and forty-something age group. Please see figure 2.

There are several reasons of critical importance given by the Foster SDA Church as to why it is trying to reach this age group:

1. The twenties-to-forties age group comprises the biggest hole in the active church membership in North America. Experts such as Monte Sahlin at the North American Division of SDAs, Paul Richardson, and others have dramatically pointed this out.[53] The average tithe payer now is 53 years of age, which already indicates that our membership is growing older and we are not meaningfully reaching the Baby Busters and Baby Boomers.

2. The second reason why Foster SDA Church feels that it should target this age group is that, according to research, such as the Barna Report, the Busters and Boomers are returning to church in increased and massive numbers. According to certain reports, there are 76 million people between 25 and 43 years of age in the United States population. This group is said to be the most reachable age group, even more so than the Hispanic population, which is growing in churches at a dramatic rate. It is also believed that most decisions for Christ are made before a person reaches his or her mid 40s. With this in mind, Foster SDA Church feels that they have an urgent mandate to strike while the iron is hot.

3. The third reason that Foster SDA Church feels that it should target this age group is that no other churches in their area are providing the Seeker Services style of evangelism. "Several churches provide evangelism opportunities focusing on traditional churched persons. There are a number of churches that offer a high church, classical music format for worship. But there are none that are using an evangelistic style worship that focuses on the contemporary unchurched person."[54]

4. The final reason that Foster SDA Church feels that it must target the Busters and Boomers in their community is that they are looking for a church. They are looking for an atmosphere where they might find a church family. The Foster SDA Church believes they are looking for spirituality and not just religion. They are looking for emphasis on relationships. They are looking for a place where they can dress more casually, drop titles and formality, and be treated as equals. They are looking for a church where worship is emphasized. They are looking for great music, a good sound system, and non-traditional forms of worship.

The Foster SDA Church states that it is adopting a vision and is endeavoring to provide a place where relevant, meaningful worship can be provided for Busters and Boomers. It is endeavoring to provide good, solid biblical principles with practical applications. It is incorporating music which is tasteful, yet appealing to the majority of the people in their target audience. It is emphasizing relational ministry. It is committed to providing an atmosphere of love, acceptance, and forgiveness.

All of this in a nutshell is part of the church's rationale for targeting Ashville Andy, who happens to be in the age group of Busters and Boomers.

ASHEVILLE ANDY

He is college educated.   He reads USA Today.

He is married to   He watches ESPN, sports,
Asheville Ann.   and CNN Headline News

He has two kids,
ages 2 and 5.   He has a white
collar job

He listens
to 102.5.   He is 32 years old.

He is athletic   He drives a Jeep
and a health   Cherokee and a
club member.   Honda Civic.

He is not   His wife is in a
affiliated with   Mom's group.
any church.

He prefers informal
He is a   over formal.
homeowner.

He is overextended in
His vacations   both time and money.
are at the Beach,
Disneyworld,
Skiing, and   He goes to the movies
camping.   twice a month.

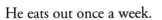

He eats out once a week.   He eats out once a week.

FIGURE 2. Ashville Andy. Greg Taylor, Building a Biblical Community Where Secular People Become Fully Devoted Followers of Christ (Asheville, NC: Foster Seventh-day Adventist Church, 1997), 10.

The Worship Services

The Foster SDA Church has two worship services on Saturday morning with a Bible lesson in between. The first service, called "Morning Worship," is designed for committed Christian believers and has a more traditional format. The second service, more of a seeker-type worship service, is called "Community Worship" and focuses on issues for the new believer or person investigating Christianity. It includes contemporary music, drama, audio and visual presentations, and an especially warm family atmosphere. The format of the two services is shown in table 2.

TABLE 2

Morning Worship at 9:15	Community Worship at 11:30
Prelude Comments Testimonials Adoration & Praise Prayer 10:30	Praise in Music Adoration & Praise Drama Announcements Offertory Message 12:30

Between 10:30 and 11:30 the Foster SDA Church has incorporated Bible classes that deal with adults seekers, called Christianity 101, with classes that explore issues for growing Christians. There is also a twenty-something class for young adults. There are also classes for children and teens ranging from Cradle Roll all the way through Earliteens. There is also a class that meets in the gymnasium for Asheville youth.[55]

Critical Analysis

Strengths

New Paradigms

One of the positive aspects of the Foster Seventh-day Adventist Church is the ability to recognize and implement the need for change. This church was established in 1906, and still could not account for more than 120 in weekly attendance 86 years later, in 1992. The underlying reason: "Our tried and true methods of evangelism were no longer effective in this area."[56] Why were they not effective? "The people around us seemed turned off to mainstream Adventist evangelism."[57]

The Foster Seventh-day Adventist Church came to the point of losing its relevance. Their old tried-and-true methods were no longer reaching the people. What was needed was not a change in the message (wine) but a change in the old wineskin. The old wineskin in this case, to quote Pastor Erin Miller, was "services that were lifeless and boring to our young people. . . . We were an older, dying church."[58] This is in keeping with Aubrey Malphurs's observation that

> "many older churches reflect the culture that surrounded them some thirty or forty years ago and clearly aren't in touch with the culture around them now. The result is that the unchurched lost in our present culture see this and reject the biblical beliefs of these churches because they sense that they're out of touch with reality and what's taking place in the world. They know a dinosaur when they see one!"[59]

The unchurched lost in the Foster SDA Church's community are clearly those (more so than any other group it would seem) they began targeting—the Baby Boomers and Busters. These are the ones, says Pastor Taylor, who "comprise the biggest hole in our active church membership in North America." They are the ones "we are not meaningfully reaching."[60]

They began transitioning to a Seeker-targeted model, such as the one in Willow Creek Church in Chicago. The result is a new way of doing church, a new way of keeping in step with the times while staying faithful to the biblical message. They are now reaching out in a creative and relevant way in addressing the concerns of the lost. Bill Hull states that "if we want people to hear, we must bring the message to life by restating the truth with great passion and in a language they understand."[61] This is a positive move and a strength of the Foster SDA Church in their new strategy.

Community Service

Besides the contemporary Seeker Service that has been implemented by the Foster SDA Church, and the process of persuasion used through music, drama, and relevant biblical preaching, there is the emphasis on contact with the community. This contact is done through their community services program. The community services program is yet another way of meeting the needs of the unchurched.

Through the community services program the Foster SDA Church is endeavoring to help answer the question, "Where is the church when it hurts?"[62]

During 1999 the Foster SDA Church members gave $40,192.81 for their outreach ministry. In addition, they brought in clothing, linens, and a variety of household items. Every Tuesday some 10 men and women come to serve clients, sort clothing, and keep order in the supply rooms.

At one point they had 32 frozen turkeys donated to them by the Merrimon House. Other donations were 80 bushel-size boxes of groceries for delivery to Head Start families. One person donated two practically new bicycles for holiday giving.

Another person and her mother-in-law took a bag of worn, bedraggled toys given to the Foster SDA Church and transformed them, washing, mending, and restoring them to bring pleasure to children. The count of families requesting assistance continues to average 30 to 35 each week. In the first two weeks of this year, they were able to minister to a lady who had lost her job. This lady of dignity and refinement told the church her story with tears in her eyes. Her bills had accumulated and were overwhelming her. The church helped to pay her electric bills. During these same two weeks the church paid six electric bills, one water bill, and provided fuel oil for seven families. The church gives assistance in other areas such as providing beds, medical supplies, and food.[63]

This aspect of reaching people who are unchurched is often overlooked and rarely emphasized. This is more than technique and strategy. It reflects Christ's method. It transcends time, culture, race, religion, and geography; it has universal appeal. "Christ's method alone will give true success in reaching the people. The Saviour mingled with men as one who desired their good. He showed His sympathy for them, ministered to their needs, and won their confidence. Then He bade them, 'follow me.'"[64]

I am happy to see that Foster SDA Church has not ignored this important aspect of its mission outreach. It is obvious that the members are touching people's lives and meeting their needs in a very personal way. This is a very positive and strong aspect of the strategy employed by the Foster SDA Church.

Weaknesses

The first weakness of the Foster SDA Church model is the lack of original research for aiding in their development of mission strategy.

The church was encouraged by the Willow Creek style of reaching the unchurched and borrowed or replicated to some extent their seven-step strategy. All this is good, for the Bible says, "Test all things, hold fast what is good" (1 Thess 5:21, NKJV).

The question remains, Will that which works for Willow Creek also work for Foster SDA Church? To attempt an answer to this question, we would need to take the following into consideration:

Megachurches are a new breed of churches that are attracting thousands. By definition they are the largest churches in North America. They are usually defined as having at least 2,000 members and may go all the way from 10,000 to 15,000. Those with 3,300 or more are among the 100 largest churches in America.[65] Willow Creek is perhaps the most well-known example of this new breed of church.[66]

This type of church is metropolitan, drawing people from way beyond its immediate community. Because of their size they offer a supermarket-like variety of choice programs geared to meet the needs of the members and those living in the surrounding community.[67]

Willow Creek is also highly intentional about meeting the religious and personal needs of its target audience. George Barna's ideas on marketing influences Willow Creek. This accounts for how well they know their target audience. They have surveyed through interviews and demographic studies, and have demonstrated their seriousness toward the agendas of the new generation. In this respect Willow Creek's strategy is tailor-made to meet the needs of unchurched Harry and Mary.[68]

The Willow Creek Seeker Service is not just another style of worship. "It is . . . not a worship service at all, but rather an evangelistic program using methods designed to reach a target group Willow Creek is determined to reach."[69]

Among the megachurches, Willow Creek is one that is copied extensively.[70] Its success in drawing large numbers of people stands in stark contrast to dying smaller churches that find it difficult to communicate with the unchurched around them. But the question is, will what works for Willow Creek work in the same way for Foster? One would have to say, not necessarily so.[71]

Church growth is a complex phenomenon. Successful models of ministry are born as specific visions (in specific contexts and with specific resources) to respond creatively to perceived needs. Thus, to copy a method without examining the context in which these methods are most successful is similar to taking medicine without knowing the thing that it is supposed to cure.[72]

In the case of the Foster SDA Church, they came to the realization that they were dying, due to the fact that they were no longer reaching the people of their community. Worship was boring and traditional. They realized they were not in step with the growing Boomer-Buster generation. They decided to change to a seeker service, to adopt a Willow Creek-type model (they are members of Willow Creek Association). All this, as I said before, is fine. What I perceive as the weakness is the fact that the same intentionality that one sees in Willow Creek (that is to say, the specific study of the Harrys and Marys in Barrington, Illinois, the extensive profiling, etc., with consequent services and ministries to meet their varied needs) is missing in the Foster model.

One of the factors in a taxonomy influencing church growth and decline is what is called "local contextual factors."[73] These factors are unique social, cultural, and demographic aspects of a local congregation's immediate environment.[74] What is unique about Asheville Andy? What unique social, cultural, and demographic characteristics does Ashville Andy have? This would mean looking at age, marital status, income, education, and occupation; also assessing values, interests, hurts, and fears as well as finding out specifically what the local people already know about religion or Christianity—getting a good feel for where they are spiritually. How do they perceive the church? What kind of church and programming will best meet their needs? This is done intentionally through a firsthand research of the community. This is what is missing in the Foster model. The intentionality that says it is all right to adopt an existing model, but how can I be intentional in order to more effectively reach my community? This requires uniqueness in research and surveys.

Mission Focus

The other weakness that I see with the Foster SDA Church model is that there is no specific or stated plan for planting other churches. The vision created seems to be strictly concerned about the growth of Foster SDA Church.

What is the mission of the church? The Seventh-day Adventist understanding of mission is that of Rev 14:6-12 and Matt 28:18-20. The gospel must go to all the world. This would mean visioning beyond the local congregation and planning for further extension of the church into new territory. Again the idea of being intentional comes into play. To be intentional in this regard we would have to determine "cultural distance." This would mean developing a clear profile of the target group in order to determine how receptive they are. Erich W. Baumgartner has rightly said that "the further the cultural distance between the target group and the church, the more intentionally cross-cultural it has to become in methodology and strategy."[75]

This could mean that consideration should be given to the possibility of different kinds of evangelism, for example, E-0, E-1, E-2, and E-3. Evangelism across a relatively small Christian distance, or of non-Christians in a similar culture, or of a strong cultural distance barrier (E-1, E-2, and E-3 respectively) may require planting new churches.[76]

This is in keeping with a healthy mission strategy and a clear vision of the gospel commission. It also is indicative of being focused on church growth and evangelism for the purpose of reaching the lost and finishing the work of the gospel. Anything short of this is truncated and eventually characterizes a myopic vision of the church's mission. Such prolonged shortsightedness that has no challenge or mission orientation beyond its immediate periphery will end up on a maintenance approach (discipling and keeping its own members). This I see as a potential weakness and could be a further hindrance to growth for the Foster SDA Church.

Rick Warren–Saddleback Community Church

Pastor Rick Warren, Senior Pastor and founder of the Saddleback Community Church of Saddleback Valley, in Orange County, Southern California, has the personal conviction that God has called him to be a pastor.

Pastor Warren states that he has been greatly influenced by both Dr. W. A. Criswell, the renowned pastor of the largest Baptist Church in the world, the First Baptist Church of Dallas, Texas, and the well-known church-growth specialist Donald McGavran.[77]

It was after reading some of McGavran's articles that Pastor Warren felt God was directing him to discover the principles–biblical, cultural, and leadership–that would produce healthy, growing churches. This was the beginning of a life-long study. It was also near the time in 1979 when Pastor Warren felt that God had, through particular providences, led him to Saddleback Valley (the fastest growing area in the fastest growing county in the United States in the 1970s) to raise up and pastor the Saddleback Community Church.[78]

Kind of Church

The kind of church that Pastor Warren had envisioned was one that would be limited to reaching the unchurched for Christ. He also determined to begin with unbelievers in the starting of Saddleback, rather than with a core of committed Christians. He never encouraged other believers to transfer their membership to his church, in fact, he openly discouraged it.[79]

Pastor Warren felt that he was following the example of Jesus, who defined His ministry target by saying, "It is not those who are healthy who need a physician, but those who are sick. I did not come to call the righteous, but sinners" (Mark 2:17, NASB). This statement of Christ helped the Saddleback leadership to stay true to their original purpose: "to bring the unchurched, irreligious people of our community to Christ."[80]

Basic Strategy

The basic strategy of Saddleback Community Church is summed up in its purpose statement. This purpose statement utilizes five key words to summarize what is considered to be Christ's five purposes for His church:

5 Circles of Commitment

CLASS 201
Discovering
Spiritual Maturity
Maturity Covenant

CLASS 101
Discovering
Membership
Membership
Covenant

CLASS 301
Discovering My
Ministry
Ministry Covenant

CLASS 401
Discovering My
Life Mission
Mission Covenant

FIGURE 3. The life development process. Rick Warren, *The Purpose Driven Church* (Grand Rapids, MI: Zondervan Publishing House, 1995), 134.

1. Magnify: Celebrating God's presence in worship
2. Mission: Communicating God's word through evangelism
3. Membership: Incorporating God's family into fellowship
4. Maturity: Educating God's people through discipleship
5. Ministry: Demonstrating God's love through service.

These key words representing five purposes are incorporated into Saddleback's mission statement which is as follows: "To bring people to Jesus and membership in his family, develop them to Christlike maturity, and equip them for their ministry in the church and life mission in the world, in order to magnify God's name." Pastor Warren believes that by balancing all five purposes, you will have a healthy church. "There is no single key," says Warren, "to church health and church growth." According to Warren there are many things the church is called to do and that is why balance is so important.[81] The Saddleback Church is organized around two concepts to ensure balance: (1) "Five Circles of Commitment" and (2) "The Life Development Process." See figure 3.

Target

Another important component of Saddleback's strategy is the clearly defined target, "Saddleback Sam." Who is Saddleback Sam? See figure 4.

At the outset Warren "focused on only one target: young, unchurched, white-collar couples. We focused on them because they were the largest group in Saddleback Valley, and because that was who I related to best." But as Saddleback has grown, Pastor Warren has added additional ministries and outreach programs to reach young adults, single adults, prisoners, the elderly, parents with ADD children, and Spanish, Vietnamese, and Korean-speaking people, as well as many other targets[82]

The Seeker Sensitive Service

Warren has developed for Saddleback Church a Seeker Sensitive Service that is intended for the members to bring their friends to. The service is designed to be attractive, appealing, and relevant to the unchurched.[83]

Two aspects of the Seeker Service are highlighted by Warren: (1) music and (2) preaching. Although music is usually the most controversial element of a Seeker Service, Warren believes that it is a critical element that cannot be ignored. He believes that the incredible power of music needs to be harnessed and understood. Warren believes

SADDLEBACK SAM

He is well educated.

He likes his job.

He likes where he lives.

Health and fitness are high priorities for him and his family.

He'd rather be in a large group than a small one.

He is skeptical of "organized religion."

He likes contemporary music.

He thinks he is enjoying life more than he did five years ago.

He is self-satisfied, even smug, about his station in life.

He prefers the casual and informal over the formal.

He is overextended in both time and money.

FIGURE 4. Our target, Saddleback Sam. From Rick Warren, *The Purpose Driven Church* (Grand Rapids, MI: Zondervan Publishing House, 1995), 170.

that one must set aside one's own personal preferences and use the music that will best reach the unchurched for Christ.[84]

The next important element of a Seeker Service that Warren stresses is the preaching of the Word. Pastor Warren discovered that the greatest complaint of the unchurched in his area was "boring, irrelevant sermons."[85]

This led Warren to reexamine his own style of preaching. He ended up throwing out his previous sermons (ten years' worth) and starting over from scratch. Warren realized that if he was going to start a church by attracting hard-core pagans, it would have to be a message to which they could relate.[86] Finding an example in the apostle Paul, who established common ground with a pagan audience at the Aeropagus in Athens, Warren now seeks to find common ground with unbelievers. "You cannot start with a text," says Warren, "expecting the unchurched to be fascinated by it. You must first captivate their attention and then move them to the truth of God's Word."[87]

Warren begins his sermons each week with a need, hurt, or interest and then moves to what God has to say about it in His Word. He believes that this is the kind of preaching that changes lives, "preaching . . . that brings the truth of God's Word and the real needs of people together through application."[88]

Aside from the element of music, preaching is considered by Warren to be the "most important element of a Seeker Service."[89] According to Warren, "There are only three non-negotiable elements of a Seeker Service:

1. Treat unbelievers with love and respect.

2. Relate the service to their needs.

3. Share the message in a practical, understandable manner."[90]

Andy Langford summarizes it well when he states that "the evangelistic task of Seeker Services provides the step up to the porch and the church household, or in the traditional theological language, a precatechesis offering of prevenient grace. The goal is to introduce Jesus to people who know nothing about him."[91]

Critical Analysis

Strengths

Discipling process

A very positive aspect of the Saddleback Community Church is its discipling process. The discipling process takes place through Saddleback's Christian education program. The goal is to help individuals develop a lifestyle of evangelism, worship, fellowship, discipleship, and ministry. This is illustrated by the "life development process."[92] See figure 3.

Saddleback uses a single diagram of a baseball diamond to visually explain its education process to the members. Each base represents a completed class and a deeper level of commitment. The goal is to have each person become a "grandslam disciple." In order for this to be realized, the members must complete sixteen hours of basic training and commit to the covenants at each base. [93]

At Saddleback it is not sufficient to receive Christ, be baptized, and join the church. They help their members develop habits that lead to spiritual maturity, and they ensure that every believer finds an appropriate ministry. They also equip every member to win others to Christ and fulfill their life mission.

It was Jesus who said, "Go therefore and make disciples of all nations" (Matt 28:19). Saddleback achieves this by attempting to bring every member around to home plate. When this is done, that person serves in the core. See five circles of commitment in figure 3. This core represents the strength of the Saddleback Church. Warren states that "a church's strength is not seen in how many show up for services (the crowd) but how many serve in the core."[94]

Preaching on purpose

Another strength that I have found in the working model at Saddleback is the emphasis on preaching with purpose. Not only does Rick Warren preach in a style that brings the truth of God's Word and the real needs of people together, he also preaches around the five purposes of his church. This does not mean that he preaches always about the church itself. What Warren does is to personalize the purposes. For example, in one title, "You Are Shaped for Significance," Warren preaches in order to mobilize people for ministry. "Answering life's toughest questions" was a series that Warren preached in order to prepare people for evangelism. Preaching around the five purposes could be done in a matter of twenty weeks, leaving much more time in the pulpit year to teach and preach on the other great themes of Scripture.[95]

The two components of discipling and preaching are in my view two of the great strengths of Saddleback's strategy for reaching and discipling unchurched people for Christ.

Weakness

The comfort zone—Reaching those to whom you relate

I have found what I consider to be a major weakness in the philosophy of Rick Warren as it relates to reaching the unchurched, those outside the fold. Over and over again Warren emphasizes that "you will best reach those you relate to." Warren states for example that "explosive growth occurs when the type of people in the community match the type of people that are already in the church, and they both match the type of person the pastor is."[96]

This may sound good, and may have some sociological value, but in God's kingdom no such artificial distinctions are allowed. Looking carefully at the above statement, one can draw several implications:

1. If what Warren proposes is true, then the church will be built on a homogeneous principle. The homogeneous principle is based on the idea that people like to become Christians, "without having to cross racial, linguistic, or class barriers to do so."[97]

2. Following Warren's argument, there is no room to "become all things to all men" (1 Cor 9:22), a very important principle laid down by Paul. Warren states that Paul's ability to relate to and

reach all classes and cultures of people is an exception. Paul had what he called the "missionary gift."[98] In other words becoming all things to all men is not a general evangelistic principle to follow, it is only for those who may be especially gifted. The rest of us must minister to others and reach others more like us.

Nowhere in the Bible does it say we should be selective about whom we carry the gospel to. Jesus said we must preach the gospel to every creature, and He promised to be with us as our help and strength (Acts 1:8; Matt 28:19-20). Paul himself said, "For as many of you as were baptized into Christ have put on Christ. There is neither Jew nor Greek, there is neither slave nor free, there is neither male nor female; for you are all one in Christ Jesus" (Gal 3:27, 28). In John 17 the burden of Christ's prayer is that His church would be one as He and the Father are one. Clearly there is no hint of the gospel being disseminated by the homogeneous principle or in accordance with our own preferences and tastes. Jesus gave no hint that the church should be built along the lines of a homogeneous principle. Ellen While states that "Jesus taught His disciples . . . that race distinction, caste, and lines of division made by men were not approved of in heaven and were to have no influence in the work of disseminating the gospel."[99]

Summary

In this chapter I have surveyed three models for reaching secular-unchurched people. Two are mega-churches–Willow Creek Community Church and Saddleback Community Church. The third is a smaller church–Foster Seventh-day Adventist Church. I surveyed their basic strategies and how they disciple and assimilate new believers. I have also highlighted what I consider to be their strengths and weaknesses.

I am happy for Pastor Hybels's openness and honesty in recognizing weaknesses and pitfalls in the Seeker Service Strategy.[100] We are all human and all have shortcomings and make mistakes. As we live in this world, we need to become accustomed to the here and not—yet quality of the Kingdom of God. We need to be willing to see weaknesses if we are to honor the Lord. I believe that Bill Hybels, Greg Taylor, and Rick Warren are truly and sincerely seeking to reach lost men and women through their respective churches. While there may be strengths and weaknesses, there is still much we can learn from these three models.

Chapter 5 Notes

1. For an understanding of the influence that Bilezikian and Schuller had on Hybels please refer to G. A. Pritchard, *Willow Creek Seeker Services* (Grand Rapids, MI: Baker Books, 1998),40-50. See also idem, "A Vision for the Church," *Willow Creek* (September/ October 1990): 20-21; Bill Hybels, *Seven Wonders of the Spirit World* (Dallas: Word Books, 1988), 9; "Into the Stratosphere," *Willow Creek*, n.d., 20; and "The Theater Days," *Willow Creek*, Special Anniversary Issue, n.d., 28.

2. See Lynne Hybels and Bill Hybels, *Rediscovering Church: The Story and Vision of Willow Creek Community Church* (Grand Rapids, MI: Zondervan Publishing House, 1995), 23-42. "Son City" -- In August of 1972, Bill Hybels began leading a group of thirty high-school students in South Park Church in Park Ridge, Illinois. The group eventually grew to seventy-five students. The group desired to reach out to non-believing friends. The music, environment, and messages were adapted to the audience. In a two-year period the group had grown to approximately one thousand young people. Later Don Cousins would suggest that in 1975 the leadership of Son City had answered God's call to carry out these biblical principles on an adult level by starting a church. Thus Willow Creek had its early beginnings in an evangelistic youth ministry. See Pritchard, 31, 32. For more details on Son City see also Don Cousins's short booklet, *Tomorrow's Church . . . Today* (South Barrington, IL: Willow Creek Publications, 1979).

3. Joe Engelkemier, "A Church That Draws Thousands," *Ministry*, May 1991, 14.

4. Hybels and Hybels, 135.

5. Ibid.

6.   Ibid., 57-59.

7.   Pritchard, 58.

8.   Ibid., 59, 61.

9.   Mark Mittleberg, "A Critical Analysis of the Epistemological Starting Points in Presuppositional Apologetics," Masters thesis, Trinity Evangelical Divinity School, 1988, 104.

10.   Pritchard, 61.

11.   The following profile of Harry and Mary is taken from G. A. Pritchard's *Willow Creek Seeker Services*, 67-75. See Strobel *Inside the Mind of Unchurched Harry and Mary: How to Reach Friends and Family Who Avoid the Church and God* (Grand Rapids: Zondervan Publishing House, 1993), 44-63. See also Gary Collins and Timothy Clinton, *Baby Boomer Blues*) Dallas: Word, 1992), 93.

12.   This profiling of Harry was taken largely from G. A. Pritchard's *Willow Creek Seeker Services*, 67-75; Lee Strobel, *Inside the Mind of Unchurched Harry and Mary: How to Reach Friends and Family Who Avoid the Church and God* (Grand Rapids: Zondervan Publishing House, 1993), 44-63. See also Gary Collins and Timothy Clinton, *Baby Boomer Blues* (Dallas: Word, 1992), 93.

Since this profiling of Harry seems to pigeon-hole unchurched people in one category, Pritchard further decided to clarify them as three different kinds: (1) "Hostile Harrys"--who are basically atheistic or agnostic in their beliefs. With over 90 percent of Americans affirming a basic belief in God, this group is very small. (2) "Curious Harrys"--are spiritually intrigued and are interested in Willow Creek's message. They have a basic belief in God and some background experience in Christianity. They do not attend church regularly. It is this group, spiritually minded and yet negative toward organized Christianity, that makes up the bulk of Willow Creek's unchurched audience. (3) The final group is the "Sincere Harrys"--they have made a commitment to investigate Christianity to see if it is really true. These are also known as "sincere seekers." Their attitude is one of checking it out, asking questions, all in their own ways. See Pritchard, 76, 77.

13. Hybels and Hybels, 169.

14. Ibid., 169-181.

15. Paul Basden, *The Worship Maze: Finding a Style to Fit Your Church* (Downers Grove, IL: InterVarsity Press, 1999), 90.

16. Pritchard, 80.

17. Hybels and Hybels, 174.

18. See Pritchard, 83, 88, 100-111.

19. Ibid., 116-183.

20. Hybels and Hybels, 174, 175.

21. Ibid., 169.

22. Pritchard, 189.

23. Jon Paulien, "Scratching Where It Itches: Ministry to the Secular," *Seeds 99: A Church Planting Conference*, Thursday, July 16, 1998, 1.

24. Pritchard, 190.

25. Paulien, *"Scratching Where it Itches,"* 1.

26. Hybels and Hybels, 174.

27. Pritchard, 190, 191.

28. Debbie Rendall, who works with the executive pastoral staff at Willow Creek and who is responsible, along with that staff, for the day to day running of the church, said that Willow Creek conducts two baptisms a year; one in June and one in December. There are no official statistics compiled from these baptisms (as of the year 2000) that give specifics of age and religious or non-religious backgrounds. Willow Creek had just begun (as of the

year 2000) the process of collecting data that would become more precise as to who among their attendees are coming to faith as a result of attending Willow Creek Community Church. Such in formation as age, unchurched status, etc. was not yet available in terms of who are successfully discipled and returned to faith among the thousands of attendees. Most of the data at that time was seen in general terms of attendance, participation, and membership in small group, church services, and so on. Debbie Hill, telephone interview by Ernan Norman, June 2000.

29.   Pritchard, 190, 191.

30.   Ibid. See also Donald K. Smith, *Creating Understanding: A Handbook for Christian Communication Across Cultural Landscapes* (Grand Rapids, MI: Zondervan Publishing House, 1992), 25-27.

31.   John R. W. Stott, *Christian Mission in the Modern World* (Downers Grove, IL: InterVarsity Press, 1975), 42.

32.   Hybels and Hybels, 184.

33.   Ibid., 185.

34.   Ibid., 186.

35.   Ibid.

36.   Basden, 94.

37.   Neil Postman, *Amusing Ourselves to Death: Public Discourse in the Age of Show Business* (New York: Penguin Books, 1985), 105.

38.   Hybels and Hybels, 185.

39.   See John McArthur, *Ashamed of the Gospel: When the Church Becomes Like the World* (Wheaton, IL: Crossway Books, 1993), 135; and George Barna, *Marketing the Church* (Colorado Springs, CO: Navpress, 1988), 33, 146. See also Pritchard, 198-201.

40.   See also Matt 9:36-38; 11:28-30; Mark 8:11-12; 10:17-31; 13:1-6; Luke 10:25-37; 14:7-11; John 3:1-13; 4:5-28.

41. Pritchard, 199.

42. Charles E. Bradford, *Preaching to the Times* (Washington, DC: Review & Herald Pub. Assn., 1975), 44.

43. Ibid.

44. Stott, 42.

45. W. A. Visser't Hooft, "Evangelism in the Neo-pagan Situation," *The International Review of Mission* 63 (January 1974): 84.

46. Ibid.

47. Stott, 43.

48. Robert M. Zamora, "The Gospel of the Abundant Life," in *Meeting the Secular Mind*, 129.

49. Russell Burrill discusses what he considers to be the four basic stages in the life cycle of all organizations. The first phase is "start up." This is the start-up phase, the birth phase, the people are together and the DNA of the future church is being incubated. The second phase is "expansion." This phase builds on the groundwork of the first phase. The church grows numerically and spiritually. In the third phase the church enters a plateau. Ministry is maintained but the church ceases to grow. It is now a mature church. Finally, phase four occurs and the church enters the period of decline. Momentum can no longer be maintained, losses occur, and the church ceases to be effective in its ministry. See Russell Burrill, *Rekindling a Lost Passion: Recreating a Church Planting Movement* (Fallbrook, CA: Hart Research Center, 1999), 101-108; see also Robert Dale, *To Dream Again: How to Help Your Church Come Alive* (Nashville: Broadman Press, 1981).

50. Greg Taylor, pastor of Foster Seventh-day Adventist Church, Ashville, North Carolina, to Ernan Norman, May 6, 1999.

51. Taylor to Norman, May 6, 1999.

52. Ibid. Those who have not been to church for anything other than a wedding or a funeral for two years or more are considered to be unchurched.

53. Monte Sahlin is a vice-president for Creative Ministries in the Columbia Union Conference of Seventh-day Adventists in Maryland, USA. Also Paul Richardson is an administrator in the School of Dentistry, Loma Linda University, Loma Linda, California.

54. Greg Taylor, *Building a Biblical Community Where Secular People Become Fully Devoted Followers of Christ* (Asheville, NC: Foster Seventh-day Adventist Church, 1999), 6-8.

55. This analysis is taken from information found in a manual titled "Building a Biblical Community Where Secular People Become Fully Devoted to Christ," Foster Seventh-day Adventist Church, Asheville, NC. See also, "Foster Seventh-day Adventist Church, available www/ fosterchurch.com/mission.html accessed 13 April 2000; Internet.

56. Taylor from Ernan Norman, May 6, 1999..

57. Ibid.

58. Ibid.

59. Aubrey Malphurs, *Planting Growing Churches for the 21st Century* (Grand Rapids, MI: Baker Books, 1998), 68, 69.

60. Taylor, *Building a Biblical Community*, 6.

61. Bill Hull, *Revival That Reforms* (Grand Rapids, MI: Fleming H. Revell, 1998), 101.

62. Foster Seventh-day Adventist Church, "When It Hurts," accessed 13 April 2000 available from www.fosterchurch.com/month.html; Internet.

63. Ibid., internet.

64. See White, *Ministry of Healing*, 143; also Rebecca Manley Pippert, *Out of the Salt Shaker*, 13; Philip G. Samaan, *Christ's Way of Reaching People*, 33, 34.

65. Erich W. Baumgartner, "Megachurches and What They Teach Us," in *Adventist Missions in the 21st Century* (Hagerstown, MD: Review and Herald, 1999), 151.

66. Ibid. See also Paul Basden, *The Worship Maze*, 88, 89.

67. Baumgartner, 152. See also Gustav Niebuhr, "American Religion at the Millennium's End," *Word and World* 18, no. 1 (Winter 1998): 10, 11.

68. Baumgartner, 152, 153; Pritchard, 59-66, 198, 245, 67-79.

69. Baumgartner, 153.

70. Ibid.

71. "What works for a church of one thousand is often not helpful to a church of four hundred or a church of thirty-five. Specific strategies for different size churches are necessary." Gary L. McIntosh, *One Size Doesn't Fit All* (Grand Rapids, MI: Fleming H. Revell, 1999), 19.

72. Baumgartner, 154.

73. Ibid., 134.

74. Ibid., 135.

75. Ibid.

76. Ibid.

77. For more details about their influence in Pastor Warren's life, see Rick Warren, *The Purpose Driven Church: Growth Without Compromising Your Message and Mission* (Grand Rapids, MI: Zondervan Publishing House, 1995), 25-30.

78. Ibid., 33-38.

79. Ibid., 39.

80. Ibid.

81. Ibid., 128.

82. Ibid., 160.

83. Ibid., 253.

84. Ibid., 293.

85. Ibid.

86. Ibid., 294.

87. Ibid., 294, 295.

88. Ibid., 295, 296.

89. Ibid., 306.

90. Rick Warren, "Worship Can Be a Witness," *Worship Leader* 6 (January-February 1997): 28.

91. Andy Langford, *Transitions in Worship: Moving from Traditional to Contemporary* (Nashville, TN: Abingdon Press, 1999), 34.

92. Warren, *The Purpose-Driven Church*, 143.

93. Ibid., 145.

94. Ibid.

95. Ibid., 149, 150.

96. Ibid., 176, 177.

97. Montgomery W. Smith, "Homogeneity and American Church Growth" Ph.D. dissertation, Fuller Institute, 1976, 49.

98. Warren, *The Purpose Driven Church, 176, 177.*

99. Ellen G. White, *In Heavenly Places* (Washington, DC: Review and Herald Publishing Association, 1967), 319.

100. See Hybles and Hybles, 184-186; also Michael G. Maudlin and Edward Gilbreath, "Selling out the House of God: Bill Hybles Answers Critics of the Seeker-Church Movement," *Christianity Today*, July 18, 1994, 21-25.

CHAPTER 6

A SUGGESTED STRATEGY TO REACH SECULAR PEOPLE

The purpose of this chapter is to present a proposed strategy for reaching secular people. This strategy is proposed in the concept of church planting. I am suggesting that the planted church should be intentional. By intentional I mean that the church should structure its outreach and inreach for the purpose of reaching and nurturing the secular-unchurched person.

The Intentional Church

The following strategy deals with planting a church that is intentional for reaching secular people. It is to the church that Christ gave the command, "Go therefore and make disciples of all nations" (Matt 28:19, NKJV). To the church with its individual members and multiplied gifts and talents is given the task of reaching the world for Christ. Paul speaks of these gifts being bestowed on the church for the work of ministry: "When He ascended on high, He led captivity captive and gave gifts to men. . . . And He Himself gave some to be apostles, some prophets, some evangelists, and some pastors and teachers, for the equipping of the saints for the work of ministry" (Eph 4:8, 11-12, NKJV; cf. Rom 12:5-8; 1 Cor 12:4-11).

Christ selected a group of men to be associated with Him. They were trained and equipped under His tutelage. They were the church. They were discipled by Christ in order that they in turn would disciple others. "These men He purposed to train and educate as the leaders of His church. They in turn were to educate others and send them out with the gospel message. . . . By these feeble agencies, through His word and Spirit, He designs to place salvation within the reach of all."[1]

Even though secular people see the church as irrelevant, and many today are down on the church, and yes, some churches are irrelevant, and it could be said that their favorite hymn is "I Shall Not Be Moved," because they will not do anything for God either intentionally or unintentionally, yet "the church is God's idea and we dear not run ahead of Him! When a local church is the church as God intended—not perfect, but functioning as the body of Christ—nothing is more powerful for reaching a (secular) community for Christ...there is nothing on earth that can substitute for it! What an awesome tool it is in the hand of God!"[2]

The church, therefore, is the best possible avenue for effective disciple making. Reaching secular-unchurched people will require the body of Christ working together. By the use of their gifts they are to bring secular people into a personal relationship with Christ and then train them to be obedient followers of their new Master. The best context for this kind of disciple making is the church, the local body of believers.[3]

Secondarily, the church must be intentional, based on whom the church is trying to reach. The church, in doing evangelism today, needs to think in terms of whom the listeners are. George Hunter contends that the first characteristic of a secular person in the modern world is that he or she is essentially ignorant of basic Christianity.[4]

The implications for mission outreach are obvious. We are living at a time when we have to do evangelism and ministry at the margins. Gone are the days when the church had the "home field advantage." There was a time when people had a basic working knowledge of Christianity. They had a positive attitude toward the faith and assumed it to be true. The witness for Christ had only to build on that and invite people to accept the faith. Today, however, after decades of secularization, most people misunderstand Christianity, are negative (if not alienated) toward the church, and do not assume the Christian message to be God's supreme revelation.[5]

Al McClure, former president of the North American Division of Seventh-day Adventists, sensing this dilemma, stated, "We must not 'expect the unchurched to come to us on our terms and adjust to our unique culture. . . . It is imperative that we be willing to devise new wineskins to serve as vehicles for the water of life. . . . We must be intentional about reaching those who speak another language—ethnically or culturally—even if it means planting a new and different kind of church."[6]

It is for this reason that I speak of being intentional. Realizing that the message of the gospel is ideally suited to the needs and concerns of secular people today leads me to suggest a strategy with the concept of the intentional church.

Planting the Intentional Church

The foregoing is a suggested series of steps for this overall strategy.

Initiating a Vision

The planting of the intentional church must begin with one's vision. Vision, says Robert E. Logan, is "the ability to see things which are not."[7] This is a vision for a new thing, a church that begins out of an understanding that there is both need and opportunity. There is the need to reach unchurched-secular people and the opportunity to do so. Such a vision is rooted in God's own example of reaching humanity.

God's method of reaching humanity did not include the sending of an angel or God coming down to us in resplendent glory. He did not speak to us in the language of heaven, but in the language of humanity. God the Son took upon Himself humanity, tabernacled with us, identified with our human needs and struggles, found pathways to us through our most familiar associations, and ultimately died for us.[8] He stepped out of His own comfort zone and became the "us" He wanted to reach. That is the reality of God's reaching humanity. In a similar sense, the vision for reaching unchurched people would mean envisioning a kind of church that goes beyond traditional forms and strategies. It has its own "authentic form, lifestyle and purpose."[9]

This kind of vision not only comes with the understanding of need—the need to reach lost souls for Christ—but it translates into an urgency and a passion—God's passion for the lost.[10] This kind of vision provides the motivation for planting a church that is intentional for reaching secular-unchurched people with the gospel.[11] Any motivation that lacks this kind of vision could be cause for frustration and failure. "When a certain godly call is absent as a motivating factor in church planting, God's blessing will not likely be on such a venture."[12]

Steps in Cultivating the Vision

Pray Concerning Vision

Pray that God will clarify the vision. Pray that your eyes be opened to see God's desire for you in the church-planting endeavor. Ask that the vision be specific and clear. Ask for the eyesalve of Rev 3:18. Our eyes, says Robert Logan, are bound earthward. We have limited vision. All that we perceive to be true is unreal in the sense that it is filtered through physical senses which tell us only partial truth about the absolute nature of our world. This kind of prayer is also like Elisha's prayer, "Lord, I pray open his eyes that he may see" (2 Kgs 6:17).[13]

Share the Vision

Share the vision with others who also have a burden for reaching unchurched-secular people. It is the personal vision of a pastor or church planter and his or her ability to communicate that vision that will inspire others to share in that vision.[14] Aubrey Malphurs states that the pastor or leader wears three hats in this process of sharing the vision:

1. Vision Cultivator: He or she initiates and develops the division, which empowers and motivates others to share in the vision.

2. Vision Communicator: The leader must keep the vision before those with whom he or she is sharing the vision.

3. Vision Clarifier: The vision clarifier focuses the vision. The leader constantly rethinks and further refines the vision.[15]

Pray With "Significant Others"

During the birthing process of the vision, the leader should pray with "significant others." These significant others are the people who will constitute the leaders or core members of the church-planting team.[16] Through intercessory prayer the leaders and team members can find mutual support and spiritual strength.

Fingerprint the Vision

The team members or significant others who share in the vision need to get their fingerprints all over the vision. This is accomplished by including them in the envisioning process. They must become a part of the process. When they feel as though they have been a part of the process because their thoughts and ideas are accurately represented in the vision, then they are more likely to strongly commit to the vision.[17]

Begin Initial Training

Once the vision has been initiated, shared, and owned by the pastor/leader and core group, the next step is training of members and the group as a whole. This approach is similar to Christ's method. His method was to choose the twelve disciples, train and equip them for service, that they might carry on the mission He started. Philip G. Samaan states that "in the construction of the edifice of His mission, much would depend on the quality training of the twelve disciples. Sublime yet simple strategy."[18] This training should have three important components:

1. Spiritual formation

2. Understanding secularization and secularism

3. On-the-job training.

Have Spiritual Formation

By spiritual formation I mean the necessity of a personal and abiding relationship with Jesus that goes beyond mere intellectual assent, but is experiential through daily personal conversion, earmarked by a devotional life of prayer and Bible study. This is an experience in which the pastor or leader must first take the journey, and then invite his team to follow him or her.

It has been suggested that in order for the pastor to be effective spiritually he must have the following in his spiritual resume:

1. He or she must learn brokenness before the Lord so God can fill him or her with His Spirit.

2. He or she must also know the word of God, which gives him or her authority in ministry.

3. He or she must be a person of intercessory prayer.

4. He or she must minister out of the calling he or she has from God; a calling which drives one to sacrifice, to take up one's cross daily, and follow Jesus Christ.[19]

The need for deep, genuine spirituality cannot be overemphasized. The pastor's own spiritual richness or lack of it will influence his or her team either positively or negatively. If it is true that "the church is the length and shadow of its pastor," then careful attention needs to be given to the character and spirituality of the minister.[20]

Ellen White states that "he who has his own heart imbued with the love of Jesus can feed the flock of God. He has a living experience and can say with the apostle John, 'that which was from the beginning, which we have heard, which we have seen with our eyes, which we have looked upon, and our hands have handled of the Word of Life; . . . that which we have seen and heard declare we unto you.'"[21]

This all-important need of Christ in the lives and hearts of pastors and leaders desirous of leading their ministry team in secular ministry is where spiritual formation begins. When pastors can successfully lead themselves and their team into this experience, success is sure to come.

Paulien highlights the fact that "those ministers, evangelists, and church members who do win secular people succeed because they have a living relationship with God. . . . A living walk with God is certainly a basic asset in anyone seeking to reach secular people. Secular ministry must begin in the devotional room."[22]

This spiritual formation which includes devotional life is the key to success or failure in this endeavor. It is clearly stated that one of the chief reasons for failure among those who witness to others is the crowding out of the devotional life. "Communion with God through prayer and a study of His Word is neglected. . . . Here is one of the chief secrets of failure in Christian work."[23]

It is imperative, therefore, that the gospel we present for the saving of souls be the gospel by which our own souls are saved. If we are going to make our influence felt in a skeptical world, we must have a living faith in Christ as a personal Savior. "If we would draw sinners out of the swift-running current, our own feet must be firmly set on the rock, Christ Jesus."[24]

Understanding Secularization and Secularism

The next step in the training should be to educate members in the understanding of secularization and secularism. Studying the process of secularization will give team members a historical perspective on the various forces and events in history that have helped to shape the present context of our society. It will raise their awareness in the reality that the West has become a vast mission field. It will help them to understand that the process of secularization has impacted our society to the point that it has affected peoples' way of living and thinking. The Christian worldview is not as potent a factor as it once was. People live unexamined lives even among Christians. Both Paulien and Rasi agree that secular culture has infiltrated the thinking of the church itself. Through television and other media, church members are subtly influenced into secular ways of thinking.[25]

Rasi goes so far as to say that "even Seventh-day Adventists are being influenced by the secular environment. We may attend church and generally follow the Adventist lifestyle, but our thought patterns, values, and priorities are not much different from those in the surrounding culture."[26]

This educating process will give the members an opportunity for introspection. Where are they in relation to the secular people whom they are desirous of reaching for Christ? Where are they in the scale of things? Are they involved in "secular drift"? Have they adopted the values and philosophies of the secular culture? Are their world views shaped by an informed biblical theology or by humanistic teachings? These are all important questions and suggest yet another reason why training in spiritual formation is so critical.

Paulien speaks persuasively to this point when he says,

> We need desperately to reflect. We need desperately to take stock. I am contending here that this is our greatest need. If you do not have a living relationship with God, please don't try to reach secular people. If you are as secular as the person you are trying to reach, you are on the same spiritual level. Like cannot elevate like. You cannot help a secular person to find God if you do not know Him for yourself.[27]

Besides studying the subjects of secularization and secularism with implications for how one's life may or may not be impacted, consideration should be given to understanding secular people themselves. A profiling of secular people along with what is considered to be their felt needs should be undertaken.

An understanding of secular people will help members to see why we need to be intentional in reaching them. It will help them to better understand why traditional approaches to propagating the gospel among secular-unchurched people are largely ineffective.[28]

At the same time, members should be made to understand that there is still hope for secular people. There are still ways to reach them, and intentional efforts should be put forth. Craig Van Gelder has stated that it is important to recognize that not everything within the postmodern condition necessarily presents a problem to Christian faith or the gospel. He mentions that the resurfacing of spirituality as a viable and necessary dimension of human existence provides a very effective bridge for communicating the gospel as good news to persons shaped by the postmodern condition.[29]

On-the-job Training

On-the-job training can begin during the planning stages. The demographic and psychographic study of the targeted community could be a point where members begin to interact intentionally with the community. At this point in time the pastor can help to supervise these members. Most of the on-the-job training will be realized during the implementation of the strategy itself.

Begin Advance Strategic Planning

The strategic planning process involves certain specifics that should be in place. They are all aspects of the strategic thinking and acting process and become vital to successful church planting. Aubrey Malphurs has done a marvelous job of articulating some basic steps for church planting and church growth that are intentional, and I have adopted them for the purposes of this study.[30]

Principles to Work By

For this strategy I present some core principles that would be helpful to those who are desirous of reaching secular-unchurched people. It is not my intention to make these principles hard and fast rules for reaching secular people. Their application will change as the mission environment changes. However, I am recommending them as a basic framework to stimulate further investigation, experimentation, and possibly further amplification.

Allow me to make a suggestion from the outset that with the exception of ministry analysis, the very first undertaking of this intentional church strategy should be a demographic study. What I am advocating is a paradigm shift in the way we have been accustomed to do evangelism and mission outreach. The assumption has been and still is that the truth that we have is what the people need. We believe, and rightly so, that the gospel is the answer to people's needs. Our approach has largely been the formulation of an evangelistic strategy based on these assumptions. This worked well in days gone by when the harvest field was more in line with that old paradigm approach. Today, however, the harvest has changed from corn to wheat. So, if we go with the old paradigm, we would be entering wheat fields with corn pickers. The result will be a failure to gather the harvest and even the possibility of destroying it while trying to gather it. That is doing ministry from the inside out, and goes with the assumption that:

1. What motivated us is what will motivate them.

2. The approach that reached us is the approach that will reach them.

3. They already know what we are talking about.

4. They like the church enough to be able to respond affirmatively.[31]

When this approach is taken we overlook the fact that we may not be scratching where it itches. We may not be addressing the real needs and concerns of the people we are trying to reach. When strategies are formulated with the assumption that what we have simply needs to be presented to the people, with no prior understanding of the needs and interests of people, we are guilty of doing a program-driven mission— mission from "the inside out."[32]

I am, therefore, suggesting that in order to be intentional we must do mission from the outside in. Mission from the outside in focuses more on what is going on with the targeted population, and what God is calling the church to do for them.[33]

Do a Ministry Analysis

The ministry analysis should focus on the spiritual and gifted resources of the church planting team. The basic question is, How equipped are we for ministry and what should we do or not do as a consequence?

Begin with Pastor/Leader

The analysis should begin with the pastor or leader. We are attempting here to look at leadership skills and styles. We are attempting to ascertain what giftedness the pastor or leader has, in order to be a successful leader in church planting. Francis contends that contemporary church planting calls for a relatively high degree of skill and commitment.[34]

Ron Gladden believes that we should "assign some of our finest, most gifted and dedicated ministers to the work of planting churches."[35] For Gladden, this comes through assessment—a process of evaluating and identifying the very best persons to lead church plants. Criteria include gift mix, personality, leadership skills, character, and denominational loyalty.[36] Particular attention should be given to leadership skills. Christian Schwartz and his team, in a recent study dealing with universally applicable church-growth principles, found that by and large leaders of successful growing churches have a leadership style expressed by the word "empowerment."[37]

The leaders of growing churches concentrate on empowering other Christians for ministry. They assist Christians to attain the spiritual potential God has for them. These pastors equip, support, motivate, and mentor individuals enabling them to become all that God wants them to be.[38] This style of leadership invests time in discipling, delegating, and multiplying. The energy they expend can be multiplied indefinitely. This is how growth occurs; God's energy, not human effort and pressure, is released to set the church in motion.[39]

In light of the above, the ministry analysis should help the pastor or leader assess their own strengths and weaknesses. It will also help in doing two things:

1. It will give the pastor or leader the opportunity to surround himself or herself with people who complement him or her.[40]

2. The pastor or leader is able to adjust to a role in the whole process of church planting that fits his or her gift mix and experience, so that his or her ministry is maximized. At the same time, it leaves room for members of the team to be placed in ministry roles for which the pastor or leader is not gifted or suited.[41]

Team Members

The ministry analysis will help church members identify their gifts and exercise them in appropriate ministries. When members can function in the area of their own giftedness, they generally serve less in their own strength and more in the power of the Holy Spirit.[42]

The results of the ministry analysis could lead to a number of questions:

1. What are our strengths as a team?

2. What are potentially our weaknesses as a team?

3. What are our unique, distinct competencies?

4. What gifts and abilities do we have that will qualify us in planting this church?

5. What (as a result of our talents and gifts) quality of ministry will we be able to offer our targeted group in the community?[43]

Do a Demographic Study

Doing a demographic study at this point of the strategy is important for beginning contact with the targeted community. Some may be concerned that the other aspects of the strategy should be developed first, such as the mission statement, proposed strategies or methods that should be used, or even the core values. There is always the possibility of allowing the targeted audience—the unchurched-secular people—

to determine or set the agenda, rather than the Word of God. Will not the agenda be driven by market forces?

This could only happen if one fails to develop the core values. Among these core values is the church's stated belief and acceptance of the inspired authority of God's Word, the guide for all evangelistic strategies. What I am proposing here is that we become intentional in formulating our approaches and strategies for reaching secular people. While the mission statement answers the question, "What has God called us to do?" and the strategy answers the question, "How will we carry out the mission?" being informed and aware of the targeted audience will be extremely helpful in formulating strategies and focusing on ways to make contact based on felt needs.

C. Peter Wagner gives three main reasons for doing a demographic study.

1. Identify target audiences: Demographics will help in knowing who lives where and how many there are. This becomes extremely helpful in planning ministry.[44] Rick Warren states that within a community there would probably be many subcultures or groups. To successfully reach each of these groups will require knowing how they think. What are their interests? What do they value? Where do they hurt? What are they afraid of? What are the most prominent features of the way they live? What are their most popular radio stations? The more you know about the targeted community, the easier it is to strategize to reach them.[45]

2. Determining receptivity: Skilled use of demographic information can help in estimating beforehand the degree of receptivity the members of the target audience will have to some methods of sharing the gospel. Paying attention to data that reveal people's mobility will be helpful because people moving into an area for the first time are ordinarily more receptive than those who have lived there a long time. Through demographics you can discover some of the felt needs. Through meeting felt needs, you will create an avenue to the soul.

3. Building confidence: A good feasibility study with up-to-date

demographics builds confidence on three sides: (a) it will help to impress those who are sponsoring you for the church- planting activity, (b) it impresses the members of the team; they will have confidence in and show a willingness to support someone who has the expertise to know the community that well, and (c) it will build your confidence; give you a handle on the targeted community and help your decision-making process.[46]

There are several sources of demographic information that one can use. Please try the following list:

12 Sources of Demographic Information

1. U.S. Census Data -You can get it from a state, a country, a standard metropolitan statistical area, a census tract, a block group or an individual block.

2. City or County Planning Commission - You can find this at the county planning office.

3. School Boards- Most school boards have updated demographic files on their districts.

4. Public Utilities- such as electric companies, gas companies, water companies, and telephone companies

5. Local Universities - Visit the sociology department or look for theses that may deal with the demographic of your area.

6. Lending Institutions - Banks, saving and loans, and finance companies usually keep their planning information close at hand.

7. Chamber of Commerce - They may have good planning information.

8. Radio Stations - Usually gather demographic information for their listening area.

9. Public Libraries - A skilled research librarian can help you.

10. Real Estate Firms - Especially the larger ones, have extensive demographic data.

11. Newspapers - Particularly in metropolitan areas, reading the daily news will give you valuable information.

12. Commercial Geodemographics - This is coordinated through a large computer complex in Ithaca, New York. Using U.S. Census data as a foundation, information is constantly updated through multiple sources of ongoing population studies.

Taken from C. Peter Wagner, Church Planting for a Greater Harvest, 83-88.

Values Discovery and Development

In this step we are dealing with what is considered core values. Core values are considered to be very important for they are at the foundation of an effective organization. Ken Blanchard and Michael O'Connor state that "perhaps more than at any previous time, an organization today must know what it stands for and on what principles it will operate. No longer is values-based organizational behavior an interesting philosophical choice—it is a requisite to survival."[47] Lyle Schaller also states that "the most important single element of any corporate, congregational, or denominational culture, however, is its value system."[48]

Malphurs defines core values as "the constant, passionate, biblical core beliefs that drive the ministry."[49] These values help to clarify what is unique and different about the ministry. They also show what the ministry will emphasize and what it will not emphasize. Some of these values are biblical absolutes, while others find their source in biblical truth. Value statements for churches include such important items as commitment to the Scriptures as God's truth, relevant Bible preaching and teaching, excellence in leadership and ministry, relevant evangelism, ministry in small groups, an emphasis on prayer, authentic and contemporary worship, lay assessment and involvement, and so on.[50]

These core values are constant; they are timeless. As a distinct aspect of the congregational soul, they remain fixed while almost everything around it is in great flux. These values dictate congregational behavior and have a strong influence on decisions made and directions taken.[51] Thus any concern for the way the strategy is shaped—what forces drive the agenda—should find an answer in the church's orientation in the shared core values.

Notice what several writers have said about the shaping power of values. James Kouzes and Barry Posner, both business consultants for organizational development at San Jose University, write:

> "Values are deep-seated standards that influence almost every aspect of our lives: our moral judgments, our responses to others, our commitment to personal and organizational goals. However silently, values give direction to the hundreds of decisions made at all levels of an organization. Options that run counter to the group's value system are seldom considered. Values constitute our personal bottom line."[52]

Peter Senge refers to values as "mental models" that shape how we act. They provide the prism through which all behavior is ultimately viewed.[53]

An example of some core values is: biblical community, biblical teaching, prayer, lost people, creativity and innovation, relevant worship, evangelism, God's grace, saving faith, etc. Do not mistake a value with its form. For example, someone may actually consider small groups as a value. Small groups are not a value, but rather a form that expresses or implements a value. You may value small groups, but that does not make them a value. Remember the definition of core values: "Constant, passionate, biblical core beliefs that drive the ministry."[54] The value behind small groups could be biblical community, or evangelism, or some other function.

Once it is clear that values are important and the team understands what they are, then identify a set of core values and develop your values statement.[55]

Mission Development

After having developed the core values for the intentional church that is to be planted, the next step is to develop the core mission statement for the ministry. The mission statement should describe the purpose and reason for the existence of the intentional church in the targeted community.

Definition: What is mission? The church's mission is a broad, brief, biblical statement of what it is supposed to be doing. It has five key elements.

1. The first element of the definition is its breadth. It is broad. It is encompassing, overarching, and comprehensive.

2. It also has the element of brevity. It should be able to be expressed in a single concise sentence. If the mission is short, the people will remember it.

3. The third element is that it is biblical. It is based on Scripture, e.g., Matt 28:19-20.

4. The fourth element is that it is a statement. It needs to be written out in the form of a mission statement.

5. The final element is that it is a statement of what the church is supposed to be doing.[56]

Kotler suggests that an organization should strive for a mission that is feasible, motivating, and distinctive.[57]

The mission statement for the intentional church should be formulated with the criteria that it is biblical, comprehensive, and brief. It should be able to state clearly what the church is supposed to be doing—reaching unchurched-secular people—in obedience to the Great Commission, and the needs to be met or service given—developing people into fully devoted followers of Christ.

Do an Environmental Scan

The environmental scan is raising the question, what is going on out there? Unlike the demographic or psychographic study of the targeted community, which seeks to understand and learn as much as possible about the persons we are trying to reach, the environmental scan is concerned with the wider context. It looks at the wider environment such as the technological, social, economic, philosophical, political, and religious. It is watching for trends and developments that could inform or impact the ministry of the church. Space and time will not allow for a listing of what could be various trends and developments in all the above categories.[58]

The Bible says that "the men of Issachar understood the time, and they knew what Israel should do" (1 Chr 12:32). In order for the intentional church to be able to use the Scriptures to address the world that its people live and work in, it must know what is going on. Practicing an environmental scan helps the leaders and members to understand the times and keeps them on the cutting edge of what the church should be doing.[59]

In his book, On Becoming a Leader, Warren Bennis reacts to our present state of recurring, disruptive change and writes, "For this reason, before anyone can learn to lead, he must learn something about this strange new world. Indeed, anyone who does not master this mercurial context will be mastered by it."[60] This is also true of the church situation in reaching the unchurched today. This goes to the matter of relevance. By understanding the culture in a radically changing world, leaders and members will be able to respond not only strategically, but also in a relevant fashion.[61]

Developing a Vision for the Ministry

In the area of demographic study I mentioned that it was strategic to do the demographic study first, since it is consistent with the idea of doing mission from the outside in. By understanding and knowing the essentials of your targeted group you are able to better plan in a way that responds strategically to their interests, needs, and concerns. So also, by doing an environmental scan, and placing it before your vision or strategy development, it is consistent with doing mission from the outside in. The environmental scan provides information and awareness of contemporary and future trends that will impact the way the leader and team members develop the vision.

The basic question that arises in the development of the vision is, "What kind of church would we like to be?"[62] What size should we be? Should we be homogenous or culturally diverse? What will our mission look like, its extent and intent?

At this point in the strategy, I would like to suggest what I have in mind for this church- planting strategy in terms of what kind of church I envision as being a part of an effective strategy for reaching secular-unchurched people. First, I am envisioning a church that is relatively small to medium—between 200 and 350 in congregational size.

Second, I am envisioning a church that should be culturally diverse and inclusive. Third, I am envisioning a mission that serves to build the planted church and further extends itself in the planting and reproducing of other churches—continual penetration. I would like to advance the following reasons for these three components, by looking at each of the above.

Small to Medium Church

Plateauing effect.

In The Pastor's Manual for Effective Ministry, Win Arn states that "In the years following World War II thousands of new churches were established. Today, of the approximately 350,000 churches in America, four out of the five are either plateaued or declining."[63] He further states that "in the normal life cycle of churches, there is birth, and in time, death. Many churches begin a plateau and/or slow decline around their 15th-18th year."[64] Russell Burrill states that many will plateau long before that time, while others may continue to ride that plateau for forty or fifty years depending on their location and ministry.[65]

One study that was done between 1965 and 1985 shows that nearly every mainline denomination is in decline. Among them are United Methodist (-16%), Episcopal (-20%), Presbyterian (-24%), and

Disciples of Christ (-42%).[66] More recent figures confirm this trend with the Presbyterian Church (U.S.A.) losing close to 10,000 members in 1995 alone and the United Church of Christ and the Christian Church (Disciples of Christ) combining for another 50,000 members lost.[67] The Southern Baptist Convention, which is considered to be one of the more evangelistic Christian denominations, is reported to have 70 percent of all Southern Baptist churches either plateaued or declining.[68] The Barna Research Group also found that attendance had dipped from a previous 40 percent to 37 percent among Americans attending a worship service.[69]

Towns, Wagner, and Rainer state that some churches reach the growth barrier between 150-200 members. These are classified as relatively small churches. Other churches reach barriers between 250-350. These are considered medium-sized churches. Some churches experience these growth barriers (declining or plateauing experiences) at less or more figures. These are not magical figures. It all depends on the dynamics involved.[70]

The 200-350-size church that I am advocating is not a magical figure, but is based on the fact that plateauing tends to come at this point for some churches. Therefore, in the proposed strategy, I am suggesting that churches that reach this size should themselves be intentional in starting and planting daughter churches that are also intentional for reaching unchurched people.

Russell Burrill says that among some of the reasons new churches should be planted today is that it will stimulate growth in an older church.

> "A church that is on a plateau or even in decline can actually be stimulated back into a growth cycle by starting a new church. . . . The start of a new church with some of its members leaving creates a void in the existing church that in turn stimulates them into action. The status quo is no longer viable. As a result, the mother church returns to a growth cycle."[71]

One reason for the choice of a small to medium-size church is that there is more effectiveness in reaching the harvest. Both Burrill and Baumgartner indicated their agreement with recent international research which shows that church growth is more effective through smaller churches that manifest high quality, steady growth, and innovative multiplication.[72]

In his study, the German missiologist Christian Schwartz revealed that large churches actually were the third most negative factor toward growth.[73] Those mega-churches that are successful were discovered to be the exception and not the rule. That is the reason everyone brags about them—they are an aberration, not a normal occurrence. Schwartz discovered that small churches were actually 1600 percent more effective in reaching the harvest than mega-churches.[74]

Another reason why I am advocating small- to medium-size churches is that they offer greater potential for relationships and belonging. Small churches, says Burrill, are a very valuable asset, especially where younger generations such as Generation X are concerned. They are said to be very relationally oriented and want small churches where relationships may be fostered.[75]

In an article, "Church Attendance Reported at Lowest Level in Two Decades," Gregg Garrison cites recent research by Penny Long Marler and other researchers, soon to be published in a book Unchurched Faith by Abingdon Press, where they have studied people under 35 who do not attend church. This 35-and-under group, who are very often children of divorced parents, according to the Marler studies, is showing that glitz—media-savvy worship—is not what they seem to want. "They were interested in a small church like the one their grandparents went to, where they can have personal relationships."[76]

Culturally diverse church

I am advocating that the church should, by its intentional strategy, be a diverse body—heterogenous. The reason for this is that we are inhabiting a sinful world where people not only experience alienation from God, but from each other. This is evident culturally and racially. The church should be in itself a witness to the world of what the power of God can do for a redeemed humanity. The secular world sees and experiences the dividing forces between various classes and groups of people. The witness that the church can offer is found in Jesus' own words in John 17:18-21, "As you sent Me into the world, I also have sent them into the world. And for their sakes I sanctify myself, that they also may be sanctified by the truth. I do not pray for these alone, but also for those who will believe in Me through their word; that they all may be one, as you, Father, are in Me, and I in you; that they also may be one in us, that the world may believe that you sent Me" (NKJV).

The SDA Bible Commentary states that "the unity springing from the blended lives of Christians would impress the world of the divine origin of the Christian Church."[77] Again, this unity is to be a demonstration of agape love, in order that the world might know that the Father sent the Son. While no biological analogy is offered here to indicate in what sense the church is to be one, Jesus did say in John 10:16 that there would be one flock. The mystical phrase used in this passage transcends even this thought. He prays for a spiritual unity, after the pattern of that spiritual unity between Himself and the Father. This unity as it pertains to Christians is not an invisible unity. It is to be such as will convince the world of the divine mission of the common Master of Christians. And, as Jesus had already explained, the badge of this unity is love, the love of Christian for Christian, which all men may see (John 13:35).[78] "The consequence of the spiritual unity of Christians, as indicated by their common love for each other, is that the world will be at last convinced that the mission of Jesus was divine, and that He is the Savior of the world."[79] Ellen White says that this is also a unity in diversity.[80]

While the passage in John 17 speaks to unity in the highest spiritual sense, it is to be expressed in the dynamics of the Christian community in terms of unity of doctrine, mission, exercise of diverse gifts, and no less so in unity of people regardless of ethnic origin or social status. Burrill has hit the nail on the head when he says that living in community with God and each other in order to increase the fellowship is at the heart of the New Testament understanding of the church as community. Fellowship thus is not a sideline of Christian activity, but biblically is the essence of what it means to be a Christian.

Again Burrill states, "A caring community where members minister to each other is itself an evangelistic tool. Non-Christians seeing people who are living in a restored community, truly caring for each other, will flock to be a part of it. Such loving, caring communities are a drawing card for evangelism."[81]

Walter Douglas spoke forcefully to this point in his article, "Multicultural Ministry: Challenges and Blessings."[82] As the then pastor of the All Nations Seventh-day Adventist Church in Berrien Springs, Michigan, Douglas stated that All Nations was intentionally established as a multi-racial, multi-ethnic, and multi-cultural congregation. He stated that it is a church born out of the biblical and theological conviction that God has made of one blood all nations of men and women (Acts 17:26), drawing them from every tribe, language, nation, and race (Rev 5:9).[83] Out of this experience of pastoring the All Nations Church, Douglas is convinced that "a culturally distinct congregation does not and cannot reflect the Kingdom of Christ so clearly portrayed in His life and teaching. Cultural difference is no legitimate basis for either inclusion or exclusion from the body of believers."[84]

Douglas states that what happened at Pentecost and what Jesus practiced in His ministry (a gathering through the Holy Spirit of "many languages, many colors, many cultures," to give testimony to the one God) was no accident. It was to be a witness to the world of the power of God.[85]

It is this witness that I speak about when I speak of being intentional. In a world that is fragmented, the church should break in with a counter-model of social life.[86]

The church-growth movement by and large has approached this from quite a different perspective. The focus is often on reaching people through social homogeneity as a necessary condition for congregational formation and growth.[87] According to the homogeneous principle, people like to become Christians "without having to cross racial, linguistic, or class barriers to do so."[88]

Hozell Francis raised the issue

"whether it is theologically tenable to promote a principle of homogeneity for the sake of expediency and comfort. Would not the unbelieving world be impressed if black and white Christians were more comfortable and cohesive in all our churches? Jesus proclaimed that the world would know that we are His disciples by the love that we have for one another (John 13:35)."[89]

While, for obvious reasons, I cannot at this juncture discuss the pros and cons of the debate, it is necessary to realize that we need not have an uncritical acceptance of all that passes in the church-growth movement. The homogeneous principle may have some promise as a tool for evangelism from the pragmatic or utilitarian perspective, but such a methodology of doing so can and should be open to scrutiny.[90]

The intentional church that is planted for the purpose of reaching secular, unchurched people is to be in itself a strategic principle. That is to say, the church demonstrating a culturally diverse community, redeemed and kept by her Lord, is a living witness to the reality of Jesus Christ. It will draw people who are longing for genuine community, a community that is not controlled by the idolatrous powers, not conformed to the practices of the surrounding culture, but shaping its life and ministry around Jesus Christ, His life, His death, and His resurrected power. Such a church lives now according to the pattern of the life in the age to come. The nature of the church's witness, though relevant and critically contextual, is a non-conformed engagement with the world. This engagement happens both through specific words and deeds performed in the world and through the witness of being a presence in the world. The church is to be different from the world in the sense that it invites questions and challenges assumptions, while at the same time it seeks to relate the gospel in a relevant and understandable way to the world.[91]

Continual church planting

It was earlier discussed that plateauing churches could be revitalized by planting other churches. This is one reason for doing so, but not the best reason. What I am proposing for this strategy is that the mission of the intentional church should be to continually seek to advance the efforts of reaching secular-unchurched people by planting other churches. This is a part of the vision for the church and should be reflected in the mission statement. This should also be developed in the core strategy.

There are at least two good reasons why such penetration by continual reproducing and planting of churches is beneficial:

1. It is a true fulfillment of the gospel commission—for the church to really have a focused mission it must look beyond itself and seek to obey the Saviour's commission mandate. To do that it becomes imperative that it start significant churches for the purpose of reaching the unchurched. For the church to penetrate across the cities of America (no one church can do it by itself) it would need to multiply itself by starting a network of biblically based intentional churches.[92] Since I am proposing that the church should not be any larger than at least 350 members, the smallest at 200 depending on the area and impact of growth rate, plans should be afoot during the 200 to 350 stage.

2. The second reason why it is beneficial to focus on continual planting is that new churches tend to evangelize better than established churches. In a study appearing in Christianity Today, Bruce Nichol states that, among evangelical churches, those under three years old will win ten people to Christ per year for every one hundred members. Those churches from three to fifteen years old will win five people per year for every one hundred church members. Those churches reaching age fifteen experience a drop in figures to three people per year for every one hundred members.[93]

Burrill states that many of the lost people are not reached because they are turned off by the existing churches, and the sad fact is that many of these churches will not change appreciably.[94] Planting new churches for reaching the unchurched is like pouring "new wine into new wineskins." Not only are those who are involved excited about the new church but they in turn attract other people who are open to change.[95] The new church will take on the characteristics of the present generation. It may itself become obsolete after many years, but it will be reaching the now generation.[96]

Strategic intent

The vision given for having the intentional church as a diverse church, a small to medium church, and a church that focuses its mission in expanding and penetrating for reaching secular people through further church planting carries with it strategic intent. Gary Hamel and C. K. Prahalad state that the dream that energizes a company is often something more sophisticated, and more positive, than a simple war cry. Strategic intent is an animating dream, providing the emotional and intellectual energy for the journey.[97] It implies significant stretch for the organization. Looking at the three areas I have outlined for the intentional church goes beyond mere human capability. It creates a tremendous challenge for the leader and members of the team. Nevertheless, as is the nature of strategic intent, it has a sense of direction, a sense of discovery, and a sense of destiny.[98]

The sense of direction will be more than just planting and growing a church, but planting and growing an intentional church that must in turn fulfill the gospel commission by continual penetration through further church planting. It presents a sense of discovery in that it emphasizes a diverse-heterogenous church as opposed to a typical homogeneous congregation. Hamel and Prahalad say that we are all seduced, to one degree or another, by the opportunity to explore the unfamiliar. Thus, it is not surprising that when a company's mission is largely undifferentiated from that of its competitors, employees may be less than inspired.[99]

What gives the differentiation is the idea of planting a church that should be heterogeneous. It has a mission that goes with the perspective that we should be an alternative community that offers the world the exciting reality of a living Christ and His power to change human lives. When the church can truly display unity in diversity in a fragmented and broken world, it is a differentiation. This anticipated and realized differentiation should fill the members with enthusiasm and emotional energy, giving them a cause to live and witness, for it also provides a sense of destiny. That destiny is to continue to fulfill the great commission of our Lord until He comes. Continue planting and reaching—focus beyond your own border. No greater ambitious and emotionally compelling strategic intent was ever articulated than Christ's command to His tiny impoverished band of followers to "go into all the world and preach the gospel" (Mark 16:15). It is full of pathos and passion; it imparts a sense of mission.[100]

Once you have a vision of what the church should be and what its ministry should be, then define the vision and communicate the vision to your team members. By definition a vision is "a clear challenging picture of the future of your ministry as it can and must be."[101]

Develop Core Strategy

Now that we have taken prior steps in our strategic planning process, it is time to develop the core strategy that answers the question, "how are we going to reach secular un-reached people for Christ?"

The prior steps in the strategic thinking and acting process will have a significant impact on the core strategy.

Your ministry analysis in terms of the giftedness and abilities of the various team members will serve to inform how and where members will serve. The demographic and psychographic study will help in profiling the targeted audience. Your core values will dictate what does and does not go into the strategy. The mission directs the strategy—it is what the strategy seeks to accomplish—and the vision provides a fresh picture of what that will look like. Also the vision will energize the strategy. And finally, the environmental scan helps in two ways:

1. It helps to keep you informed on what is taking place in and around your church and targeted community. Whether good or bad, it helps you to determine the current trends and events that affect the lives of the targeted population you are trying to reach.

2. It keeps you informed on what the other churches are doing in reaching secular people, and how what they are doing might be included in or influence your church's strategy.

Begin with Mission

In the intentional church that is to be planted, the question should be asked and answered, what is our mission? The answer to that question should provide a strong sense of direction. The mission is somewhat predetermined in that it is rooted in the Savior's Great Commission found in Matt 28:19-29; Mark 16:15; Luke 24:45-49, and Acts 1:8. This will keep the church focused on what Christ has called the church to do—make disciples. In this case, we are reaching secular—unchurched people for Christ and turning them into fully devoted followers or disciples. In order to achieve this the church's strategy must be reflective of a holistic evangelism. Avoid being a "niche church."[102] A niche church is said to be one that specializes in some aspect of the great commission (good Bible teaching or good counseling or great fellowship), at the expense of the great commission as a whole.[103]

Now that the mission is in focus and we understand what the mission is and who we are trying to reach, the next step is to define the target audience.

Focus on Target Audience

The group we are considering here is secular-unreached people. The pastor or leader and team members need to know as much as possible about the target group. Two things are helpful here:

1. The demographic/psychographic study of the community provides information in helping to more intentionally define or profile the targeted people, and as a result helps in determining how best to reach these people.

2. The previous training of team members on secularism with an intention of gaining a better understanding of secular people

will help them here in the profiling. As you profile your targeted audience, it is helpful to depict the audience in terms of a mystical figure. This could be typical of the secular-unchurched people you are trying to reach. This helps the team to know whom they have targeted. The profile should include such things as age, race, sex, income, level of education, preferred entertainment, music tastes, and financial status, to name some of the areas. The profile should also reflect attitudes, wants, needs, and values. This is just an idea of what will be in the profile. The demographic and psychographic study will give the basic information needed to develop a specific profile of the target community.[104]

Consider the Process

Once you have profiled your community and know who you are targeting, the next step is to consider the process. This concerns both the nature of evangelism and the nature of our contemporary society. Remember that people in the twenty-first century are not as pre-evangelized as they were in the early twentieth century. Most will take longer to think through the gospel and its implications and accept Christ (six to twelve months).[105]

The other aspect is to understand evangelism as process in a holistic way. Leading people to repentance in accepting Christ, and developing them into fully devoted followers (disciples), means a holistic approach to evangelism. Too often we limit our evangelism to getting people baptized: accept Christ, the twenty-seven fundamentals, get baptized, and join the church. This comes largely through proclamation of personal salvation, and a call to personal discipleship in which select sins are denounced. The wider social dimensions of the gospel are not considered in depth.[106] This understanding of evangelism as holistic is important for two reasons:

1. We have the greatest avenue to hearts of people through their felt needs. Secular people have needs that can be addressed when the social and physical aspects come into play. Pedrito U. Maynard-Reid states that this approach to evangelism will address such

205

areas as healing for daily problems; caring for personal, mental, and physical ills; and involvement with the intimate experiences of friends and neighbors and other real-life challenges in the community in which evangelistic endeavor is going forward.[107]

As we endeavor to minister to and reach secular people, matters such as personal finances, marriage and family, sex, academics, physical fitness, employment, addictions, and human rights may be addressed in the evangelistic enterprise.[108]

Maynard-Reid concludes that

> "the holistic and prophetic evangelistic task as exemplified in the ministry, life, and teaching of Jesus, John the Baptist, and the apostolic church - this is what the twenty-first century church needs. As the Holy Spirit rested upon Jesus (Luke 4:18) and the disciples (Acts 2) and anointed them to proclaim and practice the whole gospel (see Luke 4:18, 19 and Acts 2:41-47), so today we must appropriate the Holy Spirit's anointing so that when we engage in evangelism we do not do so in the narrow sense of exclusively proclaiming propositional truth. Our evangelism must meet the everyday needs of our communities in a way that will indeed make the "good news" even better."[109]

Paulien addresses this need to be more holistic in dealing with secular people. He states that the answer to the challenge of secularization is a return to the spirit of the early church as it appears in Acts 2 to 4. Paulien states that small groups, Bible seminars, and personal help for people who are struggling (physically or spiritually) are all part of the package.[110] He also says we need to address such needs as those found in Abraham Maslow's "hierarchy of needs."[111] Other needs include (a) the need to make a commitment to someone greater than oneself; (b) the need to find release from one's own failure to live up to self-imposed standards, and (c) the need for social and cosmic interconnectedness, providing relationships which are truly meaningful.[112]

Another set of basic needs involves (a) community, (b) structure, and (c) meaning. Paulien points out that the relevance of Christianity to the first and third of these needs is obvious. As regards the second, we are dealing with an area that will require seminars in time management and money management, and marriage, family, and career counseling. Secular people also need to know how to love and be loved, how to justify their existence, how to raise their self esteem, and how to relate constructively to such conditions as unemployment and social inequality.[113]

2. The second reason why evangelism should be approached holistically is that it will help us to avoid the "niche church" approach. Evangelism is to be seen as multifaceted. In reaching secular people you will want to consider various avenues and ministries that can be used to reach them where they are. As we seek to bring them to faith in Christ and develop them into full-orbed disciples, we would need to reach them physically, spiritually, and mentally. This ministry to secular people will approximate the Acts 2-4 early church model. It will reflect the way Christ and the apostles ministered holistically. Ellen White said that Christ mingled with people as one who desired their good. He met their needs, sympathized with them, won their confidence, then bade them, "Come and follow me."[114]

In considering the process of bringing a person to Christ and into maturing in Christ, think of it in three levels.

1. You are teaching a person who is at level 1 - no knowledge about Christ - unconverted person

2. Level 2 is where the person comes to faith in Christ (converted person).

3. Level 3 is where the person is committed to Christ.

The idea is to bring a person who is unconverted to conversion in Christ—they know Christ as a personal Savior. Then we want to bring them to commitment to Christ (they are committed to grow in Christ) and they are developed to make a contribution to Christ (they serve the body, share their finances, make use of their gifts in saving the lost).

In considering the various ways we are going to reach the people and bring them to full discipleship, consider the specific working strategies in three ways:

1. The church - its services, programs, facilities, etc.

2. The various outreach programs that are designed to meet needs and impact the community.

3. Training programs for equipping for service.

Develop Specific Working Strategy

The Church Services

What kind of church service shall we have? This question is asked in terms of the need to be culturally relevant in reaching the unchurched. Design the worship service. When designing the worship service two important things should be borne in mind:

1. The worship should be designed with the unchurched person in mind. You are trying to reach them where they are. Remember that the secular-unchurched person views as unintelligible the traditions, language, and worship styles so highly valued by those of us committed to the church.[115]

It means that the services should be designed with a great deal of sensitivity that takes into account where they are. Many of these people are often referred to as "strangers to the gospel," "outsiders," "the marginalized," and "the overlooked." These seekers neither understand nor appreciate liturgical or praise and worship services, which use predominantly traditional language and actions. The unchurched people want to worship anonymously and have the freedom not to participate.[116]

2. The next important thing to remember is that the worship service should be an inspiring experience for those in attendance. Schwartz has found in his study that when worship is inspiring it draws people to the service "all by itself." He has found it to be a universal church-growth principle.[117] Schwartz gives clarification to the word "inspiring" by suggesting that it be understood in the literal sense of "inspiratio," meaning "an inspiredness which comes from the Spirit of God. Whenever the Holy Spirit is truly at work (and His presence is not merely presumed), He will have a greater effect upon the way our worship service is conducted including the entire atmosphere of a gathering."[118] Therefore whether the service is traditional, praise worship, or seeker sensitive, it should be of such an inspiring nature that people will want to return.

Design two services: (1) a seeker service[119] and (2) and an inspirational service. A very important point to remember is that contemporary, culturally appropriate worship does not by itself evangelize, or necessarily attract many visitors. People are our best agencies for evangelism. Therefore the offering of two indigenous celebrative worship formats is: (1) to provide a celebration to which pre-Christians can relate and find meaning, and (2) to remove "the cringe factor" by providing a service our people would love to invite their friends to, rather than a service they would rather not bring their friends to.[120]

Sunday Morning Service. I am suggesting for purposes of strategy that the seeker service be held on Sunday. I am suggesting this for two reasons:

1. The reason for the seeker service being on Sunday is this is when the unchurched seeker is more likely to come.[121]

2. The other reason is that we have been counseled by Ellen White that "whenever possible, let religious services be held on Sunday.

Make the meetings intensely interesting. Sing genuine revival hymns, and speak with power and assurance of the Savior's love. Speak on temperance and on the religious experience."[122]

Ellen White's counsels within the context of her day that Sunday would be a good time for religious services was by all standards culturally relevant for her time. She admonished preaching on temperance issues that were current needs of the day. Why not have a seeker service in our day, on a Sunday, that is culturally relevant and have messages that are speaking to the issues of the secular minds of today? This in principle is following the advice and counsel of Ellen G. White.

Sabbath Service - An Inspirational Believers' Service.

The reason for Sabbath services is that some people will be more attracted to this kind of service— particularly the older generation. Gen-Xers and Busters and even Baby Boomers are more likely to attend the seeker services. However, some of these same ones may also attend the Sabbath service. Burrill has rightly observed that

> "While it may be true in a general sense that younger people prefer the more contemporary approach to worship, it would be a mistake to assume that all young people prefer the more contemporary style. Many of them actually prefer the traditional, and many older folk prefer the contemporary. In planning various kinds of services, realize that each service will be attended by a mix of ages but will also attract a specific generation in greater concentration."[123]

The Sabbath service while having elements of a seeker service in it will at the same time be more appropriate to the believers' walk with God. It is true that seekers and members can often have some of the same needs and issues going on in their lives. Therefore both of these groups can benefit from either service. However, the Sabbath service feeds the church on a growing level. While the service should be actually relevant and at the same time faithful to the level of consistent

Christian growth, the biblical message, the teaching, and nature of this service should be one that progresses beyond the seeker stage to maturity in grace.[124] "We cannot tolerate a church that fails to bring its members to maturity."[125]

Develop a Bible Class

Develop a beginners' Bible class. The main purpose of this Bible class is to develop in the secular-unchurched person an appreciation of and understanding of the Bible as God's inspired word. It is to bring them to an understanding that God has revealed Himself in human history to men and women, and that such revelation has been written by godly men over the centuries. It is to help them understand that the Bible testifies of Jesus Christ who came into this world and gave His life for our salvation. Therefore, a tactful clear presentation of how to accept Christ as one's personal Savior should be a part of this class, preferably just before the end of the lesson series.

Such a class is strategic and intentional for two reasons:

1. Secular-unchurched people by and large do not know the Bible very well if at all; they are basically Bible illiterate.

2. Such a Bible class, because of its content and subjects, should lead to a basic knowledge of how to accept Christ as one's personal Savior.

Similar types of classes are used by churches that are endeavoring to reach secular people. Such churches as Willow Creek Community Church and Oasis Christian Center have these beginner classes. They are called Christianity 101. I think this is a marvelous idea, but you can name your class whatever you want to—be creative and be imaginative. Make sure, however, that this idea comes across that such a class is for beginners.

The following are some suggestions for what could make up the teaching subjects:

1. Understanding the Bible - history of its development

211

2. The uniqueness of the Bible - God inspired and written by man

3. The unity of Scripture - though written by men over long periods of time it still is in agreement

4. Christ the center of Scripture

5. The plan of salvation in Scripture - the fall and God's plan to save man

6. How to be saved - simple steps, along with examples

7. How to know/love God

8. How to make the Bible relevant to daily living.

Develop Small Groups

Small groups should be developed for reaching others. These small groups should be open - anyone should be able to join. Not only should they be open, but as the groups get larger, other small groups should be formed. It has been ascertained that a church grows as the number of face-to-face groups increases and multiplies.[126] The "meta-church" and cell-based church models maintain that all small groups should be open, because these groups intentionally try to reach new members. Open groups such as those modeled by the huge churches in Korea, Singapore, and South Africa provide possibilities for growth.[127]

Notice what Ellen White says about the necessity of small groups for reaching souls. "The formation of small companies as a basis for Christian effort has been presented to me by One who cannot err."[128] Schwartz's research in growing and declining churches all over the world has shown that continuous multiplication of small groups is a universal church-growth principle. These groups should be "holistic." Holistic small groups are said to go beyond just discussing Bible passages to applying its message to daily life. In these groups members are able to bring those issues and questions that are immediate personal concerns.[129]

These small groups led by those who are pre-trained and capable, can be forums that encourage openness, caring, and belonging. In an atmosphere that is non-threatening, material sharing and addressing of needs in sensitive ways can create bonds of friendship and confidence. Through a tactful witness and modeling of one's own faithful walk with God, others in the small group can be led to accept Christ as their Savior.

Felt needs.

A number of felt needs may be addressed through small-group ministry. Such felt needs as loneliness, addictions, depression, discouragement, financial problems, anxiety, illness, family problems, and others can be ministered to. The small groups can be contexts where positive suggestions and support are given.

Listening.

These small groups are places where listening is very important. It helps to build a loving and healing atmosphere. John W. Fowler offers some suggestions on how to build a loving healing community:

1. Equip a team and draw on members' gifts. Pastors alone are not able to meet all the needs.

2. Build a solid base of trained lay listeners. They can provide pastoral care and make referrals for professional help if the situation warrants it.[130]

3. Educate members in daily living. Conduct classes in communication, time management, and emotions in the family.

4. Offer support groups and small-group Bible studies led by lay people. Hurting people need support systems and friends.

5. Be prepared for problems to surface. Once people have a warm, positive open atmosphere where it is safe, they will begin to share their pain and sorrows and express some of their needs.

6. Have a referral system for cases that may require the professional touch.

7. Be patient. It takes time to develop a social base of empathetic lay ministers. But it will be worth the effort when secular people can find hope and healing.[131]

As the open small groups expand in numbers, more and more needs and problems will need addressing. It will be good to categorize these needs in basically four areas: (1) physical needs; (2) emotional needs; (3) spiritual needs, and (4) social needs. Out of these categories, you can begin to label or name specific small groups that are designed for the various needs. For example, in the emotional needs area you may have a small group dealing with grief recovery. This can be done for all four areas.

Through the small groups we are attempting to do two things:

1. Not only are we bringing the people hope and courage, but we are helping them to cope with discouragement and doubt, fear and anxiety, anger and hatred, depression and hopelessness. Also people need help dealing with the power of temptation and addiction to habits that destroy their physical and spiritual well-being.

2. These small groups whose ministry is holistic will not stop at ministering to the felt needs, but realizing that the causes of most problems experienced by individuals are of a spiritual nature, will find and seek ways and be open to opportunities for the ministry of the Word. The teaching and application of the principles of the Word of God are the best remedy. This goes along with the findings of Schwartz, who says that the quality and numerical growth in the life of the church can be affected if small groups go beyond discussing Bible passages and apply them to daily life.[132] Bringing secular-unchurched people into a relationship with Jesus Christ and other people is our goal. We work to help people claim Christ's victory, wisdom, peace, and joy as their own.

Develop Other Programs

Seminars.

Special seminars should also be developed as a way of meeting and addressing needs. Such seminars as grief recovery seminars, stress seminars, marriage encounter and family seminars, seminars on finance and money management may all be set in motion as a way to touch and help change lives. As the needs become apparent, appropriate ways of addressing these needs should be incorporated.

Social events.

Examples of social events could be music concerts of a Christian contemporary variety. Remember we are trying to reach secular people, therefore a culturally relevant style of music should be used. Avoid triteness and extremism, but strive for relevance and depth at the same time. This will call for a strong music ministry team that knows how to put together this kind of concert.

Another social event could be a fellowship dinner or banquet. This allows for more informal association with the secular community. These are a few ideas that can be useful. As you get to know your community other social events can be selected that would meet some need for fellowship.

Other areas that may be explored are youth activities, parenting, community groups, sporting events, and special celebrations. All of these avenues should be explored and planned for as we associate and mingle with unchurched people in our target community.

Have Social and Community Outreach

This is the kind of ministry to secular people that meets them outside a congregation or church activity setting. It is meeting people with compassion, with caring, by doing something to help meet their needs. Jesus was moved many times with compassion as He ministered to human need. The Gospels introduce a word that is used only to describe the compassion of Jesus. It is the noun splagcma, from which splanchnizomai (show compassion) is translated. It literally means the heart, lungs, liver, kidney - the inward parts or "bowels" as expressed in the King James Version of the Bible. Nees states that "the word is intended to convey an identification with suffering that is so real that it produces physical effects. It is more than an intellectual understanding of sympathy. In contemporary expression one might say that compassion is to feel another's pain so deeply it produces a 'gut reaction.'"[133]

Beyond this intense feeling for the less fortunate and the weak, compassion as it is used to describe the ministry of Jesus always leads to action. It is more than empathy. It is a strong feeling and identification that produces a response to human need.[134] Ellen White stated that Christ sympathized with human beings and met their needs. Thus we have the parable of the father extending compassion to a wayward son, the Good Samaritan moved with compassion to care for a stranger robbed and beaten and left alone for dead, and Jesus Himself being stirred with compassion, fed the hungry multitude. Crowds were more than unnamed faces to Jesus. Compassion drew Him into the crowds of "harassed and helpless" people, touching and helping them one at a time (Matt 9:35-38).[135] Ellen White states that Christ went through whole villages doing nothing but healing the diseases of the people, so much so that there were no signs of sickness left after Jesus ministered in these villages.[136] He met human need. Thus in Luke 4, Jesus' commencement of His mission meant that the spreading of the good news would include healing, feeding, teaching, and forgiving. The gospel was proclaimed in deed as well as in word.[137]

When we minister in outreach ministries that meet felt needs, it is a point of contact that opens up avenues to the soul. This is important in ministering to secular people. By meeting them at their point of need and in the spirit of Jesus, we are opening up pathways by which we can say, "Come, follow me."

Getting Started

One of the ways to get started is to assess the needs of the community. Through the demographic study you would have gotten some information. You can also get it from published material, and you can talk with experts in your area, such as community development staff and city planners. Other people could be teachers and school staff, social agency workers, and community leaders. Ask which needs they think are the most serious. Include the members in your efforts. You can have an all-are-welcome outreach retreat with a good facilitator. Another way is to have a series of meetings to discuss the ideas for the outreach program.[138] Out of these meetings, key people, ideas, and various talents can emerge that would help in carrying out the outreach.

Be sure to talk to, and get feedback from, the people you might be serving. Get their understanding and perspective. Seek to know their priorities and aspirations to see how best to work together as partners to bring about results that truly meet their needs. Find out what is happening or already going on to meet these needs you are targeting. By finding out what these are, you can avoid duplicating efforts. Find out your church's skills and interests. Your members are your most important resource. These members may have skills, interests, and connections that can make outreach a reality. Choose the needs or areas of need that you would like to meet. In doing so, consider your resources. Look at your own facilities, the resources of your members,[139] and get help from sister churches and the denomination. All of these steps should be taken before formulating your approach. After you have identified the need, resources, and personnel, then begin training. After you have trained and prepared your members, then set your date and get started. With the varied gifts and talents and with the power and presence of Jesus Christ, you can successfully touch the lives in your community through meeting their needs.

Teach Relational Evangelism

The greatest resource for reaching others is people themselves. Therefore it is advantageous to develop a ministry where the very ones who are coming into the faith from a secular background are used to influence their friends and family for Jesus.

Most long-standing Christians do not have much contact with secular people. Most Christians do not have many secular friends. Hunter suggests that we need to maintain our friendships with non-Christians. Secular people can be reached better by credible Christians due to their kinship and friendship networks between believers and non-Christians, especially between new believers and non-Christians.[140]

The church should coach new believers who still have friends and relatives in the secular community on how to witness to them. These new members can maintain loving relationships with their friends and families, and influence them for Christ. People respond best to the gospel when it is presented within the context of loving relationships. There are several examples in the Bible. Andrew introduced his brother Peter to Jesus (John 1:40-42); Philip invited his friend Nathaniel to "come and see" Jesus (John 1:43-51); the Samaritan woman shared with her neighbors the new life she experienced in Jesus (John 4); the Philippian jailer told his conversion and his family joined him in the waters of baptism (Acts 16:16-34). While the message is of vital importance, it is most effectively received in the context of trusting relationships.[141]

Secular people who have become new Christians are a great evangelistic tool. They have meaningful relationships with others which mean they have frequent, caring contact with them. They have meals together, spend leisure time together, and support each other in the crises of life. They risk sharing their deepest beliefs about God, life, and spiritual reality. Jesus shared His life with the twelve disciples. He had a very meaningful relationship with them while here on earth. Therefore, we can follow His example and start with people we know and care about.[142]

There are two styles of witnessing that can be taught to new converts for the purpose of reaching their family and friends.

1. Relational or "friendship" evangelism: By being a friend and helping to meet a friend's needs, you can point that friend to God.

2. Testimonial approach: "Once I was lost, but now I'm found." The emphasis is on the contrast between the before-Christ life, and the radical transformation Christ has brought about. This testimonial approach will be very effective with friends and relatives, as they not only hear about changes Christ has made, but also see them lived out.[143] Therefore use your new believers in a strategic way to reach their secular friends and neighbors.

The above strategies that are suggested and discussed are some initial ways the intentional church can go about making contact with secular-unchurched people. The church is being intentional in bringing these people from an area in their experience where they have very little knowledge of Christ to where they have some knowledge of Him and accept Him as their Savior from sin.

As we consider moving people from where they are spiritually to where they ought to be, we need to avoid two mistakes.

The first is the sense that we must twist a decision for Christ out of everyone we have an opportunity to speak with. In this particular instance, if we extend an invitation to someone to accept Christ, and they say yes right then and there, we succeed. If the person says no we fail. There might be some "Saul to Paul" experiences, but they are the exception, especially in the secular community. Remember that people can be on the low end of the scale from 1 to 10. Still there are others whom the Holy Spirit has moved to the point of openness, people such as Cornelius and the Ethiopian eunuch, who were waiting for someone to meet their spiritual longing. Therefore, direct invitations to a Bible study group or a Bible seminar are a link to that person accepting Christ. This is why it is important to have a variety of outreach activities which meet the majority of people where they are.[144]

The second mistake we need to avoid making is the assumption that people must always progress along the spiritual interest line by numbers, the assumption that they can only be moved to the next part. Just as we can become too pushy in our outreach, we can also be overcautious. We need to realize that the Holy Spirit can move a person from a 2 or 3 on the scale to a 7 or 8 overnight. The Holy Spirit can propel people quite a long way in a short period of time. A sudden crisis or unexpected event can upset the scales of complacency and insulation and leave people open to God's intervention in their lives. We need to be ready for those moments of illumination, those times of interest and openness, when a person who has hardly given God a thought until today suddenly feels compelled to find Him. We need to move with the Holy Spirit's movements in a person's life. If they are slow and regular, then we accompany that progression patiently. If they are sudden and intense, we reinforce that movement of illumination and show how it can become a serious commitment to Christ.[145]

The church as a whole is best equipped to do this. By having various ways of ministering to people at their needs level, we are able to touch their lives and move them closer to Christ, through the various activities such as the seeker service, the various small groups, seminars, social events, and community outreach and involvement, through which we come in contact with various people. Members of the church with various gifts and talents can be used by God to minister to secular-unchurched people.

Commitment to Grow in Christ

This second level of the strategy is focused on growing, nurturing, and motivating those new believers who have come to faith in Christ, and have been baptized. This goes along with the great commission to make disciples. First, we are to baptize them, then we are to teach them whatsoever Christ has commanded (Matt 28:19, 20). Burrill points out that the understanding of the word "disciple," as used in the New Testament times, means primarily commitment to a person and living in submission to his authority in order to be taught.[146] When a person comes to faith in Christ in the initial stages, and goes on to baptism and is taught further the teachings of Christ, he or she can now grow in grace, in maturity of faith, and in obedience to God's word.

What areas of ministry and programming can be developed for discipling the new believers? Develop closed groups.[147] The small group, says Hull, is the best forum for creating community; it is also the optimum environment for making disciples.[148] In this case the small group should be closed. Previously I suggested that the small groups should be open. These are small groups that are targeting new people for the purpose of introducing them ultimately to Christ. These open groups should continue as a means of evangelizing new people. When people come to faith in Christ and have been baptized, they are now ready for further teaching and nurturing. It will also call for support and love, which a small group can provide. In order for this to happen, the small group should be a closed one.[149] The closed group is essential for this aspect of discipling for the following reasons:

1. An open group cannot provide the necessary structure and accountability. It will lead to large numbers of untrained and undisciplined people. In a closed group the members commit to such specifics as time frame, skill development, and outreach. Everyone shares the learning experience at the same time and at the same level.

2. Another reason for the closed group structure is to provide an atmosphere for mastering and living the spiritual disciplines.[150]

3. You can use those who graduate from the discipling process of the closed group to head up or lead open groups. Open groups populated by new people at different levels of their spiritual journey need a highly skilled leader to monitor and lead them.[151] The following suggestions for closed small groups are provided:

   a. Each of these small groups should encourage and support the spiritual discipline of a personal devotional life. This should include a daily systematic study of the Bible and other helpful devotional material and personal time in prayer. The group leader could give guidelines and suggestions on helpful ways to study the Bible devotionally and encourage the members to pray. Secular people who have newly come to faith need this kind of structure in order to grow spiritually. Members of the group can also share devotional experiences and hold each other accountable. The leader should also share his or her experience as an example and encouragement.

b. Each group should provide training and support for relational witnessing. These newly baptized people become the best avenues for reaching other secular people in their social networks. Two reasons are given why this is so: (a) most people who join the church (60 to 90 percent) do so as a result of the influence of neighbors, friends, and relatives;[152] and (b) the closer the relationship between a member and a nonbeliever, the less costly it is to bring that person to the church.[153]

Also, because of the friendship and close relationship of these new converts it is natural for the new believers to attend the same church. It can serve as the first step of the new believer's assimilation into the church.[154]

c. Each small group should focus on developing understanding and acceptance along cultural, racial, and ethnic lines. This model of the intentional church as racially and culturally diverse becomes in itself a witness to the world of the transforming love of Christ. Therefore the small group can become a place—a microcosm where the unity and love among members of various ethnic groups reflect the macrocosm of the larger body. The group leader should lead the group in a Bible-based study of the unity and love God wants to see in His church. Through this kind of small-group interaction, myths and stereotypes and other world views can be challenged and overcome, bringing lasting unity and healing among racial and cultural lines. Members of the group and the church should grow into understanding that God wants His church to be a public display of what His grace and love can do. Such a display becomes a powerful means of impacting the secular world. Delbert Baker has made the observation that this kind of healing and oneness is what the church needs in order to witness to the world.[155]

These small groups, meeting two or three times a month as fully functioning communities, will provide for shepherding, studying the

Bible, exercising spiritual gifts, biblical community, accountability, prayer, and evangelism.

Intermediate Bible Class

This class provides a more in-depth study of the Bible that will meet important spiritual growth needs in the new members. Many secular people have the need for a cosmic philosophy or for social and cosmic interconnectedness—knowing how everything fits together. Thus this Bible class can be a means of helping these new growing believers come to grips with a biblical world view of the order of things. The following themes from the Great Controversy Meta-Narratives should be covered.

1. The creation

2. Lucifer's rebellion

3. Humanity's fall

4. The promise of the Seed

5. The covenant promises to Noah, Abraham, Isaac, and Jacob

6. Jesus becomes a human being - the God-man - and fulfills the covenant promise to bring eternal life through His death, burial, and resurrection

7. The promise of the second coming

8. The restoration of a new heaven and a new earth.

Neither science nor technology, despite their extraordinary achievements, offers a transcendent narrative that can provide a basis for permanent values and meaning to human life. They are both morally indifferent gods, unable to provide the answers to the deeper question of life.[156] The Bible does, however, present an overarching theme of the great conflict between Christ and Satan, and their followers.[157] At stake in this great controversy are the accusations of Satan against God and His government. Satan depicts God as unjust, arbitrary, and unfair. On the other hand God has shown that He (God) is just, reasonable, and merciful. He is fair in all things.

This great conflict is played out in our world—the battle ground. The Seventh-day Adventist Church has a strong contribution to make in this area. Our teaching of the great themes in the Great Controversy metanarratives helps to bring an understanding to the cosmic order of things. This teaching when understood and accepted will help to meet that need in the lives of secular people. This class could also cover other important topics dealing with a brief history of the Christian church and the rise of the Advent movement, why there are so many denominations, basic Bible teachings on Christian lifestyle, stewardship, the gift of prophecy, God's plan for your life, and other Bible teachings that help on daily living.

Sabbath Service and Special Classes

The seeker service designed to attract and win the secular-unchurched to Christ is different from the Sabbath service. The Sabbath service is designed for those who have already made a commitment to and have joined the church. The seeker service on the other hand is intentionally designed to be an evangelistic tool for reaching the unreached. It may be held at any other time than the regular worship hour on Sabbath.

Since those who have been baptized will of necessity also be Sabbath keepers, it is necessary at this stage of the discipling process to use the Sabbath services as a means of discipling. Also special classes can be utilized as small groups for two things: 1) To provide classes that will cover more in depth than the sermon or groups, topics that are vital to commitment and spiritual growth; and 2) To provide classes that would teach principles of stewardship involving responsible use of financial resources and time. Other classes should be functioning such as youth and children's classes.

Commitment to Service

The commitment to service is the third and final phase of the discipling process. This is where members are exposed to and commit to the mission, core values, strategy, and methodology of the intentional church. To accomplish this, a special class should be organized to explore and teach in detail the various aspects of what is entailed in the entire philosophy of ministry. Since the mission is to reach secular-unchurched people for Christ, members should come away fully committed to reaching others. They should have a clear understanding of the strategy and commit to supporting it.

Spiritual Gifts Seminar

A spiritual gifts seminar should be held for the purpose of helping members find their special gift or their unique calling for service. The seminar should cover the following:

1. Discovering your spiritual gifts

2. Finding and serving in your ministry niche

3. How to give a gospel presentation

4. How to share your faith and build friendships.

The importance of this seminar is the gifts discovery and ministry placement. Very important to this process is the placement of persons in various ministries in harmony with their gifts. These seminars should be followed up by individual interviews.[158] When the church can help each of these members identify his or her spiritual gifts, the church will have successfully fulfilled a very important part of the great commission. While every member may not have the specific gift of evangelism, they will have some spiritual gifts that can be used in the endeavor to reach and disciple secular-unchurched people.[159]

Develop a support team

This support team should be made up of members of the church who are actively involved in the efforts of reaching the unchurched. This group should meet together to share experiences, ideas, encouragement, and lessons on how to communicate God's love more effectively to those they are trying to reach.

Continue to communicate

The mission and core values and the strategy should be articulated and communicated to the church through sermons, special classes, bulletins, and one on one. Let the intentional witness of the church be communicated. Also the intent of the mission is to keep on growing and reproducing by planting other churches. Keep this vision before the people and identify those who show a burden or sense a call to future church planting.

Implementation and reassessment

The planned strategy for reaching secular-unchurched people should be put into action in the targeted area, and its outcome should be assessed carefully to see if the set mission, objectives, and goals were met effectively. If these were not achieved, then there may be need for adjustment in the core strategy or tactical details or even both.

Summary

The challenge of reaching secular-unchurched people today calls for new and untried methods. This planting of the intentional church is one suggested strategy. Pastors and leaders who wish to adopt this method will find the strategic planning method helpful. As they apply these principles for reaching secular-unchurched people, they will adapt them to their own unique context.

Chapter 6 Notes

1.   White, *Acts of the Apostles*, 17, 18.

2.   Alvin Reid, *Introduction to Evangelism* (Nashville, TN: Broadman and Holman Publishers,1998) 94.

3.   Robert E. Logan, *Beyond Church Growth: Action Plans for Developing a Dynamic Church* (Grand Rapids, MI: Fleming H. Revell, 1998), 193.

4.   Hunter, 44. For an understanding of the life and mind of the secular, unchurched, see chapter 2 of this present study. For wider insight, see George Barna, *Virtual America: The Barna Report, 1994-1995* (Ventura, CA: Regal, 1994); Phillip L. Berman, *The Search for Meaning: Americans Talk About What They Believe and Why* (New York: Ballentine, 1990); William D. Hendricks, *Exit Interviews: Revealing Stories of Why People Are Leaving the Church* (Chicago: Moody, 1993); James Patterson and Peter Kim, *The Day America Told the Truth*; Wade Clark Roof, *Spiritual Market Place: Baby Boomers and the Remaking of American Religion* (Princeton, NJ: Princeton University Press, 1999); Lee Strobel, *Inside the Mind of Unchurched Harry: Why People Steer Clear of God and the Church and How You Can Respond*; Andres Tapia, "Reaching the First Post-Christian Generation," in *Christianity Today*, September 12, 1994, 18; Richard N. Ostling, "America's Ever- Changing Religious Landscape: Where We've Come From and Where We're Going," *Brookings Review* (Spring 1999): 13.

5.   Hunter, 107.

6.   Alfred McClure, "Planting and Harvesting," *Review and Herald*, December 5, 1996, 17-18.

7.   Logan, 24.

8.   White, *Ministry of Healing*, 22-24.

9. Bruce Larson and Ralph Osborne, *The Emerging Church* (Waco, TX: Word Books, 1970), 11.

10. Burrill, 23.

11. Hozell C. Francis, *Church Planting in the African American Context* (Grand Rapids, MI: Zondervan, 1999), 26.

12. Ibid., 25.

13. Logan, 26.

14. Ibid., 34.

15. Malphurs, 50.

16. Ibid., 51, 52.

17. Ibid., 52.

18. Samaan, 17.

19. Elmer Towns, C. Peter Wagner, and Thom S. Rainer, *The Every Church Guide to Growth: How Any Plateaued Church Can Grow* (Nashville, TN: Broadman and Holmes, 1998), 5, 6.

20. Ibid., 6.

21. White, *Gospel Workers*, 105.

22. Paulien, 90.

23. White, *Christ's Object Lessons*, 52.

24. Ellen G. White, *Counsels on Sabbath School Work* (Washington, DC: Review and Herald, 1966), 100.

25. Jon Paulien, "The Gospel in a Secular World," in *Meeting the Secular Mind: Some Adventist Perspectives* (Berrien Springs, MI Andrews University Press, 1985), 26. See also, Humberto M. Rasi, "The Challenge of Secularism," in *Adventist Mission in the*

21ˢᵗ Century (Hagerstown, MD: Review and Herald Pub. Assn., 1999), 69.

26. Rasi, "The Challenge of Secularism," 69.

27. Paulien, *Present Truth in the Real World*, 89.

28. Hunter, *Church for the Unchurched*, 24, 25. See also James Emery White, *Rethinking the Church*, 14-21; Rasi, "The Challenge of Secularism," 62-70.

29. Craig Van Gelder, "Reading Postmodern Culture Through the Medium of Movies," in *Confident Witness--Changing World*, 62. Also the postmodern condition is said to include such dimensions as: urbanized life with its complex patterns of social relationships, multiple tasks and responsibilities that fragment time and space, an economy shaped and driven by technology and its advances, job, career, and identity defined by professionalized roles and skills, submerged racial and ethnic identities in a stew-pot society, the pervasive influence of change and rapid obsolescence, bureaucratic organizations run by rules and policies, individualized moral values concerning such matters as divorce and sexuality, radical forms of individuality producing isolation and aloneness, and hunger for overarching story to give meaning and structure to life. *Missional Church: A Vision for the Sending of the Church in North America*, ed. Darill L. Guder (Grand Rapids, MI: Wm. B. Eerdmans, 1998), 20. Denzin has also referred to the postmodern condition in similar terms as: a nostalgia, conservative longing for the past, coupled with an erasure of the boundaries between past and the present, a pornography of the visual, the commodification of sexuality and desire, a consumer culture which objectifies a set of masculine cultural ideals, resentment and a detachment from others. See Norman K. Denzin, *Images of Postmodern Society: Social Theory and Contemporary Cinema* (Newbury Park, CA: Sage Publications, 1991), viii.

30. See Aubrey Malphurs, *Advance Strategic Planning: A New Model for Church and Ministry Leaders* (Grand Rapids, MI: Baker Books, 1999).

31. Hunter, *Church for the Unchurched*, 24.

32. Ruthven Joseph Roy, "Marketing and Mission: Applying Marketing Principles to Seventh-day Adventist Mission in the Virgin Islands" D.Min. dissertation, Andrews SDA Theological Seminary, 1999, 125, 126.

33. Ibid.

34. Francis, 25.

35. Ron Gladden, "Evangelism and Church Planting," *Ministry*, October 1999, 9.

36. Ibid.

37. Christian A. Schwartz, *National Church Development: A Guide to Eight Essential Qualities of Healthy Churches* (Carol Stream, IL: Church Smart Resources, 1996), 22.

38. Ibid.

39. Ibid.

40. Logan, 54.

41. J. Robert Clinton, *The Making of a Leader* (Colorado Springs, CO: NavPress, 1988), 46.

42. Schwartz, 24.

43. Malphurs, *Strategic Planning*, 64.

44. C. Peter Wagner, *Church Planting for a Greater Harvest* (Ventura, CA: Regal Books, 1990), 81.

45. Warren, *The Purpose Driven Church*, 165.

46. Wagner, 81, 82.

47. Ken Blanchard and Michael O'Connor, *Managing by Values* (San Francisco: Berrett-Koehler Publishers, 1996), 3.

48. Lyle E. Schaller, *Getting Things Done* (Nashville: Abingdon Press, 1986), 152.

49. Malphurs, *Strategic Planning*, 83.

50. Malphurs, *Vision for Ministry*, 74.

51. Malphurs, *Strategic Planning*, 83; see also Merton P. Strommen, *The Innovative Church* (Minneapolis: Augsburg, 1997), 99.

52. James M. Kouzes and Barry Z. Posner, *The Leadership Challenge* (San Francisco: Jossey-Bass, 1991), 190-201.

53. Peter M. Senge, *The Fifth Discipline* (New York: Doubleday, 1990), 175.

54. Malphurs, *Strategic Planning*, 96.

55. You can find a step-by-step process of how to develop a good values statement or credo in Aubrey Malphurs's *Advance Strategic Planning*, 93-97.

56. Malphurs, *Strategic Planning*, 105-107.

57. Philip Kotler and Alan R. Andreasen, *Strategic Marketing for Nonprofit Organizations* (Englewood Cliffs, NJ: Prentice Hall, 1991), 72.

58. Malphurs, *Strategic Planning*, 117-123. Belasco and Stayer suggest a system called scan, clip, and review, one that they borrowed from the CIA, that will help in the environmental scan. It is also known as content analysis. Using this system, members and leaders who agree to be scanners or watchers of the culture, scan newspapers, a certain number of periodicals and books consistently every month. Each clips articles that he or she considers important to what is taking place now and what could

be a future trend or a shaping event. These are collected in files and folders. Some culture watchers could read trendy authors such as John Naisbitt, Faith Popcorn, Alvin Toffler, and others. They are looking for information that could affect the church now or in the future, no matter how remote it may seem. Periodic meetings should be held to review materials for recurring trends in areas like secularizationing, unchurched people, technology, mission paradigms, etc. After eliminating the non-essential material, the rest should be brought to the leadership and questions should be asked such as, What are the one, two, or three future events that will have the most effect on our church or ministry? What will happen when these events occur? What can we do now in preparation for them? James A. Belasco and Ralph C. Stayer, *Flight of the Buffalo* (New York: Warner, 1993), 129.

59. Malphurs, *Strategic Planning*, 117.

60. Warren Bennis, *On Becoming a Leader* (New York: Addison Wesley, 1989), 2.

61. Malphurs, *Strategic Planning*, 117.

62. Ibid.

63. Arn, *The Pastor's Manual for Effective Ministry*, 41.

64. Ibid., 43.

65. Burrill, *Rekindling a Lost Passion*, 103.

66. This came from statistics compiled by Les Parrot III and Robin D. Perrin, "The New Denominations," *Christianity Today*, 11 March 1991, 20. Also a 1994 report shows that few of the ten largest U.S. denominations reported increases in membership or drops of more than 1 percent. On this, see *The Yearbook of American and Canadian Churches 1994*, as reported in *National and International Religion Report* 8 (4 April 1994): 3.

67. Ken Garfield, "Some Churches Losing Members," *The Charlotte Observer*, 30 March 1996, 2G.

68. As noted in the *SBC Handbook* (Nashville: Convention Press, 1991), produced by the Church Administration Department of the Sunday School Board of the Southern Baptist Convention).

69. George Barna, *Virtual America: The Barna Report 1994-1995* (Ventura, CA: Regal, 1994), 46-53.

70. Towns, Wagner, and Rainer, 2-5.

71. Burrill, *Rekindling a Lost Passion*, 93.

72. Burrill, *Rekindling the Passion*, 24; Baumgartner, "Megachurches," 158.

73. Schwartz, 46. For an explanation of Schwartz's findings, see 46-48.

74. Ibid., 48.

75. Burrill, 68.

76. Gregg Garrison, "Church Attendance Reported at Lowest Level in Two Decades," *Presbyterian Outlook*, available from www.personalpastor.org/ppo3020.htm, accessed 13 April 2000; Internet.

77. "May We Be One," *Seventh-day Adventist Bible Commentary*, ed. Francis D. Nichol (Washington, DC: Review & Herald, 1980), 5:1053.

78. See J. H. Bernard, *A Critical and Exegetical Commentary on the Gospel According to St. John* (Edinburgh: T & T Clark, 1972), 576, 577; Joseph H. Mayfield, "The Gospel According to John," *Beacon Bible Commentary* (Kansas City, MO: Beacon Hill Press, 1965), 7:195.

79. "May We Be One," *SDABC*, 5:1148.

80. Russell C. Burrill, *Recovering an Adventist Approach to the Life and Mission of the Local Church* (Fallbrook, CA: Hart Research Center, 1998), 129.

81. Ibid.

82. Walter Douglas, "Multicultural Ministry: Challenges and Blessings," *Ministry*, July 1999, 8.

83. Ibid.

84. Ibid., 9.

85. Ibid.

86. Charles Scriven, *The Transformation of Culture* (Scottdale, PA: Herald Press, 1988), 136.

87. *Missional Church*, 73.

88. Smith, "Homogeneity and American Church Growth," 49.

89. Francis, 100.

90. Ibid., 102.

91. *Missional Church*, 117.

92. Malphurs, *Planting Growing Churches*, 45; Burrill, *Rekindling a Lost Passion*, 101.

93. "Churches Die with Dignity," *Christianity Today*, June 14, 1991, 68-70.

94. Burrill, *Rekindling a Lost Passion*, 101.

95. Malphurs, *Planting Growing Churches*, 46.

96. Burrill, *Rekindling a Lost Passion*, 95.

97. Gary Hamel and C. K. Prahalad, *Competing for the Future* (Boston: Harvard Business School Press, 1996), 141.

98. Ibid., 142.

99. Ibid., 145.

100. Ibid., 146.

101. Malphurs, *Advanced Strategic Planning*, 140. A vision statement can take several forms. I have included in the appendix a few samples of vision statements.

102. Malphurs, *Advanced Strategic Planning*, 156, 157.

103. Ibid., 157.

104. Ibid., 160, 161. See also *Planting Growing Churches*, 271-274.

105. *Planting Growing Churches*, 276.

106. Pedrito U. Maynard-Reid, "Holistic Evangelism," *Ministry*, May, 2000, 22.

107. Ibid.

108. Ibid.

109. Ibid.

110. Paulien, *The Gospel in a Secular World*, 34.

111. Ibid., 37.

112. Ibid.

113. Ibid., 38.

114. White, *Ministry of Healing*, 143.

115. Wright, 47.

116. Andy Langford, *Transitions in Worship: Moving from Tradition to Contemporary* (Nashville, TN: Abingdon Press, 1999), 32, 33.

117. Schwartz, 30, 31.

118. Ibid., 31.

119. For an example of a seeker service please see Appendix C.

120. Hunter, *Church for the Unchurched*, 77.

121. Ibid., 74.

122. Ellen G. White, *Christian Service* (Takoma Park, Washington, DC: General Conference of Seventh-day Adventists, 1947), 164. Burrill points out that "holding a service on Sunday morning does not deny Sabbath- keeping unless one is neglecting Sabbath worship. Conducting a Sunday service to attract visitors is no different from holding an service on Sunday night, as done by Adventists in times past. The only difference is that the service is in the morning instead of in the evening. Since Sunday evening is no longer a major church night, Saturday night or Sunday morning can work well for this seeker service." Burrill, *Rekindling a Lost Passion*, 145.

123. Burrill, *Rekindling a Lost Passion*, 131.

124. Ibid., 145

125. Ibid.

126. Bob Gillian, *Infrastructure Lecture Notes*, The Vision 2000 Training Network, Evangelical Free Churches of America, 1-3.

127. Bill Hull, *Seven Steps to Transform Your Church* (Grand Rapids, MI: Fleming H. Revell, 1993), 142.

128. Ellen G. White, *Testimonies to the Church* (Mountain View, CA: Pacific Press Publishing Association, 1948), 7:21, 22.

129. Schwartz, 32.

130. I am suggesting that the purpose for small groups is to provide fellowship, encouragement, and support along with meeting spiritual needs, not in-depth counseling or therapy.

131. John W. Fowler, *Evangelism Two Thousand: Proclaiming Christ in the 21ˢᵗ Century* (Boise, ID: Pacific Press Publishing Association, 1994), 64, 65.

132. Fowler, 68. See also Schwartz, 32.

133. Nees, 20.

134. Ibid.

135. Ibid., 20, 21.

136. Ellen White, *Steps to Christ* (Washington, DC: Review and Herald Publishing Association, 1981), 12.

137. Nees, 21.

138. Victor N. Coleman, David E. Butler, and Jessica A. Boyatt, *Acting out Your Faith: Congregations Making a Difference* (Boston: Insights, 1994), 136.

139. Ibid., 136-139.

140. Hunter, *How to Reach Secular People*, 65.

141. Wright, 29.

142. Randy Beaton, *Everyday Evangelism: Making a Difference for Christ Where You Live* (Grand Rapids, MI: Baker Books, 1997), 52.

143. Ibid., 57.

144. Mark A. Finley, *Fulfilling the Gospel Commission* (Fallbrook, CA: Hart Research Center, 1989), 44, 46.

145. Ibid., 45-47.

146. Russell Burrill, *Radical Disciples for Revolutionary Churches* (Fallbrook, CA: Hart Research Center, 1996), 29, 30.

147. Hull, *Seven Steps to Transform Your Church*, 136.

148. Ibid.

149. Once a small group has set its goal and reached the desired number, it is closed to further membership. If someone or more

than one leaves the group, it can open up again to others until the number is reached.

150. Hull, 143.

151. Ibid.

152. Donald G. McGavran, *Understanding Church Growth* (Grand Rapids, MI: Eerdmans, 1990), 225.

153. Win Arn and Charles Arn, *The Masterplan for Making Disciples*, 165.

154. Win Arn, *The Church Growth Ration Book* (Pasadena, CA: Church Growth, 1987), 23.

155. Delbert W. Baker, *Make Us One: Celebrating Spiritual Unity in the Midst of Cultural Diversity* (Boise, ID: Pacific Press Publishing Asociation, 1995), 162.

156. Rasi, *The Challenge of Secularism*, 68.

157. Ellen G. White, articulated this theme in her five- volume *Conflict of the Ages* series, published by the Pacific Press Publishing Association.

158. Burrill, *Rekindling a Lost Passion*, 204, 205.

159. Arn and Arn, *The Master's Plan for Making Disciples*, 124.

CHAPTER 7

REFLECTIONS

The massive impact of secularization has effectively undercut the role of religion as a definitive authority in the postmodern world view. The West (and that, of course, would include America) has become vastly secularized. Evidence of this is seen in the increasing difficulties of evangelizing the unchurched population. While the tried and true traditional methods of the past have been successful, and while they may still have success in reaching certain populations,[1] the challenge of reaching a growing secular-unchurched community will demand untried and innovative strategies. This would mean becoming culturally relevant, while at the same time preserving uncompromisingly the integrity of the gospel.

If churches are to be effective in reaching secular unchurched people, they will have to minister in a relevant fashion by addressing the needs and issues facing post-modern men and women. While theologically the presentation of the gospel is to be uncompromisingly biblical, it is at the same time to be culturally relevant. The gospel is unchanging by nature. The great inspired truths of God's word are non-negotiable. However, the way we present these truths, can be out of sync with an increasingly secular world. Times have changed.

The present context (21st-century post-modern society) would suggest that old wineskins should be replaced by new ones. One must keep in mind that forms and structures which serve as vehicles in carrying out the mission are not sacred in and of themselves. They are subject to and must be altered when the situation or circumstances demand it. On the other hand, when forms and structures are treated as sacrosanct, they remain constant in a mercurial context. They become stale, stiff, and inflexible. The end result is irrelevance.

To be relevant in this generation is to follow Paul's principle. Paul, for the sake of the gospel, became "all things to all men" in order to save some. It is to be imitators of God, who adjusted the content of dreams for the purpose of reaching two different individuals with the same message (Dan 2 and 7). It is to follow Christ's example, whose ministry necessitated putting new wine into new wineskins. It is also to emulate John (evangelist and revelator) and the rest of the apostles who wrote the New Testament in the *Koine* Greek. They addressed their audiences in language they could understand and appreciate. They used key phrases and familiar expressions that were relevant to the context and people of the time.

To be relevant will also necessitate moving beyond the cherished forms and traditions of the past. Our evangelistic successes of yesteryear are to be applauded. There are, however, new challenges in an increasingly secular society. The old swords of yesteryear have become rusty and worn. The strategies to be employed now must not be limited to traditional forms. Now is the time to seek out and study new and untried ways of reaching a vast mission field in our post-modern West. Under the guidance of the Holy Spirit, new ways may be devised for reaching secular men and women for Christ.

In this suggested strategy, I have proposed that the intentional church be a different kind of church in the sense that it puts aside its own cultural and individual preferences in order to reach secular people. I have suggested that the intentional church be a diverse (heterogeneous) worshiping community. It is the kind of church that challenges the values of the dominant culture—a culture especially characterized by race distinction, caste, and lines of division. Into this fragmented and broken world, the church unfurls the unifying banner of Prince Immanuel. Under this banner the poor and the rich sit together, the Black and White embrace each other, and the least has a place at the head of the table. This kind of witness transcends homogeneous units and socially selective groups.

When secular men and women, who themselves experience the divisive forces of society as out of control, witness a redeemed and transformed humanity, that loves and cares for each other, they encounter the reality of the living Christ and are convinced. The greatest witness the church can give in favor of the gospel is to be a loving and united community. Jesus said, "by this shall all men know that you are my disciples if you have love one for another" (John 13:35).

It is my contention that the church can bear a potent testimony to a secular world by being spiritually and ethnically united. Such a harmonious community is evidence that transformation has taken place, not by a sociological or an anthropological or theological principle, but by the power of the living Redeemer. This ontological display of oneness in the midst of a fragmented and racially divided world becomes the incontrovertible argument and an undisputable witness for Christ (John 13:35).

The intentional church will therefore be strategic in its worship and ministry. Through meeting the felt needs of its targeted community, and through culturally relevant worship, witness, and service, the church is to reach secular men and women for Christ.

This study, with its suggested strategy, is presented with the hope that it will be a help and a source of encouragement to those desirous of reaching secular people. It is not presented or intended to be taken as the definitive answer or as a panacea for all the challenges in reaching secular people. It is an attempt to help find the answers. The study itself is subject to the changing times and should not be treated as the ultimate solution to the secular challenge facing Christianity. There will be and must be various methods and strategies for reaching secular people. It is my hope that this project will serve to stimulate further investigation and study.

So where do we go from here?—

The biblical narrative that comes to mind is that of Moses and the children of Israel caught between a rock and a hard place at the

Red Sea. They could not advance due to the Red Sea directly in their pathway. They could not go back because Pharaoh and the armies of Egypt were at their backs. They could not turn to the left because there was no outlet at the rock, and they could not turn to the right because there was no way around the mountain. What should they do? Where do they go from here? The command was to stand still and witness the salvation of the Lord (Exodus 14: 13-14). All Moses had to do was to stretch out his rod. What's that in your hand Moses? Make use of it! Stretch it out! Now stand still and see the power of Omnipotence at work. The first thing God did was to interpose between the armies of Egypt and the children of Israel (Exodus 14: 19-20). The pillar of fire (a bright cloud) and the pillar of darkness (a dark cloud) stood back to back between Pharaoh and Moses. The Pillar of fire gave light and protection to God's people while the pillar of darkness prevented the advance of the Egyptian armies. Meanwhile, Moses made use of what was in his hands and God did the rest (Verses 20-22).

What's that in your hand, O Church of God? Use it! Stretch it out! The God who was with Moses is the same God who is with us. He is the same who said, "As I was with Moses, so I will be with you; I will never leave you nor forsake you." (Joshua 1: 4). He is the same that said, "And surely I am with you always, to the very end of the age." (Matthew 28: 20). In the mighty providence of God we have been lead to the red sea of our mission endeavors. The task before us is formidable and we are at a standstill. We are at a lost for a solution as to how to advance successfully in a secular post-modern age. We cannot go back because the past has been swallowed up in the present mega-shifts of a secular age. The wolves of an ever changing world are at our backs. We cannot turn to the left because there is no outlet in traditions of yesteryear. We cannot turn to the right because the liberal philosophies of this age are incompatible with the cause of Christ. So where do we go from here? Look up! Listen for the clear council and direction of God. This is God's mission, the *Missio Dei*. His question to us is "what's that in your hands?" why don't you use it, stretch it out, and stand still and witness the mighty acts of God in this secular post-modern age? It is my humble opinion that God has placed in the hands of His Church all that is needed to accomplish the task and finish the work in this final hour of Earth's history.

It is for this reason that I have emphasized the "Intentional Church" as a working strategy for reaching secular people. We do not need to reinvent the Church. The Church is the Church precisely because Christ has called us out of the world unto Himself by means of His redemptive act that established the New Covenant between Himself and His people. The Church is not man's creation but God's. The Church, of which Christ is the Head, is a communal society that has been transformed and not conformed to the idolatrous powers of this age. The church therefore is not subject to man's manipulations nor is it's identity derived from institutional and beaurocratic structures. The Church finds its identity in its relationship with Christ. This important truth must not be lost to the consciousness of those practitioners in the church growth movement, who spare no pains in their attempts to reinvent the church in order to establish relevance in a secular age. Some misguided attempts at establishing relevance have often resulted in a syncretism that makes the message of the gospel indistinguishable from the voice of the dominant culture. This kind of "syncretism develops because the Christian community attempts to make its message and life attractive, alluring, and appealing to those outside the fellowship. Overtime the accommodations become routinized, integrated into the narrative story of the Christian community, and inseparable from its life. When major worldview changes occur within the dominant culture, the church has difficulty separating the eternals from the temporals. When it is swept along with the ebb and flow of cultural currents, the church looses its moorings."[2]

As a Seventh-day Adventist biblical community we are not immune to the subtle forms of syncretism that we have witnessed among some of our Christian friends—particularly when we engage in an uncritical acceptance of those forms and modalities that lends to said syncretism. This is not to suggest that we are better or smarter than others, or that there are no church growth practices that are unworthy of our emulation and adaptation. There is much that we can learn from others who have been successful in their attempts in reaching secular people— there is much that we can learn from our Christian friends.

We must also admit that we share much in common with traditional evangelical beliefs. We hold for example, to the all sufficiency of scripture as God's inspired Word, normative for all Christians, and the test of all religious experience and doctrine. We also hold to the biblical narrative of the Fall in Eden, and the resulting sinful nature of man that is in rebellion against God and His holy law. We believe unequivocally in the necessity of man's need of a Savior, that Savior being the Lord Jesus Christ, the one unique and only Son of God who is also Son of Man— fully God and fully man. We believe that salvation is by faith alone in the atoning sacrifice of Christ on the cross, and that this good news of a crucified and risen Christ must be preached among all nations, inviting men and women everywhere to repent and confess their sins to God whose law they have broken, and exercise the free gift of faith in Christ, their sin pardoning Redeemer. All this and more we share in common with other fellow churches, particularly those of the evangelical persuasion.

The key of narrative—

It is to be noted however, that God has given to us as a Seventh-day Adventist Church a very important key to reaching this post-modern secular culture with the gospel. So what do we have in our hands? "The key," says Martin Webber "is *narrative.* 'Tell me your story' is a favorite conversation starter for postmodernists. They care more about human experience more than impersonal propositional truth."[3] In the modern world, says Sweet, abstract principles were privileged over "stories." The intellectual was simply the nonvisual person.[4] Sweet suggest that "storytelling" is "the third upgraded avenue of ministry…. the narrative quality of experience is a deeply religious issue. We inhabit a storied reality. Human cognition is based on storytelling…. stories are 'the fundamental instrument of thought'….the language of scripture is story. You can tell stories and never use words….the stories of the Gospels are told most effectively with bread and wine—images and elements of the earth, images and elements you can taste, touch, see, smell, and hear. Postmoderns need to be able to taste, touch, hear, smell, and see this story of Jesus."[5]

At first glance this seems like bad news for us Seventh-day Adventists, who have been generally propositional in our presentation of the gospel, and very cerebral in our evangelistic preaching, whether in more traditional or contemporary satellite Net series. We do hold however, a very important key in our hands—*the key of the great controversy narrative.* Like no other, we Seventh-day Adventists have in our hands a unique God-given biblical narrative that, if properly presented, unlocks the secret to reaching a secular-postmodern generation effectively and convincingly. This overarching story of Eden lost to Eden restored in the earth made new, synchronizes well every Adventist belief, characterizing the Great Controversy narrative as uniquely Adventist in both content and scope.[6]

While this is noteworthy of itself, there is an element that has to be rediscovered and applied if we are to be effective communicators of this grand gospel narrative in a postmodern culture. That element to which I refer is *story telling.* The gospel must be storied. The great controversy narrative, as understood within the parameters of the "Third Angels Message," must be storied. Every facet of Adventist teaching that holds within itself the answer to many of the questions of the postmodern mind (Christ and His High Priestly Ministry, Heaven and the Future—The Earth Made New, the Sabbath, the Nature of Humans and the State of the Dead, the Punishment of the Wicked and the Eternal reward and Home of the Righteous, the story of our Health Message, etc.) must be storied. "Everything Adventists believe can be framed in the context of story," says Weber, "Everything! Even prophecy is narrative in advance, a spotlight into future events from a loving God who guides the universe."[7]

While we can truly say that "no other church can offer what Adventists have for the postmodern world," our test will be our ability "to shift emphasis away from presenting doctrine as a series of propositions, which appeal only to modernists," to the task of evangelizing a postmodern world by presenting "our fundamental beliefs in the context of our unique Great Controversy narrative."[8]

Part of that challenge, as noted by Reinder Bruinsma, is the need for us as Adventists to present "the 'grand story'" not as facts of Adventist history and doctrine, but as the meta-narrative of Jesus Christ.[9] This approach will resonate well with the post-modernists, primarily with the Gen-Xers (born 1965 to 1983) and with Millenials (born 1984 to today), whose orientation to learning and to the discovery of truth is of an experiential and preferential nature. These post-modernists will be effectively influenced by the storied gospel, if it is presented in an experiential, dynamic, interactive, relational, and engaging way. As Jimmy Long has rightly observed:

> "The key question for X'ers today is: 'Is it real?' not 'Is it true?' Their lives are more likely to be changed through the heart than through the mind. They need to see the incarnation of the gospel in people's lives more than to hear the proclamation of the gospel through our words. Do we have places where seekers can see the gospel in action? Do we invite them into our community? They need to experience the love of Jesus more than they need to be informed that Jesus is love."[10]

Up-close and relational—

This brings us to another critical element in engaging the secular-postmodern mind. That element is the operative word "*relational.*" The gospel, by its very nature, is relational—it is not merely propositional. To our great discredit we have been lacking (especially as concerns non-members, non-Christians, non-Adventists) in meaningful sustained contact through friendships or community involvement with those we are unsuccessfully trying to reach with "our story." Yes, we have much to offer this generation, and much that if rightly presented will meet felt needs, and provide definite answers to the longings of many a man or woman in our postmodern culture. Take for example "our story" that not only surrounds the history and origin of our health message, but that is made evident in the experiences and lives of hundreds of Seventh-day Adventist Christians—the evidence of a healthy lifestyle that has been documented in *National Geographic Magazine* as "the prescribed lifestyle" providing "a testimony perhaps, to the power of mixing health and religion."[11]

This story that is ongoing amongst Adventists has been highlighted as a healthy lifestyle that has raised the level of Adventists' life expectancy, while lowering their risks of such diseases as heart attacks, obesity, and cancer. In the end the average Adventist lives four to ten years longer than the average person in their community. "That," according to *National Geographic*, "makes the Adventists one of the nation's most convincing cultures of longevity."[12] Does such an observation by a world renowned, culturally-based magazine tickle your sense of pride at being an Adventist? It should. What tempers such pride, however, is our failure to be a relational biblical community, a resident model of community engagement in the everyday life and experience of everyday people—the people who need to know and understand what *National Geographic* underscores as one of "the secrets of living longer"— not to mention a happier and more fulfilled life. Ask yourself, "Do we have something unique as a Christian community to offer a postmodern-secular world that is seeking a more fulfilling, healthier and longer life?" For an answer to that question you need only to read the article entitled, "Adventists," in the November, 2005 special issue of *National Geographic* titled, "The Secrets of Living Longer." In this article *National Geographic* States that:

> "The Adventist Church…has always preached and practiced a message of health. It expressly forbids smoking, alcohol consumption, and eating biblically unclean foods, such as pork. It also discourages the consumption of other meat, rich foods, caffeinated drinks, and 'stimulating' condiments and spices. 'Grains, fruits, nuts, and vegetables constitute the diet chosen for us by our Creator,' wrote Ellen White, an early figure who helped shape the Adventist Church. Adventists also observe the Sabbath on Saturday, socializing with other church members and enjoying a sanctuary in time that helps relieve stress. Today most Adventists follow the prescribed lifestyle—a testimony, perhaps, to the power of mixing health and religion."[13]

Our problem is clearly not one of having what it takes to meet the felt needs of people in the world around us. No, ours is rather a need of a relational model in ministry, one that brings us up-close to people—so close that they are influenced from real life contact rather than from impersonal and secondhand approaches. What was it that made Christ successful with the people whose lives He touched and transformed for the better? It was His up-close and personal mingling with them. His familial contact with tax collectors and sinners drew criticism from the religious elite of His day. Jesus was careful to point out, however, that those that are sick are in need of the personal touch of the health practitioner. No isolationist methods would do. What was needed was the familiar touch of a friend—a friend who mingled with men as one who desired their good.

In the article under discussion, this is clearly the missing peace of the puzzle in the story of one Marge Jetton, the featured Adventist centenarian. Marge like so many of us Seventh-day Adventists "spends most of her time with other Adventists. 'It's difficult to have non-Adventist friends,' she says, 'where do you meet them? You don't do the same things. I don't go to movies or dances.' As a result, researchers say, Adventists increases their chances for long life by associating with people who reinforce their healthy behaviors."[14] This may be commendable as far as our lifestyle goes. What is less commendable, however, is our lack of friendships with non-Adventists. Researchers have shown that most Adventists have very few secular friends outside of their immediate circle of belonging. Our healthy life style is kept and practiced amongst ourselves, while a dying and perishing world is held at arms length because we are either afraid to mingle or simply unwilling to develop meaningful relationships with others beside our own kind. Whatever may be our reason(s) for isolating ourselves from the real world and the people around us, one thing is certain, the present posture will not get the job done in a secular-postmodern world. Without the same personal contact with people as exhibited by Jesus our example, we are bound to fail. Once again it bears repeating, "Christ's method alone will prove successful in reaching the people. *He mingled with men as one who desired their good....*"[15]

In a most recent issue of *Adventist World,* dated January 2007, a featured article titled, "Reaching the Secular Mind," by Sarah K. Asaftei, highlights the missing piece of the puzzle (up-close relationships, friendships, etc.) as clearly the key to reaching secular people across the Trans-European Division (TED). According to Sarah K. Asaftei, "LIFEdevelopment.info (LDi) is a fresh biblical concept that has proven successful…" in reaching postmoderns. This innovative approach to reaching postmoderns was developed by Miroslav Pujic (TED director of Ministry to postmoderns) and "equips lay members for engaging with their communities to share the story of Jesus (see Mark 5:19)."[16] This unique ministry concept teaches lay members how to develop close meaningful friendships with others, with the goal of gradually presenting important truths the way Jesus did—"within the context of trust and relationships."[17]

This fresh evangelistic approach focuses on the value of up-close relationships rather than public campaigns. It views evangelism as a process rather than an isolated event. LDi stresses the idea that witnessing is a narrative between two people who become friends and share experiences, leading to a connectedness that breathes common ground other than shared religion. Out of this relationship between friends opportunities arise to share religious beliefs and spiritual values that eventually lead to Bible studies—"forty Bible studies bring out every aspect of Seventh-day Adventist doctrine, using postmodern language and nonthreathening vocabulary. This stage brings the decision for baptism into the Seventh-day Adventist Church."[18]

According to Sarah Asaftei, "Stories and testimonies come pouring in from across the TED as LDi centers and LIFEdevelopment groups are gaining momentum." This "integrated approach to witnessing, is turning friends into believers." Interest in and other ministries of LDi are springing up in many countries in Europe and the Middle East. Interest in this new approach to reaching secular postmodern people has also been shown in "Australia, Japan, Korea, South America, Brazil, and the United States."[19] There seems to be a new awareness to the importance of carrying out the council so often sited in the statement by Ellen G. White that Christ method alone will give true success in reaching the people. This very important paradigm shift in reaching secular postmodern people is proving to be one of the secrets to our success as a Seventh-day Adventist Church. This need to be up-close and relational is also echoed in another statement by Ellen

White which says, "Your success will not depend so much upon your knowledge and accomplishments, as upon your ability to find your way to the heart. By being social and coming close to the people, you may turn the current of their thoughts more readily than by the most able discourse."[20]

For such a time as this—

Not only is there a need to be relational in a postmodern world, but how satisfying it is to be a part of an apocalyptic generation! This secular-postmodern world of ours is inescapably caught up in events of a nature that is altogether shocking, unimaginable, and terrifying. The high watershed has been the unforgettable horrors of 9-11, and the subsequent mystical forebodings that something big, something other-worldly, something cosmic is about to happen. Postmodern people are now asking a familiar question to the bearers of apocalyptic news—the prophetic spokespersons. That question had been asked of Jesus concerning future events. It is a question recorded in Matthew, the twenty fourth chapter: "Tell us," they said, "when will this happen, and what will be the sign of your coming and of the end of the age?" The minds of the disciples had been agitated by a previous statement of Jesus that was a prophetic forecast of the desolations and terrors that would befall the much revered temple. The Bible says, "Jesus left the temple and was walking away when his disciples came up to him to call his attention to its buildings. 'Do you see all these things?' he asked. 'I tell you the truth, not one stone here will be left on another, every one will be thrown down.'" Wow! Imagine that! Any allusions to the destruction of the Jewish temple (in the mind of a Jew) were synonymous to the end of the age, to the end of the world itself. This was clearly reflected in the question posed to Jesus. Postmodern people are asking a similar question, prompted by minds that have been agitated by recent terrifying events. The terrorist attacks on the twin towers of the world trade center in New York City, followed by the horrifying implosion of both towers, conjured up and continues to conjure up images of an apocalyptic nature, that seem to suggests a coming global crisis of apocalyptic proportions.

We noted earlier that this postmodern generation is a generation that is open to spirituality and religion. This postmodern search for the spiritual, this return to the supernatural, is tied to our present culture's preoccupation with the end of the world—with apocalypticism. The questions posed by postmodern people are not of the mundane intellectual variety. They are the questions that reveal a searching for answers to the terrifying events of our day. They are trying to make sense of the present madness. How popular are the predictions and the so-called prophecies of Nostradamus since 9-11? Buzz words such as Armageddon, Doomsday, and Apocalypse Now; fill the airwaves and the Hollywood movie theatres. What an opportunity to bear testimony to the great prophetic and apocalyptic books of Daniel and Revelation! Who better than Seventh-day Adventists to bear such a testimony? To paraphrase the heavenly messenger in the book of Daniel: There is none that holdeth with us in these things—not Hollywood, not Nostradamus, or any other. This postmodern time is our time. Any recorded failure to address the deep spiritual longings of a secular-postmodern generation will be due to our ineptitude. We are the people of prophecy. We are the bearers of the apocalyptic wine skins. The key—the great controversy narrative—is in our hands. The opportunity for using that key is knocking incessantly at our door. We have been called to the kingdom for such a time as this.

A call to prayer—

The words of Jesus in Matthew 9: 35-37 now become extremely relevant for our time: "Jesus went through all the towns and villages, preaching the good news of the kingdom and healing every disease and sickness. When He saw the crowds, he had compassion on them, because they were harassed and helpless, like sheep without a shepherd. Then he said to his disciples, 'The harvest is plentiful but the workers are few. Ask the Lord of the harvest, therefore, to send out workers into his harvest field.'" (NIV). This is a call to prayer, not only for workers, but for the harvest itself. Every great religious awakening, every major breakthrough in soul winning that has been recorded, has always been preceded and/or accompanied by earnest, persevering prayer to God by His people. Take for example, the day of Pentecost in Acts 2. The Bible says, "They were together in one place."(Verse1). This coming together of the early disciples was characterized by deep soul searching and earnest, incessant prayer to God. The resultant display of spiritual renewal accompanied by the infilling of the Holy Ghost that was experienced by the disciples is unparalleled thus far in the Church's history. Not only was there a manifestation of the outpouring of the Holy Spirit, but there was also the conviction, repentance, and baptism of about three thousand souls in one day, with others being added to their number daily. (See verses 41& 47). Amazing! Oh, for that flame of living fire in our postmodern age! In an age when we must admit that our Church growth, in terms of numbers added, is not only on plateau, but in decline. What happened in Acts 2 (early rain outpouring) is what it took then, and that (later rain outpouring) is what it will take now, in order to reach secular-postmodern men and women with the everlasting gospel.

The gathering of the harvest in our secular age is directly related to the call to prayer. There are two focal points to this prayer offensive: 1. the call to prayer for the needed laborers, and 2. the call to prayer for the harvest itself. One thing must be borne in mind— this call to prayer for laborers to enter the harvest field in our secular-postmodern time, is not the same as a personal ministries announcement for a general gathering of everyone on a Sabbath afternoon for the purpose of handing out tracks or "going out in the field." This is a call for intentional laborers, to engage in intentional ministry, by an intentional church, with an intentional mission strategy for reaching secular-postmodern people. Prayer in this instance is not an appendage to a long strategic list of how to's and what to's. This prayer offensive is foundational to the entire enterprise. Everything and every step must be bathed in prayer. In the first instance we are to pray for willing laborers to enter the ripened harvest field. Obviously, this is not to convince God of the need or to remind Him to supply the willing, but rather it is a call for us through much prayer to awaken to our own responsibility in working for the harvest, and thus to share with Christ the burden for reaching souls for the Kingdom of God. It is also for us, by our example and encouragement, to pray that others will open their hearts to that same call and that same burden for the lost. Laborers thus awakened through prayer will be attuned to the unique challenges for entering a postmodern-day harvest field. It is a unique call to a unique challenge. It is not just that laborers are needed, but also the kind of laborers or person(s) God can use for reaching a secular mindset. Ministry to secular people is not for everyone. Some of us will never be comfortable or be mentally or spiritually prepared to step outside our comfort zone. This is a call to work and think outside the box, and to exchange the inflexible wineskins of tradition for new wine skins. It takes a specially prepared kind of person who will make his or herself available to be used by the Lord of the harvest. This may or may not include you, dear reader. One thing is for certain, all that I have discussed or suggested in this book, concerning our need to reach secular people, cannot be accomplished without prayer or merely by status quo. The church must be deadly in earnest in prayer before the Lord of the harvest or the plans, the laborers, and the efforts put forth may bring more harm than good.

In the final instance we must pray for the harvest itself. In our day, in this context, the harvest is the secular-postmodern men and women who constitute a majority in our culture. Indeed, they are like sheep without a shepherd. Secular-postmodern men and women are tossed to and fro on a sea of relativism. Nothing holds a capital. Their minds are held captive to a philosophy that denies any absolutes; nothing is true in itself, and there is no central meaning and no certain outcomes. Despite their claims to spirituality and their return to a quest for the supernatural, secular-postmodern people are as confused as ever. Our prayers must be for a breakthrough that overrides the litany of voices—the plurality of suitors that confuse their thinking. The prayer offensive for the harvest is a battle against spiritual forces that hold men and women captive to the will of the prince of darkness. Our prayers, offered in faith, are spiritual weapons that attack strongholds. The apostle Paul states it this way: "For though we live in the world, we do not wage war as the world does. The weapons we fight with are not the weapons of the world. On the contrary, they have divine power to demolish strongholds. We demolish arguments and every pretension that sets itself up against the knowledge of God, and we take captive every thought to make it obedient to Christ." (2 Cor.10: 3-5).

There are certain realms where strategy in and of itself is impotent to effect change in people's hearts. There are chains that can only be broken by means of importunate prayer—prayer that moves the mighty arm of God. The harvest field, though ripe for the taking, is still populated with those people that need more than a common touch. Prayer brings them and us into the realm of the supernatural, where scales fall from blind eyes, where fetters are broken at the touch of Omnipotence, where spiritual darkness flees at the presence of the Light, and where the impossible becomes possible. This power from above, and from outside of man, operates in response to unceasing intercessory prayer. There must be a prayer offensive if the harvest is to be gathered in.

Prayer offensives were the order of the day in the early beginnings of the Gospel. Often when the believers prayed there were demonstrations of Divine power among them. It is stated for example that, "After they prayed, the place where they were meeting was shaken. And they were all filled with the Holy Spirit and spoke the word of God boldly." The record also states that they prayed for the miraculous to accompany their efforts as they preached the good news that Jesus was the Christ. Here is a sample from one such prayer in the book of Acts: "...enable your servants to speak your word with great boldness. Stretch forth your hand to heal and perform miraculous signs and wonders through the name of your holy servant Jesus" (Acts 4: 31, 29 & 30). Such a prayer releases the power of God against "the god of this age" who "has blinded the minds of unbelievers, so that they cannot see the light of the gospel of the glory of Christ, who is the image of God" (2 Cor. 4: 4). When God's power is released through mighty prevailing prayer for the harvest, God "open(s) their eyes and turns them from darkness to light, and from the power of Satan to God, so that they may receive forgiveness of sins and a place among those who are sanctified by faith in me" (Acts 26: 18).

This "everlasting gospel" which opens blinded eyes, and turns people from the bondage of Satan to the freedom and joy of new life in Christ Jesus, has been entrusted to us—the embattled missional Church of

God—in a secular-postmodern age. Success is sure to come; we will triumph! The carefully laid plans and strategies that find their echo in Christ, the greatest strategist of all, when united with Divine power, become an unstoppable force in advancing the Gospel. The greatest days are just ahead for God's faithful witnesses. My appeal in this book is for intentional ministry, carried forward by intentional people, through the support and auspices of an intentional church, bathed in incessant importunate prayer, and empowered by the promise of an Almighty God who says to us what He said to the first little band of disciples: "All authority in heaven and on earth has been given to me. Therefore go and make disciples of all nations, baptizing them in the name of the Father and of the Son and of the Holy Spirit, and teaching them to obey everything I have commanded you. And surely I am with you always, to the very end of the age" (Matt. 28: 18-20). Amen.

Chapter 7 Notes

1. Normally, the traditional approach to proclamation of the gospel reaches individuals who are already Christians and attending other churches or some close friends or family members who have orientations toward the church and Christianity. These populations typically accept further light on the Sabbath, health, state of the dead, mode of baptism, or some other doctrinal point. They can easily identify with the basic Christian beliefs of salvation by grace through faith, man's lost condition, the need for repentance, and other cardinal Christian teachings. The traditional approach, therefore, calls these ones to further repentance based on the "new light" they have heard, and the need to "come out of Babylon." This approach to evangelism will always have its place and will be effective for these kinds of populations. The unchurched population, however, will need to be approached differently. Nevertheless, the traditional approach still has its unique place in fulfilling the gospel commission.

2. Michael Pocock, Gailyn Van Rheenen, Douglas McConnell, *The Changing Face of World Missions: Engaging Contemporary Issues*

and Trends, (Grand Rapids, MI: Baker Academic, 2005) 102, 103.

3. Martin Weber, "Reaching Postmodern Society" in *Outlook, (September*, 2006) 7.

4. Leornard Sweet, *Postmodern Pilgrims: First Century Passion For The 21ˢᵗ Century World,* (Nashvillee, TN: Broarman & Holman Publishers, 2000) 123.

5. Ibid. 123, 124.

6. Weber, "Reaching Postmodern Society", 7.

7. Ibid. 9.

8. Ibid.

9. Riender Bruinsma, "The Quest for Integrity: Facing the Key Challenges of Postmodernism," in *The Journal of Adventist Education.* October/November 2006. p.21

10. Jimmy Long, *Generating Hope: A Strategy for Reaching the Postmodern Generation* (Downers Grove, Ill.: InterVarsity Press, 1997), p. 210.

11. Dan Buettner "Adventists" in *National Geographic,* November, 2005 pp. 22-25.

12. Ibid. 25.

13. Ibid. 22-25.

14. Ibid. 26.

15. White, *The Ministry of Healing,* 143.

16. Sarah K. Asaftei "Reaching the Secular Mind" in *Adventist World,* January, 2007 16.

17. Ibid. Ibid.

18. Ibid. 16,17.

19. Ibid. 18.

20. Ellen G. White, *Gospel Workers*, (Washington, D.C.: Review and Herald Publishing Association, 1948) 193.

APPENDIX A

SECULAR MIND GROUPING AND CHARACTERISTICS OF SECULAR PEOPLE

SECULAR MIND GROUPING AND CHARACTERISTICS OF SECULAR PEOPLE

Secular Mind Groupings

The suggested grouping of the secular mind that follows is based on Russell Hale's findings, resulting from interviews with unchurched people in the United States. There are ten groups of unchurched, seven of which are substantially secular. Added insights come from George Hunter and Mark Finley, each of whom has provided further knowledge of these groups.

1. The Anti-institutionalist: These are defectors from the church who see the church as primarily preoccupied with its own self-maintenance. Such persons do not accept formal organizational structures as germane to "true religion." They object to the church's emphasis on finances, buildings, and property. They decry the disunity of the churches, each claiming to have the keys to the kingdom. They fault the churches from their own Scriptures that say "that they all may be one." The competition they observe is manifested in what they call "knifing" and "knocking" one another. The churches, they feel, compete to build and protect their own empires. Anti-institutionalists are considered to be "solitary Christians or unaffiliated travelers" who avoid membership in the institutionalized church, thus escaping "contamination" to remain "purer."

2. The Boxed In are those who characterized their past experiences with churches as too confining. They resist being controlled by doctrines, ethics, people, and leaders. They want space for moving and breathing.

Halle recognizes three subtypes:

   a. The Constrained: Inside the church they felt smothered and cramped in boxes that were characterized by ethics and doctrines that were too narrow; but now outside the church they are free; fresh air, freedom, and the walls have crumbled.

b. <u>The Thwarted</u>: These felt stifled in their growth toward maturity. They resent being treated as children or adolescents. "They reject what they perceive as the church's excessive emphasis on passivity, quietism, and dependence."

c. <u>The Independent</u>: They are considered fierce individuals. The church is to them as a prison or strait-jacket. Their mental outlook is capsulated in such phraseology as "Don't fence me in" or "Unhand me" or "Let me go!" They want no external constraints. They will be captive to no one. They have taken charge of their own lives. They desire their freedom to move in and out of the boxes at will, in their own time and way. They move in to get what satisfies them at the moment and then leave at will. The independent view the church as a box that limits their freedom to "do my own thing" or to "do it my way."

3. <u>The Burned Out</u> are those who have spent their energies working in the church. Their fuel is gone. Two classes of the unchurched are noted here:

a. <u>The Used</u> have feelings of having been exploited or manipulated. They were once church leaders or had been extremely active participants in church programs and activities; they had no time to come aside and rest awhile. They accepted too much, and having been "worked out," they adopt a stance of "never again."

b. <u>The Light Travelers</u> have "an exaggerated consequence of having first felt used; although (and they do admit it) they brought that use on themselves." There was a time when church involvement was useful for them and their families; for "praying together" . . . which meant "staying together." They were setting a right example for their children, sharing in their values and beliefs. They do not regret the experience, but feel such baggage is optional or dispensable. "With fewer years remaining they want to travel more lightly. 'An overnight bag will do. You can't fit the church into that', they say."

4. <u>The Floaters</u>: These were never really committed to the church to begin with. They never really stayed and functioned in any church; they drifted and floated on the surface with their peripheral involvement.

Again there are two subtypes:

   a. <u>The Apathetic</u>: These floaters lack any deep feelings for or sensitivity toward what the church stands for or does. They have an attitude that says "I couldn't care less" or even "whatever." They have a take-it or leave-it posture, which is extremely superficial. No serious church involvement exists anywhere.

   b. <u>The Marginal</u> are those whose associations with churches have been so superficial that drifting from place to place without ever establishing any strong ties has become habitual. They never stay by to own up to responsibility for anything, whether to people or to what the church teaches. They move with ease from group to group and belief to belief, playing it "loose and thin." They are similar to the "box-ins" in that respect. With no commitments, involvements, or meaningful ties, they are essentially floaters.

5. <u>The Hedonists</u> are those who indulge and prize leisure pursuits. They find satisfaction and fulfillment in pleasure satisfying activities.

6. <u>The Locked Out</u> are those who feel locked out by the churches, and have no authorized way of entering in. They feel as though the churches have closed their doors against them, "via formal excommunication, slight, disregard, or discrimination, whether overt or covert."[1] They feel that the church does not want them

263

inside. Even though some might have locked themselves out, the effect is the same.

There are three subtypes:

a. The Rejected have deep hurt that their desire for communion or fellowship has been limited. This might have been due to some disobedience to or involvement in some disapproved behavior, such as divorce or certain birth-control practices. Some see themselves as "not good enough" as they measure their own behavior against expectations of holiness or perfection.

b. The Neglected: Many of these (the poor, the ethnic minorities, and the aging) feel that their needs are being ignored and overlooked. They feel forgotten and lost.

c. The Discriminated can often cite specific acts of prejudice against them. They are the most hostile of the locked out. They feel the churches do not care for or want their kind. They feel snubbed and openly excluded.

7. The Nomads change residence often and attend church wherever they live, but avoid deep involvement now to avoid grief later.

8. The Pilgrims view all knowledge as incomplete. They are on an ideological pilgrimage, seeking for satisfying meanings and values. Their central characteristic is tentativeness--a provisional stance toward final or ultimate truth.

9. The Publicans are the largest group of the unchurched. The churches are perceived as populated by Pharisees. They label those in the church as phonies, hypocrites, fakers, and persons living double lives. This dissonance, for them, becomes a scandal. Perceiving themselves as not being able to live up to the teachings of the church, they opt to remain on the outside.

10. The True Unbelievers are subdivided into other categories as: Atheists-Agnostics, Deists-Rationalists, and Humanists-Secularists. Except for the latter subclass, Halle found few

authentic unbelievers in his sample. He believes that this accords with polling data that show 95 percent of Americans saying that they believe in God, even though (as I have discussed in chapter 3) many have differing perspectives on the image of God and thus one cannot readily qualify what that belief entails or what, if any, effect it has on lives. There are relatively few who are considered true unbelievers.

The subcategories are:

a. <u>Agnostics-Atheists</u>: those who deny the existence of any ultimate reality (as God) or hold such reality as known or even knowable.

b. <u>Deists-Rationalists</u> comprise those whose theology, whether articulated or unarticulated, is based on human reason rather than revelation.

c. <u>Humanists-Secularists</u> are those who embrace worldliness in the sense that the dignity and worth of a human being lies in their own capacity for self-realization through reason, without benefit of any supernatural revelation, or clergy, or church.

These ten distinct types revealed by Halle are substantially secular and fit alongside other designations by George Hunter and Mark Finley. George Hunter sees three categories that represent a third each of the secular classes:

1. <u>Ignostics</u> have no Christian memory; they do not know what Christians are talking about.

2. <u>The Notional</u> are Christians who think of themselves as more or less Christian because they assume their culture is more or less Christian.

3. <u>The Nominal</u> are Christians who are somewhat active in churches, but their religion is civil religion, which they might mistake for Christianity, and most gospel washes past them. All three groups are considered secular since their lives are not substantially

impacted by the Christian faith. They have lifestyles that reflect assumptions, vocabularies, and decision making that lacks a Christian agenda. Many in the first two groups have not been "church broke"--that is to say, they do not know how to act in church--they would feel incompatible and alienated in a typical church service. The nominals, says Hunter, are church broke and pass themselves off as believers, but they are driven by doing their own thing and their culture's values.

Mark Finley also categorizes four types of secularists, with some general characteristics found in both Halle's and Hunter's groups:

1. The Secular Materialist is typified as the young business executive for whom the *summum bonum* of life is his job. His goals are a house in the suburbs, wall-to-wall carpeting, nice furniture, television, swimming pool, two or more late-model cars, and vacations in Bermuda and the Bahamas. Material values and possessions are his chief concern and his driving passion. He keeps an eye on the stock markets; his chief concern is economics, even though he may be concerned for his family.

2. The Religious Dropout no longer attends religious services. He or she is concerned with social issues and is turned off by organized religion. He has his own value system, being interested in social and philosophical issues. She is also attracted to the party life (smoking, drinking, etc.). He is reflective about life, but has no foundation, nothing to grasp.

3. The Secular Hard Hat is essentially the all-American person, working hard from dawn to dusk. He is happy with the sports page, television, and his attitude about religion is "don't bother me about that stuff." She reflects the "me" generation, where everyone thinks only of themselves.

4. The Secular Philosopher is introspective and thoughtful. He has rejected Christianity as a viable option. He has a naturalistic worldview. He or she believes in Darwin and Freud, believing that the world came into being through randomness, and that

human beings are largely the product of their own environment and heredity, over which they have no control.[2]

Characteristics of Secular People

1. Secular people are essentially ignorant of basic Christianity.

2. Secular people are seeking life before death.

3. Secular people are conscious of doubt more than guilt.

4. Secular people have a negative image of the church.

5. Secular people have multiple alienations.

6. Secular people are untrusting.

7. Secular people have low self-esteem.

8. Secular people experience forces in history as "out of control."

9. Secular people experience forces in personality as "out of control."

10. Secular people cannot find "the door."

11. Secular people, though increasingly ignorant of Christianity, are highly spiritual.

12. Secular people are hungry for intimacy.

13. Secular people lack life skills.

14. Secular people long for dignity.

15. Secular people are world-wise.

APPENDIX B

FORCES IN HISTORY AFFECT THE SECULARIZATION PROCESS

FORCES IN HISTORY AFFECT THE SECULARIZATION PROCESS

1. The European Renaissance (14th to 15th centuries). This marked a shift from theocentrism to anthropocentrism, placing new emphasis on human values, creativity, and achievements. It also brought philosophy out from under the tutelage of theology. Within the span of a generation the Renaissance had shown diversity of expressions and their unprecedented quality--such men as Leonardo da Vinci, Michelangelo, and Raphael produced their master works; Columbus discovered the New World; Luther rebelled against the Catholic Church and began the Reformation; and Copernicus hypothesized a heliocentric universe and commenced the scientific revolution. Polyphonic music, tragedy and comedy, poetry, painting, architecture, and sculpture all achieved new levels of complexity and beauty. Individual genius and independence were widely in evidence. No domain of knowledge, creativity, or exploration seemed beyond man's reach. From its beginning with Petrarch, Boccaccio, Bruni, and Alberti, through Erasmus, More, Machiavelli, and Montaigne, to its final expression in Shakespeare, Cervantes, Bacon, and Galileo, the Renaissance did not cease producing new paragons of human achievement. Such a prodigious development of human consciousness and culture had not been seen since the ancient Greek miracle at the very birth of Western civilization. Western man was indeed reborn.

   Some technical inventions were also pivoted in the making of the new era: a) The magnetic compass, which permitted the navigational feats that opened the globe to European exploration; b) Gunpowder, which contributed to the demise of the old feudal order and the ascent of nationalism; c) The mechanical clock, which brought about a decisive change in the human relationship to time, nature, and work, separating and freeing the structure of human activities from the dominance of nature's rhythms; d) The printing press, which produced a tremendous increase in learning made available both ancient classics and modern works to an

271

ever broadening public, and eroded the monopoly on learning long held by the clergy. All of these inventions were powerfully modernizing and ultimately secularizing in their effects.

2. The Reformation (16th century) emerged as a result of open criticism of the Christian Church's deviation from its original principles and condemnation of its blatant abuses. The Reformers emphasized a personal faith, individual study of the Bible, and direct access to God through prayer and meditation.

Armed with the thunderous moral power of an Old Testament prophet, Luther defiantly confronted the Roman Catholic papacy's patent neglect of the original Christian faith revealed in the Bible. Sparked by Luther's rebellion, an insuperable cultural reaction swept through the sixteenth century, decisively reasserting the Christian religion while simultaneously shattering the unity of Western Christendom.

Perhaps the most fundamental spirit in the genesis of the Reformation was the emerging spirit of rebellion, self-determining individualism, and particularly the growing impulse to intellectual and spiritual independence which had now developed to that crucial point where a patently critical stand could be sustained against the West's highest cultural authority, the Roman Catholic Church.

The Protestant spirit prevailed in half of Europe, and the old order was broken. Western Christianity was no longer exclusively Catholic, not monolithic, nor a source of cultural unity.

The Protestant Reformation was at once a conservative religious reaction and a radically libertarian revolution. Yet, for all the Reformation's conservative character, its rebellion against the church was an unprecedentedly revolutionary act in Western culture--not only as a successful social and political insurgency against the Roman papacy and ecclesiastical hierarchy, with the Reformation supported by the secular rulers of Germany and other northern countries, but first and foremost as an assertion of the individual conscience against the established church framework of belief, ritual, and organizational structure.

The Reformation was a new and decisive assertion of rebellious individualism--of personal conscience, of "Christian Liberty," of critical private judgment against the monolithic authority of the institutional church--and as such further propelled the Renaissance's movement out of the medieval church and medieval character. Although the conservative Judaic quality of the Reformation was a reaction against the Renaissance in the latter's Hellenic and pagan aspects. On another level, the Reformation's revolutionary declaration of personal autonomy served as a continuation of the Renaissance impulse--and was thus an intrinsic, if partially antithetical, element of the overall Renaissance phenomenon. There is that extraordinary paradox of the Reformation, for while its essential character was so intensely and unambiguously religious, its ultimate effects on Western culture were profoundly secularizing. By overthrowing the theological authority of the Catholic Church, the intentionally recognized supreme court of religious dogma, the Reformation opened the way in the West for religious pluralism, then religious skepticism, and finally a complete breakdown in the until then relatively homogeneous Christian worldview. As time passed, the average Protestant, no longer enclosed by the Catholic womb of grand ceremony, historical tradition, and sacramental authority, was left somewhat less protected against the vagaries of private doubt and secular thinking. From Luther on, each believer's belief was increasingly self-supported; and the Western intellect's critical faculties were becoming even more acute.

The Reformation also contributed to such aspects as biblical theology vs. scholastic theology, thus supporting a different view of nature as purely mundane. God was seen as operating the world fully distinctly from His own infinite divinity. The world could be analyzed as dynamic material processes, without any reference to God and His transcendent reality. The way became clear for a naturalistic view of the cosmos, moving first to the remote rationalist Creator of Deism, finally to secular agnosticism's elimination of any supernatural reality.

The Reformation also helped in the realignment of personal loyalties and in the rise of the various nation states in Europe, marked by aggressive competition. There was a succession of increasingly secularizing political and social consequences: first the establishment of the individual state-identified churches, then the division of church and state, religious toleration, and finally the predominance of secular society. Out of the exceedingly illiberal dogmatic religiosity of the Reformation eventually emerged the pluralistic tolerant liberalism of the modern era.

3. The Enlightenment or Scientific Revolution (17th and 18th centuries). Here we have the enthronement of the primacy of reason in opposition to organized religion. The scientific method became the principal means of discovering truth, and divine revelation was gradually sidelined. Such men as Copernicus, Kepler, Galileo, and Newton had helped to advance the scientific revolution based on the heliocentric model and a moving Earth. What would emerge from these scientific discoveries was an intricate and orderly universe, where God seemed to have removed Himself from further active involvement or intervention in nature. It was assumed now that God allowed the universe to run on its own according to perfect immutable laws. The new image of the Creator was that of a divine architect, a master mathematician and clock worker, while the universe was viewed as a uniformly regulated and fundamentally impersonal phenomenon. Man's role in that universe could best be judged on the evidence that, by virtue of his own intelligence, he had penetrated the universe's essential order and could now use that knowledge for his own benefit and improvement. One could scarcely doubt that man was the crown of creation. The scientific revolution--and the birth of the modern era--was now complete.

4. Socialism and Marxism (19th and 20th centuries). During these two centuries, you have the promotion of scientific materialism

and secular state ownership as the best method to analyze the world and to solve the problems of humanity. In this perspective, religion was seen as "the opium of the people"--something to be rejected and crushed in order to awaken human reason so it could grapple with the new world that Marxism promised.

For Karl Marx, religion was an illusion. He saw it as a kind of symptom of social disorder which sustains and aggravates that disorder. It expresses pathological alienation. To attain social freedom and maturity, religion has to be shaken off. Marx thought of religion as a poor substitute for action, which would become obsolete as that (revolutionary) action came into its own, and as a society was born without the need for religion. Marx did acknowledge that religion could yield a sense of human self-awareness, and a means of interpreting the world. But he believed it to be mistaken and misleading. Religion obscured reality. When reality was unveiled, religion would be unnecessary. Darwin also arose to challenge the doctrine of creation by postulating that human beings were essentially little more than advanced rational animals.

Freud also arose and questioned the doctrine of conversion and religious experience by providing a psychological explanation for these phenomena, making any supernatural experience superfluous.

5. Postmodernism and Urbanization (late 20th century). Although postmodernism is considered to be a reaction against the nationalistic and progressive premises of modernism, it has nonetheless pushed forward secularization by maintaining that human beings cannot have access to reality and therefore have no means of perceiving truth.

Urbanization, with its vast transportation and media culture and sense of anomie, has seen people flock to the cities to be uprooted from their traditional religious moorings. As a result, a consciousness of God is "reduced." All these developments have given humankind increased autonomy, longevity, and greater control of their lives, the environment, and even outer space.

The foregoing was adapted from Richard Tarnas, *The Passion of the Western Mind: Understanding the Ideas That Have Shaped Our World View*, (New york: Ballantine Books, 1991) pp. 224-323.

APPENDIX C

A SAMPLE SEEKER SERVICE

A SAMPLE SEEKER SERVICE

Order of Service - The elements of a seeker service follow a logical flow, as seen in the following service.

1. The Opening - Someone enters the stage and gives a short opening remark and welcome.

2. Band Warmup - The band would usually play a contemporary gospel song to warm up the audience.

3. Solo - An individual sings another contemporary song, such as "My Father's Eyes" or "Unbelievable Love" or "Morning Star," etc.

4. Announcements - are usually given at this time. Most of these will focus on the various programs and services designed to meet specific needs of the unchurched or seekers.

5. Drama - Drama is used as a visual and creative way of presenting biblical messages and themes to the unchurched. They also set the stage for the talk or message of the night. An example of this kind of drama is that sponsored by the Andrews University Student Activities Department--a contemporary musical drama entitled "Divine Reign--The Story of Esther." The upbeat, entertaining production is being used as a tool for friendship and evangelism with Gen-Xers and secular audiences. It is targeted to those who may not feel comfortable in a "church" setting. The goal is to build relationships while opening the doors for spiritual exploration and discussions on Bible topics.[3]

6. Offering - The one who calls for the offering usually states that the visitors or guests are not pressured or expected to give. This is in keeping with the idea that unchurched people negatively view the idea of the church asking for money.

7. Testimony - This is usually a real-life testimony, about five minutes in length. It is usually about what Christ has done in someone's life.

8. Song - Usually another contemporary gospel song, usually sung by a group or choir accompanied by either recorded music or the band or orchestra.

9. Scripture - The Scripture is read, using a more modern translation of the Bible and is related to the talk or message for the evening.

10. Talk or Message - is usually on an issue or topic that relates to the felt needs of the audience or seekers.

11. Question and Answer - This could follow a brief talk or message and relates to the subject. It creates an atmosphere of openness and invites questions that people may need answers to on the subject or areas that may need clarification.

12. Closing Prayer - Before the closing prayer, a reminder of the services and programs offered for guests is given along with next week's topic. Then people are asked to stand for a closing prayer.[4]

Other services can also be developed and conducted at different times from the seeker type service. These services are usually for more mature believers and will be more in keeping with their spiritual growth and needs.

Appendices Notes

1   J. Russell Halle, *The Unchurched: Who They Are and Why They Stay Away* (San Francisco: Harper and Row, 1980), 104.

2   The foregoing categories were largely taken from J. Russell Halle, *The Unchurched: Who Are They and Why They Stay Away* (San Francisco: Harper & Row, Publishing, 1980), 99-108. See also George Hunter III, *How to Reach Secular People*, 41, 42, and Mark Finley, "Targets and Tactics," in *Meeting the Secular Mind*, 101, 102.

3   The Andrews University Student Activities Department, "Divine Reign - The Story of Esther," bulletin insert at Pioneer Memorial Seventh-day Adventist Church, May 13, 2000.

4   See Ed Dobson, *Starting a Seeker Sensitive Service: How Traditional Churches Can Reach the Unchurched* (Grand Rapids, MI: Zondervan Publishing House, 1993), 114-133.

GLOSSARY OF TERMS

Amoral: That which is neither moral nor immoral. Persons considered amoral are believed to be unable to distinguish right from wrong and thus to have no sense of moral responsibility.

A priori: From the former; a Latin term referring to thought or knowledge arising from a concept or principle that precedes empirical verification, or that occurs independently of experience.

Baby Boomer: Technically refers to those people born between 1946 and 1964, representing over 76 million Americans.

Baby Buster: Broadly defined, a Baby Buster is a person born between 1965 and 1983 and represents at least 66 million Americans. They are called Busters because they represent a smaller (bust) generation compared to their Boomer parents who make up the largest single generation in United States history.

Builders Generation: Made up of people who were born prior to 1946.

Church Growth: As a technical term, church growth is the discipline in missiology which studies the multiplication of the qualitative growth of the church. It addresses itself to the strategic issue of how to win the most people to Christ in the most direct way in the shortest time possible with the highest quality of result in faithfulness to God, in individuals' lives, and in the corporate life of the church and its ministry in the world. Modern church-growth theory dates from 1955, when Donald A. McGavran published *The Bridges of God* and initiated the structural framework which characterizes the church-growth movement. His definitive statement is found in the 1980 revision of *Understanding Church Growth*, which has an extensive bibliography. Though general church-growth theory grew out of the Third World mission research, it has now been contextualized for American church growth (by such as C. Peter Wagner) and applied to such issues as church planting and the communication of the gospel.

Context: The social location of a group or class (from Lat. *contextus*, "a weaving together").

Contextualization: To translate the unchanging gospel of the kingdom into verbal forms meaningful to their particular existential situation. It also means to discover the legitimate implications of the gospel in a given situation. It goes deeper than application and calls for a proper exegesis of the text. Contextualization refers to more than just theology; it also includes developing church life and ministry that are biblically faithful and culturally appropriate.

Epistemology: From the Geek *episteme,* "knowledge," plus *logos,* "theory." A theory of knowledge. In philosophy, epistemology examines how we gain knowledge, investigating the origin, structure, methods and validity of knowledge. It studies how we know what we know.

Evangelism: From the Greek noun *evangelion*, "good news," and the verb *evangelizomai*, "to proclaim good news." Evangelism is the active preaching or presentation of the gospel through a variety of means with the goal of bringing the hearer, through the power of the Holy Spirit, to faith in Jesus Christ and thus into a right relationship with God (see Luke 15; John 3:13; Rom 5:8; 10:14-15; 2 Pet 3:9). God has given all believers the privilege and responsibility of being ambassadors of Christ, ministers of reconciliation in the world (2 Cor 5:17-21).

Globalization: The trend toward an increasing interdependence of economies and businesses on a global scale, especially in trade, the movement of money, manufacturing (e.g. outsourcing the manufacture of consumer goods), and service provision (e.g. computer technicians living in India answering questions from people in the United States).

Marginalized: The marginalized are individuals and groups who live on the margins of a society. "Not able to participate in its socioeconomic, political, or religious life, due to cultural, political, religious, or socioeconomic differences."

Missional: Being oriented toward mission in thinking, acting, and living. Missional churches are churches that have mission as their heartbeat.

Modernity: A term often used to designate the post-Enlightenment period in Europe and North America in which people turned to a scientific culture and its promises in order to fill a void left by a decline in religion. The values of the secular culture and rejection of religious authority are primary as well as belief in knowledge as certain, objective, and good.

Moral Relativism: The value of "moral relativism" states that what is moral is dictated by a particular situation in light of a particular culture or social location. The usual phraseology is "what is true for you is true for you, and what is true for me is true for me."

Mysticism: The Greek *mysterion,* from *mystes,* "one initiated in the secrets of a truer reality." Mystics stress direct apprehension of God, direct communication or revelation from God, and salvation on the basis of this direct relationship. One strand of mysticism tends toward occultism, stressing magic, parapsychology and a preoccupation with visions and supernatural powers and revelations. Historic biblical Christianity stands opposed to this type of mysticism, arguing that the text of scripture is all any person needs to discover God's will for his or her life. God has objectively revealed the truth equally for all.

Naturalism: The philosophical idea that the system of nature we observe and experience is the whole of reality, the sum total of existence. Everything that exists—matter, nature, life, mind, creativity—is explained in terms of a mechanistic materialism. To a naturalist the human mind, for example, is nothing more than an electrical-chemical machine, a product of the evolutionary process. Naturalism dismisses the existence of any spiritual realm, thus ruling out the existence of God, spirit, immortality, and human freedom. It is the fundamental tenet of atheism.

Nihilism: A philosophical view that rejects all authority, tradition, and morality (from Lat. *nihil,* "nothing"). As a nineteenth century social and political philosophy, it rejected religious and moral values.

Pluralism: The idea that there is more than one correct approach to truth or reality. In their most extreme form pluralists advocate the blending of all sets of competing ideas, each only having a portion of the whole and each true in its own way. In religious terms, those who promote pluralism claim that no religion has an exclusive hold on religious truth; all are legitimate in their own sphere of influence.

Postmodernism: A description of a contemporary intellectual and cultural climate as a stage beyond the "modernism" introduced by the Enlightenment. It is marked by a rejection of "objective truth," the powers of reason, and claim of universality. Texts and symbols are emphasized together with a corporate understanding of truth that is relative to each community in which one participates.

Religious a priori: A term in philosophical theology since the time of F. D. E. Schleiermacher (1768-1834), who argued that there is an innate capacity within humans for religion that can be the presupposition for all particular religions.

Religiosity: An excessive or affected religious zeal. It connotes an outward display of actions without a correspondingly genuine valuing of religion.

Religious experience: A special sense of the presence of the divine or of one's relationship to the holy. It is an experience or aspect of experience that one believes possesses religious significance or meaning.

Secular: In common usages, that which is worldly, earthly, and temporal and thus not religious or spiritual (Lat. *saecularis* from *saeculum*, "age," "generation"); Also used to describe those who are not bound by monastic rules, vows, or church authority.

Secularism: A term that relates human viewpoints, beliefs, values, actions, or institutions to the world in contrast to relating them to religious dimensions beyond the natural order (Lat. *saecularis*, "age," "generation," "the world").

Secularity: A method of thought and way of perceiving reality that disregards religious claims and processes purely on the basis of the perceived (natural) world (Lat. *saecularis*, from *saeculum*, "age," "generation," "the world").

Secularization: The process of moving from an orientation that includes a religious dimension for thought and action to one that is forced on the world itself as the only perceived reality (Lat. *saecularis*, from *saaeculum*, "age," "generation," "the world").

Secular people: People who are not substantially influenced by Christianity. It does not mean that they are irreligious. They may have once attended church but drifted away. Secular people vary in ethnicity, culture, age, needs, education, socioeconomic class, etc. See chapter 2.

Secular-unchurched: A term for unchurched, non-Christians or unchurched-preChristians. Of course, there are some people who may be considered unchurched but yet not secular, e.g., Hindus, Muslims, Jews, etc. Secular people and unchurched people are used interchangeably. Hunter raises the question, What kind of church reaches secular, unchurched non-Christians? In the same breath he refers to these as secular people, secular seekers, unchurched-non-Christians, or unchurched preChristians.

Seekers: Used for those who may attend a church seeking for something, and thus not having made a commitment to Jesus Christ.

Sitz im Leben: A term used in biblical interpretation that seeks to ascertain the particular context or circumstances in which a certain passage originated (Ger. "setting in life").

Social ministry: Service offered in ministry by churches and individuals to relieve human suffering and provide for the needs of the community. It often focuses on issues of justice in society as well as being concerned with the basic necessity of life for those without resources.

Syncretism: The replacement of core or important truths of the Gospel with non-Christian elements.

Unchurched: Those who do not belong to or participate in the life of a Christian church.

World view: A world view is a set of presuppositions (assumptions which may be true, partially true, or entirely false) which we hold (consciously, subconsciously, consistently, or inconsistently) about the basic makeup of our world.[1]

Glossary Note

1. The glossary of terms are credited to: Donald K. McKim, *Westminster Dictionary of Theological Terms* (Louisville, KY: Westminster/John Knox Press, 1996); Terry L. Miethe, *The Compact Dictionary of Doctrinal Words* (Minneapolis: Bethany House Publishers, 1988); Walter A. Elwell, *The Concise Evangelical Dictionary of Theology* (Grand Rapids, MI: Baker Book House, 1991); Richard S. Taylor, *Beacon Dictionary of Theology* (Kansas City, MO: Beacon Hill Press, 1983); David J. Hesselgrave and Edward Rommen, *Contextualization: Meanings, Methods, and Models* (Grand Rapids, MI: Baker, 1992); Gary L. McIntosh, *Three Generations: Riding the Waves of Change In Your Church* (Grand Rapids, MI: Fleming H. Revell, 1997); Hunter, *How to Reach Secular People and Church for the Unchurched*; James W. Sire, *The Universe Next Door* (Downers Grove, IL: InterVarsity Press, 1997); Michael Pocock, Gailyn Van Rheenen, and Douglas McConnell, *The Changing Face of World Missions: Engaging Contemporary Issues and Trends* (Grand Rapids, MI: Baker Academic, 2005); *The Challenge of Postmodernism*, David S. Dockery, editor. (Grand Rapids, MI: Baker Academics, 2001).

SUGGESTED
BIBLIOGRAPHY/RESOURCES

Adventist Development and Relief Agency. *ADRA Today*. Washington, DC: ADRA International, 1985.

Arn, Win. *The Church Growth Ration Book*. Pasadena, CA: Church Growth, 1987.

_____. *The Pastor's Manual for Effective Ministry*. Monrovia, CA: Church Growth, Inc., 1988.

Arn, Win, and Charles Arn. *The Master's Plan for Making Disciples*. Grand Rapids, MI: Baker Books, 1998.

Aune, David. "Revelation 1-5." *Word Biblical Commentary*. Dallas, TX: Word Books, 1997.

Baker, Delbert W. *Make Us One: Celebrating Spiritual Unity in the Midst of Cultural Diversity*. Boise, ID: Pacific Press Publishing Association, 1995.

Barna, George. *Absolute Confusion: How our Moral and Spiritual Foundations Are Eroding in this Age of Change*. Ventura, CA: Regal Books, 1993.

_____. "The Case of the Missing Baby Boomers." *Ministry Currents* 2, no. 1 (January-March 1992): 2-5.

_____. *Evangelism That Works: How to Reach Changing Generations with the Unchanging Gospel.* Ventura, CA: Regal Books, 1995.

_____. *The Frog in the Kettle.* Ventura, CA: Regal Books, 1990.

_____. *Marketing the Church.* Colorado Springs, CO: NavPress, 1988.

_____. *The Second Coming of the Church.* Nashville: Word Publishing, 1998.

_____. *User-Friendly Churches.* Ventura, CA: Regal Books, 1991.

_____. *Virtual America: The Barna Report, 1994-1995.* Ventura, CA: Regal Books, 1994.

Barr, Browne. "Finding the Good at Garden Grove." *Christian Century,* May 4, 1977, 424-427.

Basden, Paul. *The Worship Maze: Finding a Style to Fit Your Church.* Downers Grove, IL: InterVarsity Press, 1999.

Baumgartner, Erich W. "Megachurches and What They Teach Us." In *Adventist Missions in the 21st Century.* Hagerstown, MD: Review and Herald Publishing Association, 1999.

Beach, Bert B. "Adventism and Secularism." *Ministry,* April 1996, 22-25.

Beaton, Randy. *Everyday Evangelism: Making a Difference for Christ Where You Live.* Grand Rapids: MI: Baker Books, 1977.

Belasco, James A., and Ralph C. Stayer. *Flight of the Buffalo.* New York: Warner, 1993.

Bennis, Warren. *On Becoming a Leader.* New York: Addison Wesley, 1989.

Berger, Peter L. *The Sacred Canopy: Elements of a Sociological Theory of Religion.* Garden City, NY: Doubleday, 1967.

Berger, Peter L. "Some Second Thoughts On Substantive versus Functional Definitions of Religion." *Journal for the Scientific Study of Religion* 13, no. 1 (June 1974): 125-133.

Berger, Peter L., Briggette Berger, and Hansfield Kellner. *The Homeless Mind: Modernization and Consciousness.* New York: Random House, 1973.

Berman, Philip L. *The Search for Meaning: Americans Talk About What They Believe and Why.* New York: Ballentine, 1990.

Bernard, J. H. *A Critical and Exegetical Commentary on the Gospel According to St John.* Edinburgh: T & T Clark, 1972.

Bibby, Reginald W. *Fragmented Gods: The Poverty and Potential of Religion in Canada.* Toronto: Irwin Publishing, 1990.

Biggs, David. "Study: Ex-Protestants Not Returning to Fold." *Dallas Morning News,* June 5, 1992, 27.

Bilezikion, Gilbert. "A Vision for the Church." *Willow Creek,* September/October 1990, 20-21.

Birchell, Mark. "The Case for Corporate Leadership in the Local Church." In *All Are Called: Toward a Theology of the Laity. Essays from a Working Party of the General Synod Board of Education.* London: CIO Publilishing, 1985.

Blamires, Harry. *The Christian Mind: How Should a Christian Think?* Ann Arbor, MI: Servant Books, 1963.

Blanchard, Ken, and Michael O'Connor. *Managing by Values.* San Fransisco: Berrett-Koehler Publishers, 1996.

Bockelman, Wilfred. "Pros and Cons of Robert Schuller." *Christian Century,* August 20-27, 1975, 732-735.

Bork, Robert H. *Slouching Towards Gomorrah: Modern Liberalism and American Decline.* New York: Regan Books/Harper Collins Publishers, 1996.

Bosch, David J. *Transforming Mission: Paradigm Shifts in Theology of Mission.* Maryknoll, NY: Orbis Books, 1998.

Bradford, Charles E. *Preaching to the Times.* Washington, DC: Review and Herald Publishing Association, 1975.

Brimsmead, Robert D. *This Is Life.* Fallbrook, CA: Verdict Publications, 1978.

Bruce, Steve. *Religion in the Modern World: From Cathedrals to Cults.* New York: Oxford University Press, 1996.

Buntain, Ruth Jaeger. *Empties Drifting By.* Boise, ID: Pacific Press Publishing Association, 1985.

Burrill, Russell. *Radical Disciples for Revolutionary Churches.* Fallbrook, CA: Hart Research Center, 1989.

_____. *Recovering an Adventist Approach to the Life and Mission of the Local Church.* Fallbrook, CA: Hart Research Center, 1998.

_____. *Rekindling a Lost Passion: Recreating a Church Planting Movement.* Fallbrook, CA: Hart Research Center, 1999.

Bush, Rush L. "What Is Secularism?" *Southwestern Journal of Theology* 26 (1984): 5-14.

Cameron, Earl P. W. *Evangelism in Today's World: Attracting Evangelistic Audiences in a Secular Society.* Oshawa, ON, Canada: Maracle Press, 1996.

Campolo, Anthony. "Strategies for Ministry in a Secular Society" (sound recording). Silver Spring, MD: North American Youth Ministries, 199 .

Celek, Tim, and Dieter Zander. *Inside the Soul of a New Generation: Insights and Strategies for Reaching Busters.* Grand Rapids, MI: Zondervan Publishing House, 1996.

Chalfont, Paul H., Robert E. Beckley, and Eddie C. Palmer. *Religion in Contemporary Society.* Sherman Oaks, CA: Alfred Publishing Company, 1981.

Chandler, Russell. *Racing Toward 2001: The Forces Shaping America's Religious Future.* Grand Rapids, MI: Zondervan Publishing House, 1992.

Cherry, Kittridge, and James Mitulski. "Raising Lazarus: Can Liberal Churches Grow?" *Witness* 72 (March 1989): 12-15.

Christian Witness to Secularized People. Lausanne Occasional Papers No. 8. Wheaton, IL: Lausanne Committee for World Evangelization, 1980.

"Churches Die with Dignity." *Christianity Today,* January 14, 1991, 68-70.

Claman, Victor N., and David E. Buttler. *Acting on Your Faith: Congregations Making a Difference: A Guide to Success in Service and Social Action.* Boston, MA: Insights, 1994.

Clinton, Robert J. *The Making of a Leader.* Colorado Springs, CO: NavPress, 1988.

Coleman, Victor N., David E. Butler, and Jessica A. Boyatt. *Acting Out Your Faith: Congregations Making a Difference.* Boston: Insights, 1994.

Collins, Gary, and Timothy Clinton. *Baby Boomer Blues.* Dallas, TX: Word Books, 1992.

Cousins, Don. *Tomorrow's Church . . . Today.* South Barrington, IL: Willow Creek Publications, 1979.

Crippen, Alan, ed. *Reclaiming the Culture: How You Can Protect Your Family Future.* Colorado Springs, CO: Focus on the Family Publishing, 1996.

Dale, Robert. *To Dream Again: How to Help Your Church Come Alive.* Nashville, TN: Broadman Press, 1981.

Denzin, Norman K. *Images of Postmodern Society: Social Theory and Contemporary Cinema.* Newbury Park, CA: Sage Publications, 1991.

Douglas, Walter B. T. "Multicultural Ministry: Challenges and Blessings." *Ministry*, July 1999, 8-12.

Downing, Christine. "Hekate." *The Encyclopedia of Religion.* New York: Collier Macmillan Publishers, 1987.

"Dream Dreams." *Seventh-day Adventist Bible Commentary.* Edited by Francis D. Nichol. Hagerstown, MD: Review and Herald Publishing Association, 1977.

Duckworth, George E. "Greek Language." *Encarta Encyclopedia*, available from http://encarta.msn.com/index/conciseindex/04/00403000htm, accessed 9 January 2001; Internet..

Elwell, Walter A. *The Concise Evangelical Dictionary of Theology.* Grand Rapids, MI: Baker Book House, 1991.

_____, ed. Evangelical Dictionary of Theology. Grand Rapids, MI: Baker Book House, 1984.

Engelkemier, Joe. "A Church that Draws Thousands." *Ministry,* May 1991, 14-17.

Erickson, Millard J. *Does It Matter if God Exists? Understanding Who God Is and What He Does for Us.* Grand Rapids, MI: Baker Books, 1996.

Fackre, Gabriel, Ronald H. Nash, and John Sanders. *What about Those Who Have Never Heard? Views of the Destiny of the Unevangelized.* Downers Grove, IL: InterVarsity Press, 1995.

Finley, Mark. *Fulfilling the Gospel Commission.* Fallbrook, CA: Hart Research Center, 1989.

_____. "Targets and Tactics." In *Meeting the Secular Mind: Some Adventist Perspective,* ed. Humberto M. Rasi and Fritz Guy. Berrien Springs, MI: Andrews University Press, 1985.

Foster Seventh-day Adventist Church. "When It Hurts." Available from www.fosterchurch.com/month.html. Accessed 13 April, 2000; Internet.

Fowler, John W. *Evangelism Two Thousand: Proclaiming Christ in the 21ˢᵗ Century.* Boise, ID: Pacific Press Publishing Association, 1994.

Francis, Hozell C. *Church Planting in the African-American Context.* Grand Rapids, MI: Zondervan Publishing House, 1999.

Frost, Rob. "The Process of Secularization." In *Evangelical Forum of Theology* accessed 16 August 1999; available from www.ox-west. ac.uk/wmsc/eft/secular/html; Internet.

Fuller, Robert C. "Religion and Empiricism in the Works of Peter Berger." *Zygon* 22 (1987): 497-510.

Gallup, George. "Church-Going in United States Has Remained Remarkably Constant Since 1971." In *Religion in America: Who Are the "Truly Devout" Among Us?* Princeton, NJ: Princeton Religion Research Center, 1982.

Gallup, George, and D. Michael Lindsay. *Surveying the Religious Landscape: Trends in U.S. Beliefs.* Harrisburg, PA: Moorehouse Publishing, 1999.

Gallup, George, and Jim Castelli. *The People's Religion: American Faith in the 90s.* New York: Macmillan Publishing Company, 1989.

Gallup, George, and Robert Besilla. "More Find Religion Important." *Washington Post*, January 22, 1994, 3B.

Gallup, George, and Timothy Jones. *The Saints Among Us: How the Spiritually Committed Are Changing Our World.* Harrisburg, PA: Moorehouse Publishing, 1993.

Gallup Surveys of 1980-1984. *Unsecular America.* Edited by Richard J. Neuhaus. Grand Rapids, MI: Eerdmans, 1996.

Garfield, Ken. "Some Churches Losing Members." *The Charlotte Observer*, 30 March 1996, 2G.

Garraty, John A., and Peter Gay. *A History of the World: The Modern World.* Vol. 2. New York: Harper and Row, 1972.

Garrison, Gregg. "Church Attendance Reported at Lowest Level in Two Decades. *Presbyterian Outlook.* Available from www.personalpastor.org/ppo3020.htm; accessed April 13, 2000; Internet.

Gay, Craig M. *The Way of the (Modern) World: Or, Why It's Tempting to Live as if God Doesn't Exist.* Grand Rapids, MI: Eerdmans Publishing Company, 1998.

General Conference of Seventh-day Adventists, *Sara's Dress.* Video recording. Silver Spring, MD: ADRA International, 1991.

Gilkey, Langdon. *Naming the Whirlwind: The Renewal of God Language.* Indianapolis: Bobbs-Merrill Company, 1969.

Gillian, Bob. Infrastructure Lecture Notes, The Vision 2000 Network, Evangelical Free Churches of America, 1-3.

Gladden, Ron. "Evangelism and Church Planting." *Ministry*, October 1999, 5-9.

Glassner, Peter E. *The Sociology of Secularization: A Critique of a Concept.* London: Routledge and Kegan Paul, 1997.

Gonzalez, Cesar. "A Sinner Among Saints: Is There Room for Me in Your Church?" *View* (1999): 15-22.

Goulding, Courtney. "Reaching the Secular Person in Urban Areas." Term paper, Andrews University Seventh-day Adventist Theological Seminary, Berrien Springs, MI, 1988.

"Greek, (Language)." *Seventh-day Adventist Bible Commentary.* Edited by Francis D. Nichol. Hagerstown, MD: Review and Herald Publishing Association, 1979.

Greeley, Andrew M. *Religious Change in America.* Cambridge, MA: Harvard University Press, 1989.

Griffin, David Ray. *God and Religion in the Postmodern World.* Albany, NY: State University of New York Pressm 1989.

Hadaway, C. Kirk. *Church Growth Principles.* Nashville, TN: Broadman Press, 1991.

Hadaway, C. Kirk, Penny Long Marler, and Mark Chaves. "Over-Reporting Church Attendance That Demands the Same Verdict." *American Sociological Review* 63 (1998): 122-130.

_____. What the Polls Don't Show: A Closer Look at U.S. Church Attendance." *American Sociological Review* 58 (1993): 741-752.

Halle, Russell R. *The Unchurched: Who Are They and Why They Stay Away.* San Francisco: Harper and Row Publishing, 1980.

Hamel, Gary, and C. K. Prahalad. *Competing for the Future.* Boston: Harvard Business School Press, 1996.

Harris, Steve. "Helping People Help You." *Leadership: A Practical Journal for Church Leaders* 9 (Winter 1988): 98-102.

Hazel, Gerhard F. *The Covenant in Blood.* Mountain View, CA: Pacific Press Publishing Association, 1982.

Hays, Richard B. *The Moral Vision of the New Testament.* San Francisco: Harper-San Francisco, 1996.

Hertel, Bradely R., and Hart M. Nelson. "Are We Entering a Post-Christian Era? Religious Belief and Attendance in America, 1957-1968." *Journal for the Scientific Study of Religion* 13 (1974): 409-419.

Hendricks, William D. *Exit Interviews: Revealing Stories of Why People Are Leaving the Church.* Chicago: Moody Press, 1993.

Hesselgrave, David J., and Edward Rommen. *Contextualization: Meanings, Methods, and Models.* Grand Rapids, MI: Baker Book House, 1992.

_____. *Three Generations: Riding the Waves of Change in Your Church.* Grand Rapids, MI: Fleming H. Revell, 1997.

Hill, Douglas John. "Metamorphosis: From Christendom to Diaspora." In *Confident Witness, Changing World: Rediscovering the Gospel in North America,* ed. Craig van Gelder. Grand Rapids, MI: Eerdmans, 1999.

Hofstachter, Richard. *Academic Freedom in the Age of the College.* New York: Columbia University Press, 1955.

Hollinger, David A. *Science, Jews and Secular Culture: Studies in Mid-Twentieth Century American Intellectual History.* Princeton, NJ: Princeton University Press, 2000.

Hooft, W. A. Visser't. "Evangelism in the Neo-Pagan Situation." *The International Review of Mission* 63 (1974): 81-86.

Horrocks, Geoffrey. *Greek: A History of the Language and Its Speakers.* White Plains: Longman Publishing Group, 1998.

Hull, Bill. *Jesus Christ, Disciple Maker: Rediscovering Jesus' Strategy in Building His Church.* Grand Rapids, MI: Fleming H. Revell, 1994.

_____. *Revival That Reforms.* Grand Rapids, MI: Fleming and Revell, 1998.

_____. *Seven Steps to Transform Your Church.* Grand Rapids, MI: Fleming H. Revell, 1993.

Hunter, George G. *Church for the Unchurched.* Nashville, TN: Abingdon Press, 1996.

_____. *How to Reach Secular People.* Nashville, TN: Abingdon Press, 1992.

Hutchins, Frank C., and Marcus M. Silver. *Position Statement to the GC Committee on the Secular Mind.* Human Destiny No. 5. Mount Lake Terrace, WA: The Human Destiny Foundation, 1983.

Hybels, William. *Rediscovering Church: The Story and Vision of Willow Creek Community Church.* Grand Rapids, MI: Zondervan Publishing House, 1995.

_____. *Seven Wonders of the Spiritual World.* Dallas, TX: Word Books, 1988.

_____. "Speaking to the Secular Mind: What Does It Take to Preach Convincingly to Today's Non-Christians?" *Leadership* 9 (1988): 28-34.

Hyde, William T. "Is an Irreligious Society the Result of the Outgrowth of the Idea of the Separation of Church and State?" An Essay Presented to the Faculty of the Seventh-day Adventist Theological Seminary as an Entry in the Context Sponsored by the POAH. Berrien Springs, MI: Andrews University Seventh-day Adventist Theological Seminary, 1950.

"Into the Stratosphere." *Willow Creek,* Special Anniversary Issue, 20. (n.d.).

Jackson, Phil. *Sacred Hoops: Spiritual Reflections of a Hardwood Warrior.* New York: Hyperion, 1995.

Johnson, Benton. "The Denominations: The Changing Map of Religious America." *The Public Perspective: A Roper Center Review of Public Opinion and Polling* 4 (March/April 1993): 3-6.

Jurrison, Cynthia A. "Pop Spirituality: An Evangelical Response." *Word and World* 28 (1998): 14-23.

Kaiser, Christopher B. "From Biblical Security to Modern Secularism: Historical Aspects and Stages." In *The Church Between Gospel and Culture: The Emerging Mission in North America,* ed. R. George Hunsberger and Craig van Gelder. Grand Rapids, MI: Eerdmans Publishing Company, 1996.

"Keys." *Seventh-day Adventist Bible Commentary.* Edited by Francis D. Nichol. Hagerstown MD: Review and Herald Publishing Association, 1980.

Kotler, Philip, and Allan R. Andreasen. *Strategic Marketing for Nonprofit Organizations.* Englewood Cliffs, NJ: Prentice Hall, 1991.

Kouezes, James M., and Barry Z. Posner. *The Leadership Challenge.* San Francisco: Jossey-Bass, 1991.

Kozman, Barry A., and Semour P. Lachman. *The Barna Report 1992-1993.* Ventura, CA: Regal Books, 1992.

_____. *One Nation Under God: Religion in Contemporary American Society.* New York: Crown Trade Paperbacks, 1993.

Kretschmar, Juanita. *The Ministry of E-Van-gelism.* Manhasset, NY: Community Health Services Department of the Greater New York Conference of Seventh-day Adventists, 1984.

Kretschmar, Juanita, and Merlin Kretschmar. *The Mustard Seed Ministry.* Video recording. New Hyde Park, NY: Power to Cope Broadcast Ministries, 1992.

Langford, Andy. *Transitions in Worship: Moving from Traditional to Contemporary.* Nashville: Abingdon Press, 1999.

LaRondelle, Hans K. *Light for the Last Days: Jesus' End Time Prophecies Made Plain in the Book of Revelation.* Nampa, ID: Pacific Press Publishing Association, 1999.

Larson, Bruce, and Ralph Osborne. "Primary Sources." In *The Emerging Church*, ed. Richard Engquist. Waco, TX: Word Book Publishers, 1970.

Lewis, C. S. *Mere Christianity*. New York: Macmillan, 1960.

Lewey, Guenter. *Why America Needs Religion: Secular Modernity and Its Discontents*. Grand Rapids, MI: William B. Eerdmans Publishing Company, 1996.

Logan, Robert E. *Beyond Church Growth: Action Plans for Developing a Dynamic Church*. Grand Rapids, MI: Fleming H. Revell, 1998.

Logan, Robert E., and Larry Short. *Mobilizing for Compassion: Moving People into Ministry*. Grand Rapids, MI: Fleming H. Revell, 1994.

Luckman, Thomas. *The Invisible Rebellion: The Problem of Religion in Modern Society*. New York: Macmillan, 1967.

_____. "The Structural Conditions of Religious Consciousness in Modern Societies." *Japanese Journal of Religious Studies* 6 (1979): 121-137.

McClure, Alfred. "Planting and Harvesting." *Review and Herald*, December 5, 1996, 14-19.

MacMillan, Conway. "The Scientific Method and Modern Intellectual Life." *Science*, n.s., 1 (1895): 537-542.

Magnum, Eve Arnold. "Spiritual America." *U.S. News and World Report*, 1994, 48-59.

Malphurs, Aubrey. *Advance Strategic Planning: A New Model for Church and Ministry Leaders*. Grand Rapids, MI: Baker Books, 1999.

_____. *Planting Growing Churches for the 21ˢᵗ Century*. Grand Rapids, MI: Baker Books, 1998.

_____ *Pouring New Wine into Old Wineskins: How to Change a Church Without Destroying It.* Grand Rapids, MI: Baker Books, 1997.

Marcum, John P. "Measuring Church Attendance: A Further Look." *Review of Religious Research* (1999-2000): 122-130.

Marler, Penny Long, and C. Kirk Hadaway, "Did You Really Go to Church This Week? Behind the Poll Data." *Christian Century* 115 (1998): 472-475.

_____. "Testing the Attendance Gap in a Conservative Church." *Sociology of Religion* 60 (1999): 175-176.

Marsden, George. *The Outrageous Idea of Christian Scholarship.* New York: Oxford University Press, 1998.

_____. *The Soul of the American University: From Protestant Establishment to Established Nonbelief.* New York: Oxford University Press, 1994.

Marsden, George M., and Bradley G. Longfield, eds. *The Secularization of the Academy.* New York: Oxford University Press, 1992.

Martin, David. *A General Theory of Secularization.* New York: Harper & Row, 1978.

Marty, Martin E. *Verities of Unbelief.* New York: Holt, Rinehart, & Winston, 1964.

_____. "Where the Energies Go." *Annals of the American Academy of Political and Social Science* 527 (1993): 11-26.

Maudlin, Michael G., and Edward Gilbreath. "Selling Out the House of God: Bill Hybels Answers Critics of the Seeker-Church Movement." *Christianity Today,* July 18, 1994, 21-25.

Maxwell, C. Mervyn. *God Cares.* Nampa, ID: Pacific Press Publishing Association, 1981.

"Maybe One." *Seventh-day Adventist Bible Commentary*. Edited by Francis D. Nichol. Hagerstown, MD: Review and Herald Publishing Association, 1980.

Mayfield, Joseph H. "The Gospel According to John." *Beacon Bible Commentary*. Kansas City, MO: Beacon Hill Press, 1965.

Maynard-Reid, Pedrito U. "Holistic Evangelism." *Ministry*, May 2000, 20-22.

McArthur, John. *Ashamed of the Gospel: When the Church Becomes Like the World*. Wheaton, IL: Crossway Books, 1993.

McClory, Robert. "Super Church: We Have Seen the Future of Religion, and It Is Slick." *Reader* 21 (1992): 22-24.

McGavran, Donald G. *Understanding Church Growth*. Grand Rapids, MI: Eerdmans Publishing Company, 1990.

McGrath, Allister E. *Intellectuals Don't Need God and Other Modern Myths*. Grand Rapids, MI: Zondervan Publishing House, 1993.

McIntosh, Gary L. *One Size Doesn't Fill All*. Grand Rapids, MI: Fleming H. Revell, 1999.

McKim, Donald K. *Westminster Dictionary of Theological Terms*. Louisville, KY: Westminster/John Knox Press, 1996.

Miethe, Terry L. *The Compact Dictionary of Doctrinal Words*. Minneapolis: Bethany House Publishers, 1988.

Missional Church: A Vision for the Sending of the Church in North America. Edited by Darrill R. Guder. Grand Rapids, MI: William B. Eerdmans, 1998.

Mittleberg, Mark. *Building a Contagious Church: Revolutionizing the Way We View and Do Evangelism*. Grand Rapids, MI: Zondervan Publishing House, 2000.

_____. "A Critical Analysis of the Epistemological Starting Points in Presuppositional Apologetics." Master's thesis, Trinity Evangelical Divinity School, Deerfields, IL: 1988.

Monroe, Kelly. *Finding God at Harvard*. Grand Rapids, MI: Zondervan Publishing House, 1996.

Mwansa, Pardon Kandanga. "A Training Program in Pastoral Responsibilities for Church Elders in Lusaka, Zambia." D.Min. dissertation, Andrews University, 1993.

Naisbitt, John. *Megatrends*. New York: Warner Books, 1982.

Newbegin, Leslie. *A Word in Season: Perspectives on Christian World Missions*. Grand Rapids, MI: William B. Eerdmans Publishing Company, 1994.

_____. *Foolishness to the Greeks: The Gospel and Western Culture*. Grand Rapids, MI: William B. Eerdmans Publishing Company, 1991.

Neuhaus, Richard John. *American Apostasy: The Triumph of "Other" Gospels*. Grand Rapids, MI: William B. Eerdmans Publishing Company, 1989.

Neuhaus, Richard John, gen. ed. *Unsecular America*. Grand Rapids, MI: William B. Eerdmans Publishing Company, 1986.

Niebuhr, Gustav. "American Religion at the Millennium's End." *Word and World* 18 (1998):

5-13

Nikolalopoulous, Konstantine. "The Language of the New Testament and an Example for the Historical Unity of the Greek Language." *Greek Orthodox Theological Review* 42 (1997): 259-271.

Nord, Warren A. *Religion and American Education: Rethinking a National Dilemma*. Chapel Hill, NC: University of North Carolina, 1995.

Norton, Charles Eliot. "Religious Liberty." *North American Review* 104 (1867): 586-597.

Oates, Wayne E. *Luck: A Secular Faith.* Louisville, KY: Westminster John Knox Press, 1995.

Oosterwal, Gottfried. "Faith and Mission in a Secularized World." Department of World Mission, Andrews University Theological Seminary, April 5, 1993.

_____. "The Process of Secularization." In *Meeting the Secular Mind: Some Adventist Perspectives.* Ed. Humberto M. Rasi and Fritz Guy. Berrien Springs, MI: Andrews University Press, 1985.

Ostling, Richard N. "America's Ever-Changing Religious Landscape: Where We've Come from and Where We're Going." *Brookings Review* (1999): 11-13.

Parrot, Les, and Robin D. Perrin. "The New Denominations." *Christianity Today,* 11 March, 1991, 29-33.

Patterson, James, and Peter Kim. *The Day America Told the Truth.* New York: Prentice Hall, 1991.

Paulien, Jon. *The Abundant Life Amplifier--John.* Boise, ID: Pacific Press Publishing Association, 1995.

_____. "The Gospel in a Secular World," in *Meeting the Secular Mind: Some Adventist Perspectives.* Berrien Springs, MI: Andrews University Press, 1985.

_____. Present Truth in the Real World: The Adventist Struggle to Keep and Share Faith in a Secular Society. Boise, ID: Pacific Press Publishing Association, 1993.

_____. "Scratching Where It Itches: Ministry to the Secular." *Seeds 99: A Church Planting Conference,* July 16, 1998.

Pearson, Michael. "The Problem of Secularism." In *Cast the Net on the Right Side . . . Seventh-day Adventists Fase the "Isms,"* ed. Richard

Lehmann, Jackson Mahon, and Borge Schantz. Bracknell, England: European Institute of World Missions, 1993.

Pippert, Rebecca Manley. *Out of the Salt-Shaker and Into the World: Evangelism as a Way of Life*. Downers Grove, IL: InterVarsity Press, 1979.

Postman, Neil. *Amusing Ourselves to Death: Public Discourse in the Age of Show Business*. New York: Penguin Books, 1985.

Presser, Stanley, and Linda Stinson. "Data Collection Mode and Social Desirability Bias Self-Reported Religious Attendance." *American Sociological Review* 63 (1998): 137-145.

Pritchard, G. A. "The Theater Days." *Willow Creek,* Special Anniversary Issue, 28.

_____. *The Willow Creek Seeker Services*. Grand Rapids, MI: Baker Book House, 1998.

Ramachandra, Vimoth. *The Recovery of Mission: Beyond the Pluralist Paradigm*. Grand Rapids, MI: Eerdmans Publishing Company, 1997.

Rasi, Humberto M. "The Challenge of Secularism," in *Adventist Mission in the 21ˢᵗ Century*. Hagerstown, MD: Review and Herald Publishing Association, 1999.

Rasi, Humberto M., and Fritz Guy, ed. *Meeting the Secular Mind: Some Adventist Perspectives*. Berrien Springs, MI: Andrews University Press, 1985.

Religion in America--50 Years: 1935-1985. Princeton, NJ: Gallup Organization, 1985.

Roberts, John H., and James Turner. *The Sacred and the Secular University*. Princeton, NJ: Princeton University Press, 2000.

Roof, Wade Clark. *A Generation of Seekers: The Spiritual Journeys of the Baby Boom Generation.* New York: Harper Collins Publishers, 1993.

_____. *Spiritual Market Place: Baby Boomers and the Remaking of American Religion.* Princeton, NJ: Princeton University Press, 1999.

Roy, Ruthven Joseph. "Marketing and Mission: Applying Marketing Principles to Seventh-day Adventist Mission in the Virgin Islands." D.Min. dissertation, Andrews University, 1999.

Samaan, Philip G. *Christ's Way of Reaching People.* Hagerstown, MD: Review and Herald Publishing Association, 1990.

"Save Some." *Seventh-day Adventist Bible Commentary.* Edited by Francis D. Nichol. Washington, DC: Review and Herald Publishing Association, 1980.

SBC Handbook. Nashville, TN: Convention Press, 1991.

Schaller, Lyle. *Create Your Own Future!* Nashville, TN: Abingdon Press, 1991.

_____. *Getting Things Done.* Nashville, TN: Abingdon Press, 1986.

Schuller, Robert H. *Your Church Has Real Possibilities.* Glendale, CA: G/L Publications, 1974.

Schwartz, Christian A. *National Church Development: A Guide to Eight Essential Qualities of Healthy Churches.* Carol Stream, IL: Church Smart Resources, 1996.

Scott, Drusilla. *Everyman Revived: The Common Sense of Michael Polanyi.* Chippenham, England: Anthony Rowe, 1995.

Scott, Nathan A. *The Broken Center: Studies in the Theological Horizon of Modern Literature.* New Haven, CT: Yale University Press, 1966.

Scriven, Charles. *The Transformation of Culture.* Scottdale, PA: Herald Press, 1988.

Senge, Peter M. *The Fifth Discipline.* New York: Doubleday, 1990.

Senior, Donald, and Carroll Stuhlmueller. *The Biblical Foundations for Mission.* Maryknoll, NY: Orbis Books, 1989.

Seventh-day Adventist Bible Commentary. 10 vols. Edited by Francis D. Nichol. Washington, DC: Review and Herald Publishing Association, 1980.

Seventh-day Adventist Theological Seminary Bulletin 1994-1995. Berrien Springs, MI: Andrews University Press, 1994.

Shea, William H. *The Abundant Life Amplifier.* 2 vols. Boise, ID: Pacific Press Publishing Association, 1996.

_____. "Unity of Daniel." In *Symposium on Daniel,* 3 vols., ed. Frank B. Holbrook. Washington, DC: Biblical Research Institute, 1986.

Sider, Ronald J. *One-Sided Christianity? Uniting the Church to Heal a Lost and Broken World.* Grand Rapids, MI: Zondervan Publishing House, 1993.

Sims, Jack. "Baby Boomers: Time to Pass the Torch." *Christian Life,* January 1986, 22-25.

Singer, David. "The Crystal Cathedral: Reflections on Schuller's Theology." *Christianity Today,* August 8, 1980, 28-29.

Sire, James W. *The Universe Next Door.* Downers Grove, IL: InterVarsity Press, 1997.

Smith, Donald K. *Creating Understanding: A Handbook for Christian Communication Across Cultural Landscapes.* Grand Rapids, MI: Zondervan Publishing House, 1992.

Smith, Gary Scott. *The Seeds of Secularization: Calvinism, Culture, and Pluralism in America*. Grand Rapids, MI: Christian University Press, 1985.

Smith, Montgomery W. "Homogeneity and American Church Growth." Ph.D. dissertation, Fuller Institute, 1976.

Smith, Tom. W. "A Review of Church Attendance Measures." *American Sociological Review* 63 (1998): 131-136.

Staples, Russell Lynn. *Transmission of the Faith in a Secular Age*. New Orleans, LA: Andrews Society for Religious Studies, 1990.

Stark, Rodney, and William Sims Bainbridge. *The Future of Religion: Secularization, Revival and Cult Formation*. Berkeley and Los Angeles: University of California Press, 1985.

_____. *The Index of Leading Spiritual Indicators*. Dallas: Word Publishing, 1996.

Stark, Rodney, and Lawrence R. Iannaccone. "A Supply-Side Reinterpretation of the 'Secularization of Europe.'" *Journal for the Scientific Study of Religion* 33 (1994): 230-232.

_____. *Creation and the History of Science*. Grand Rapids, MI: Eerdmans Publishing Company, 1991.

Stearns, Amy, and Bill Stearns. *Catch the Vision 2000*. Minneapolis, MN: Bethany House Publishers, 1991.

Steinborn, Melvin G. *Can the Pastor Do It Alone? A Model for Preparing Lay People for Lay Pastoring*. Ventura, CA: Regal Books, 1987.

Stott, John R. W. *Christian Mission in the Modern World*. Downers Grove, IL: InterVarsity Press, 1975.

Strobel, Lee. *Inside the Mind of Unchurched Harry and Mary: How to Reach Friends and Family Who Avoid God and the Church*. Grand Rapids, MI: Zondervan Publishing House, 1993.

Strommen, Merton. *The Innovative Church*. Minneapolis, MN: Augsburg Press, 1997.

"A Study of Christ: The Prologue to John," *A Journal of Exposition* 3, no. 4 (May 1996), [journal on-line]; available from: http://www: scripturestudies.com/indes.html; Internet; accessed 12 January 2001.

Sweeten, Gary Ray. "The Development of a Systematic Human Relations Training Model for Evangelical Christians." Ed.D. dissertation, University of Cincinnati, 1975.

Szczesny, Gerhard. *The Future of Unbelief*. New York: George Braziller, 1961.

Tapia, Andres. "Reaching the First Post-Christian Generation." *Christianity Today*, September 12, 1994, 18-23.

Tarnas, Richard. *The Passion of the Western Mind: Understanding the Ideas that Have Shaped Our World View*. New York: Ballatine Books, 1993.

Taylor, Greg. "Building a Biblical Community Where Secular People Become Fully Devoted Followers of Christ." Ashville, NC: Foster Seventh-day Adventist Church, 1997.

_____ to Ernan Norman, May 6, 1999.

Taylor, Richard S. *Beacon Dictionary of Theology*. Kansas City, MO: Beacon Hill Press, 1983.

The Oxford Encyclopedic English Dictionary. Edited by Joyce M. Hawkins and Robert Allen. Oxford: Clarendon Press, 1991.

"Theater Days." *Willow Creek,* Special Anniversary Issue (n.d.), 28.

Thorne, Norman E., ed. *Classic Texts in Mission and World Christianity*. Maryknoll, NY: Orbis Books, 1998.

Towns, Elmer, C. Peter Wagner, and Thom S. Rainer. *The Every Church Guide to Growth: How Any Plateaued Church Can Grow.* Nashville, TN: Broadman and Holman, 1998.

U. S. Department of Health and Human Services. *Taking Time.* Bethesda, MD: National Institute of Health, 1982.

Van Gelder, Craig. "Reading Postmodern Culture Through the Medium of Movies." In *Confident Witness - Changing World*, ed. Craig van Gelder. Grand Rapids, MI: Eerdmans Publishing Company, 1999.

Van Gelder, Craig, and George R. Hunbugh. *The Church Between Gospel and Culture: The Emerging Mission in North America.* Grand Rapids, MI: William B. Eerdmans Publishing Company, 1996.

Wagner, Peter C. *Church Planting for a Greater Harvest.* Ventura, CA: Regal Books, 1990.

Walker, Larry Lee. "Biblical Languages." *Baker Encyclopedia of the Bible.* Edited by Walter A. Elwell. Grand Rapids, MI: Baker Book House, 1988.

Walker, Richard. "Trends: More Christians Saying No to Church." *Christianity Today*, September 2, 1988, 56, 57.

Wallis, Roy. "Secularization." *The International Encyclopedia of Sociology.* Edited by Michael Man. New York: Continuum, 1984.

Walsh, Andrew. "Church Lies and Polling Data." *Religion in the News* 1 (1998): 1-7.

Walton, John H., Victor H. Matthews, and Mark W. Chavalas. *The IVP Bible Background Commentary: Old Testament.* Downers Grove, IL: InterVarsity Press, 2000.

Warren, Rick. *The Purpose-Driven Church: Growth Without Compromising Your Message and Mission.* Grand Rapids, MI: Zondervan Publishing House, 1995.

_____. "Worship Can Be a Witness." *Worship Leader* 6 (1997): 28, 29.

Watkins, Derrel R. *Christian Social Ministry.* Nashville, TN: Broadman and Holman Publishers, 1994.

White, Ellen G. *Christian Service.* Takoma Park, Washington, DC: General Conference of Seventh-day Adventists, 1947.

_____. *Counsels on Sabbath School Work.* Washington, DC: Review and Herald, 1966.

_____. *The Desire of Ages.* Mountain View, CA: Pacific Press Publishing Association, 1940.

_____. *Evangelism.* Washington, DC: Review and Herald Publishing Association, 1973.

_____. *Gospel Workers.* Washington, DC: Review and Herald Publishing Association, 1974.

_____. *The Great Controversy.* Boise, ID: Pacific Press Publishing Association, 1950.

_____. *In Heavenly Places.* Washington, DC: Review and Herald Publishing Association, 1967.

_____. *The Ministry of Healing.* Mountain View, CA: Pacific Press Publishing Association, 1942.

_____. *Positive Christian Living.* Washington, DC: Review and Herald Publishing Association, 1952.

_____. *Selected Messages.* 2 vols. Washington, DC: Review and Herald Publishing Association, 1958.

_____. *Steps to Christ.* Washington, DC: Review and Herald Publishing Association, 1981.

_____. *Testimonies to the Church.* 9 vols. Mountain View, CA: Pacific Press Publishing Association, 1948.

White, James Emery. *Rethinking the Church*. Grand Rapids, MI: Baker Books, 1997.

Willimon, William H. *The Intrusive Word: Preaching to the Unbaptized*. Grand Rapids, MI: William B. Eerdmans Publishing Company, 1994.

Willow Creek Resources. "An Inside Look at the Willow Creek Seeker Service: Show Me the Way." Video recording. Grand Rapids, MI: Zondervan Video, 1992.

_____. "An Inside Look at the Willow Creek Worship Service: Building a New Community." Video recording. Grand Rapids, MI: Zondervan Video, 1992.

Wilson, Bryan. *Religion in Secular Society: A Sociological Comment*. Middlesex, England: Penguin Books, 1969.

"Word" (Gr. *Logos*). *Seventh-day Adventist Bible Commentary*. Edited by Francis D. Nichol. Hagerstown, MD: Review and Herald Publishing Association, 1980.

Wright, Chris. "The Case Against Pluralism." In *The Unique Christ in Our Pluralist World*, ed. Bruce J. Nicholls. Grand Rapids, MI: Baker Book House, 1994.

Wright, Tim. *Unfinished Evangelism: More Than Getting Them in the Door*. Minneapolis, MN: Augsburg Press, 1995.

The Yearbook of American and Canadian Churches, 1994. Quoted in *National and International Religion Report*, April 4, 1994, 3.

Zamora, Robert M. "The Gospel of the Abundant Life." In *Meeting the Secular Mind: Some Adventist Perspectives* ed. Humberto M. Rasi and Fritz Guy. Berrien Springs, MI: Andrews University Press, 1985.

Dr. Ernan Norman may be reached via email for request of his services in church growth seminars dealing with how to reach secular people or how to develop strategy in ministry in a post-modern age. Please contact him at pastore36@msn.com or ernan.norman@atlanticuc.edu.

ABOUT THE AUTHOR

Dr. ERNAN A. NORMAN has served as a minister of the gospel with the Seventh-day Adventist Church for more than 26 years, and during that time has been actively involved not only in the pastoring of churches, but also in the work of evangelism, of discipling and of nurturing those under his care. He has served both within the Caribbean and the United States. Dr. Norman also holds the degrees M.Div., and D.Min. from the Seventh-day Adventist Theological Seminary, Andrews University, Berrien Springs, MI. Currently Dr. Norman is serving as an assistant professor of Theology and Religion at Atlantic Union College, South Lancaster, Massachusettes, where he also teaches the class "Witnessing to the Secular Mind."

CPSIA information can be obtained at www.ICGtesting.com
Printed in the USA
BVOW010859160212

283049BV00001B/102/A